Glencoe
# CHEMISTRY
## MATTER AND CHANGE

# Laboratory Manual

## Student Edition

**Glencoe**
**McGraw-Hill**

New York, New York    Columbus, Ohio    Woodland Hills, California    Peoria, Illinois

Glencoe
# CHEMISTRY
MATTER AND CHANGE

## Hands-On Learning:
Laboratory Manual, SE/TE
Forensics Laboratory Manual, SE/TE
CBL Laboratory Manual, SE/TE
Small-Scale Laboratory Manual, SE/TE
ChemLab and MiniLab Worksheets

## Review/Reinforcement:
Study Guide for Content Mastery, SE/TE
Solving Problems: A Chemistry Handbook
Reviewing Chemistry
Guided Reading Audio Program

## Applications and Enrichment:
Challenge Problems
Supplemental Problems

## Assessment:
Chapter Assessment
MindJogger Videoquizzes (VHS)
TestCheck Software, Windows/Macintosh

## Teacher Resources:
Lesson Plans
Block Scheduling Lesson Plans
Spanish Resources
Section Focus Transparencies and Masters
Math Skills Transparencies and Masters
Teaching Transparencies and Masters
Solutions Manual

## Technology:
Chemistry Interactive CD-ROM
Vocabulary PuzzleMaker Software,
    Windows/Macintosh
Glencoe Science Web site:
**science.glencoe.com**

Send all inquiries to:
Glencoe/McGraw-Hill
8787 Orion Place
Columbus, OH 43240-4027

ISBN 0-07-824524-9
Printed in the United States of America.
.7 8 9 10 045 09 08 07 06 05 04

# Contents

## Laboratory Activities

### CHAPTER 1  Introduction to Chemistry

### CHAPTER 2  Data Analysis

### CHAPTER 3  Matter—Properties and Changes

### CHAPTER 4  The Structure of the Atom

### CHAPTER 5  Electrons in Atoms

### CHAPTER 6  The Periodic Table and Periodic Law

# How to Use This Laboratory Manual

Chemistry is the science of matter, its properties, and changes. In your classroom work in chemistry, you will learn a great deal of the information that has been gathered by scientists about matter. But, chemistry is not just information. It is also a process for finding out more about matter and its changes. Laboratory activities are the primary means that chemists use to learn more about matter. The activities in the *Laboratory Manual* require that you form and test hypotheses, measure and record data and observations, analyze those data, and draw conclusions based on those data and your knowledge of chemistry. These processes are the same as those used by professional chemists and all other scientists.

# Organization of Activities

- **Introduction**  Following the title and number of each activity, an introduction provides a background discussion about the problem you will study in the activity.

- **Problem**  The problem to be studied in this activity is clearly stated.

- **Objectives**  The objectives are statements of what you should accomplish by doing the investigation. Recheck this list when you have finished the activity.

- **Materials**  The materials list shows the apparatus you need to have on hand for the activity.

- **Safety Precautions**  Safety symbols and statements warn you of potential hazards in the laboratory. Before beginning any activity, refer to page xiv to see what these symbols mean.

- **Pre-Lab**  The questions in this section check your knowledge of important concepts needed to complete the activity successfully.

- **Procedure**  The numbered steps of the procedure tell you how to carry out the activity and sometimes offer hints to help you be successful in the laboratory. Some activities have **CAUTION** statements in the procedure to alert you to hazardous substances or techniques.

- **Hypothesis**  This section provides an opportunity for you to write down a hypothesis for this activity.

- **Data and Observations**  This section presents a suggested table or form for collecting your laboratory data. Always record data and observations in an organized way as you do the activity.

- **Analyze and Conclude**  The Analyze and Conclude section shows you how to perform the calculations necessary for you to analyze your data and reach conclusions. It provides questions to aid you in interpreting data and observations in order to reach an experimental result. You are asked to form a scientific conclusion based on what you actually observed, not what "should have happened." An opportunity to analyze possible errors in the activity is also given.

- **Real-World Chemistry**  The questions in this section ask you to apply what you have learned in the activity to other real-life situations. You may be asked to make additional conclusions or research a question related to the activity.

# Writing a Laboratory Report

When scientists perform experiments, they make observations, collect and analyze data, and formulate generalizations about the data. When you work in the laboratory, you should record all your data in a laboratory report. An analysis of data is easier if all data are recorded in an organized, logical manner. Tables and graphs are often used for this purpose.

**Title:** The title should clearly describe the topic of the report.

**Hypothesis:** Write a statement to express your expectations of the results and as an answer to the problem statement.

**Materials:** List all laboratory equipment and other materials needed to perform the experiment.

**Procedure:** Describe each step of the procedure so that someone else could perform the experiment following your directions.

**Results:** Include in your report all data, tables, graphs, and sketches used to arrive at your conclusions.

**Conclusions:** Record your conclusions in a paragraph at the end of your report. Your conclusions should be an analysis of your collected data.

Read the following description of an experiment. Then answer the questions.

All plants need water, minerals, carbon dioxide, sunlight, and living space. If these needs are not met, plants cannot grow properly. A scientist wanted to test the effectiveness of different fertilizers in supplying needed minerals to plants. To test this idea, the scientist set up an experiment. Three containers were filled with equal amounts of potting soil and one healthy bean plant was planted in each of three containers. Container A was treated with Fertilizer A, Container B was treated with Fertilizer B, and Container C did not receive any fertilizer. All three containers were placed in a well-lit room. Each container received the same amount of water every day for 2 weeks. The scientist measured the heights of the growing plants every day. Then the average height of the plants in each container each day was calculated and recorded in **Data Table 1.** The scientist then plotted the data on a graph.

**1.** What was the purpose of this experiment?

_____

**2.** What materials were needed for this experiment?

_____

**3.** Write a step-by-step procedure for this experiment.

_____

_____

_____

_____

_____

_____

_____

_____

_____

_____

| Data Table 1: Average Height of Growing Plants (in mm) | | | | | | | | | | |
|---|---|---|---|---|---|---|---|---|---|---|
| Container | Day | | | | | | | | | |
| | 1 | 2 | 3 | 4 | 5 | 6 | 7 | 8 | 9 | 10 |
| A | 20 | 50 | 58 | 60 | 75 | 80 | 85 | 90 | 110 | 120 |
| B | 16 | 30 | 41 | 50 | 58 | 70 | 75 | 80 | 100 | 108 |
| C | 10 | 12 | 20 | 24 | 30 | 25 | 42 | 50 | 58 | 60 |

**4. Data Table 1** shows the data collected in this experiment. Based on this data, state a conclusion for this experiment.

_____

_____

**5.** Plot the data in **Data Table 1** on a graph. Show average height on the vertical axis and the days on the horizontal axis. Use a different colored pencil for the graph of each container.

# Laboratory Equipment

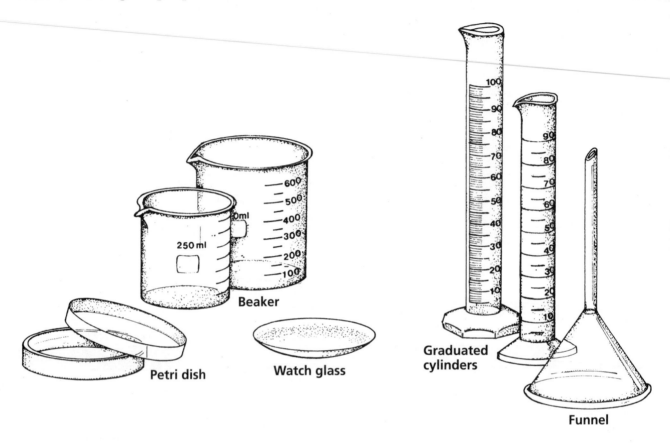

Beaker

Petri dish

Watch glass

Graduated cylinders

Funnel

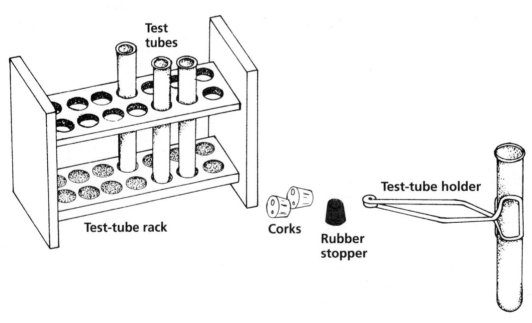

Test tubes

Test-tube rack

Corks

Rubber stopper

Test-tube holder

# Laboratory Equipment, *continued*

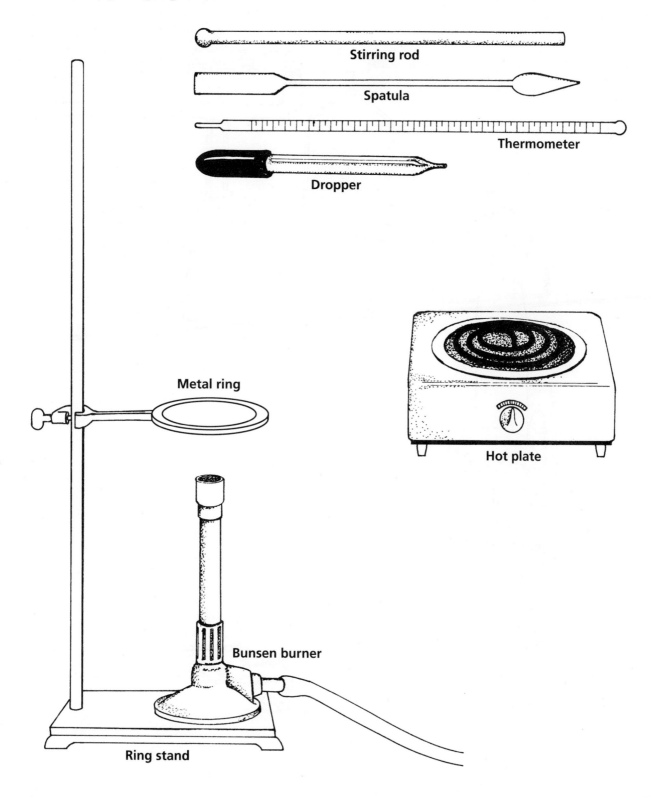

Stirring rod

Spatula

Thermometer

Dropper

Metal ring

Hot plate

Bunsen burner

Ring stand

# Laboratory Equipment, *continued*

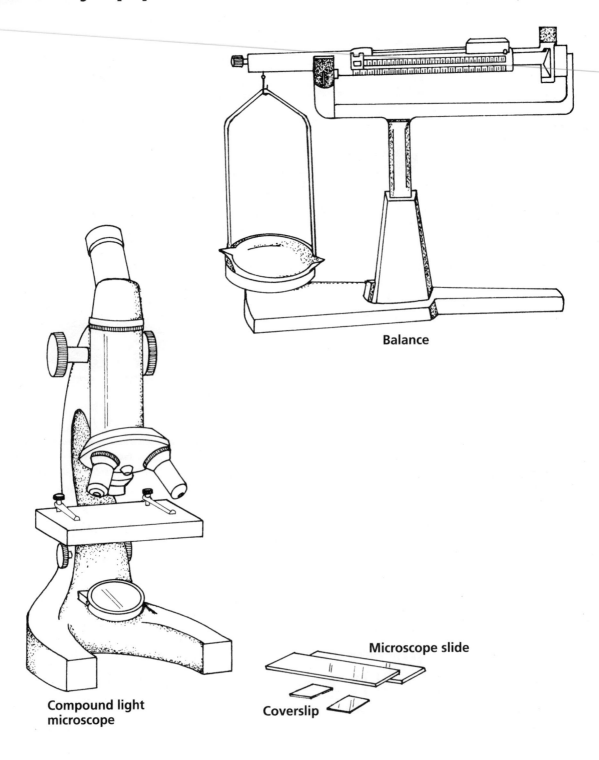

Balance

Compound light
microscope

Microscope slide

Coverslip

# Safety in the Laboratory

The chemistry laboratory is a place to experiment and learn. You must assume responsibility for your own personal safety and that of people working near you. Accidents are usually caused by carelessness, but you can help prevent them by closely following the instructions printed in this manual and those given to you by your teacher. The following are some safety rules to help guide you in protecting yourself and others from injury in a laboratory.

1. The chemistry laboratory is a place for serious work. Do not perform activities without your teacher's permission. **Never** work alone in the laboratory. Work only when your teacher is present.

2. Study your lab activity **before** you come to the lab. If you are in doubt about any procedures, ask your teacher for help.

3. Safety goggles and a laboratory apron must be worn whenever you work in the lab. Gloves should be worn whenever you use chemicals that cause irritations or can be absorbed through the skin.

4. Contact lenses should not be worn in the lab, even if goggles are worn. Lenses can absorb vapors and are difficult to remove in an emergency.

5. Long hair should be tied back to reduce the possibility of it catching fire.

6. Avoid wearing dangling jewelry or loose, draping clothing. The loose clothing may catch fire and either the clothing or jewelry could catch on chemical apparatus.

7. Wear shoes that cover the feet at all times. Bare feet or sandals are not permitted in the lab.

8. Know the location of the fire extinguisher, safety shower, eyewash, fire blanket, and first-aid kit. Know how to use the safety equipment provided for you.

9. Report any accident, injury, incorrect procedure, or damaged equipment immediately to your teacher.

10. Handle chemicals carefully. *Check the labels of all bottles* **before** *removing the contents.* Read the labels three times: before you pick up the container, when the container is in your hand, and when you put the bottle back.

11. Do **not** return unused chemicals to reagent bottles.

12. Do **not** take reagent bottles to your work area unless specifically instructed to do so. Use test tubes, paper, or beakers to obtain your chemicals.

Take only small amounts. It is easier to get more than to dispose of excess.

13. Do **not** insert droppers into reagent bottles. Pour a small amount of the chemical into a beaker.

14. **Never** taste any chemical substance. **Never** draw any chemicals into a pipette with your mouth. Eating, drinking, chewing gum, and smoking are prohibited in the laboratory.

15. If chemicals come into contact with your eyes or skin, flush the area immediately with large quantities of water. Immediately inform your teacher of the nature of the spill.

16. Keep combustible materials away from open flames. (Alcohol and acetone are combustible.)

17. Handle toxic and combustible gases only under the direction of your teacher. Use the fume hood when such materials are present.

18. When heating a substance in a test tube, be careful not to point the mouth of the tube at another person or yourself. Never look down the mouth of a test tube.

19. Use caution and the proper equipment when handling hot apparatus or glassware. Hot glass looks the same as cool glass.

20. Dispose of broken glass, unused chemicals, and products of reactions only as directed by your teacher.

21. Know the correct procedure for preparing acid solutions. *Always add the acid slowly to the water.*

22. Keep the balance area clean. Never weigh chemicals directly on the pan of the balance.

23. Do **not** heat graduated cylinders, burettes, or pipettes with a laboratory burner.

24. After completing an activity, clean and put away your equipment. Clean your work area. Make sure the gas and water are turned off. Wash your hands with soap and water before you leave the lab.

The *Chemistry: Matter and Change* program uses safety symbols to alert you and your students to possible laboratory hazards. These symbols are provided in the student text inside the front cover and are explained below. Be sure your students understand each symbol before they begin an activity that displays a symbol.

| SAFETY SYMBOLS | HAZARD | EXAMPLES | PRECAUTION | REMEDY |
|---|---|---|---|---|
| DISPOSAL | Special disposal procedures need to be followed. | certain chemicals, living organisms | Do not dispose of these materials in the sink or trash can. | Dispose of wastes as directed by your teacher. |
| BIOLOGICAL | Organisms or other biological materials that might be harmful to humans | bacteria, fungi, blood, unpreserved tissues, plant materials | Avoid skin contact with these materials. Wear mask or gloves. | Notify your teacher if you suspect contact with material. Wash hands thoroughly. |
| EXTREME TEMPERATURE | Objects that can burn skin by being too cold or too hot | boiling liquids, hot plates, dry ice, liquid nitrogen | Use proper protection when handling. | Go to your teacher for first aid. |
| SHARP OBJECT | Use of tools or glassware that can easily puncture or slice skin | razor blades, pins, scalpels, pointed tools, dissecting probes, broken glass | Practice common-sense behavior and follow guidelines for use of the tool. | Go to your teacher for first aid. |
| FUME | Possible danger to respiratory tract from fumes | ammonia, acetone, nail polish remover, heated sulfur, moth balls | Make sure there is good ventilation. Never smell fumes directly. Wear a mask. | Leave foul area and notify your teacher immediately. |
| ELECTRICAL | Possible danger from electrical shock or burn | improper grounding, liquid spills, short circuits, exposed wires | Double-check setup with teacher. Check condition of wires and apparatus. | Do not attempt to fix electrical problems. Notify your teacher immediately. |
| IRRITANT | Substances that can irritate the skin or mucus membranes of the respiratory tract | pollen, moth balls, steel wool, fiber glass, potassium permanganate | Wear dust mask and gloves. Practice extra care when handling these materials. | Go to your teacher for first aid. |
| CHEMICAL | Chemicals that can react with and destroy tissue and other materials | bleaches such as hydrogen peroxide; acids such as sulfuric acid, hydrochloric acid; bases such as ammonia, sodium hydroxide | Wear goggles, gloves, and an apron. | Immediately flush the affected area with water and notify your teacher. |
| TOXIC | Substance may be poisonous if touched, inhaled, or swallowed | mercury, many metal compounds, iodine, poinsettia plant parts | Follow your teacher's instructions. | Always wash hands thoroughly after use. Go to your teacher for first aid. |
| OPEN FLAME | Open flame may ignite flammable chemicals, loose clothing, or hair | alcohol, kerosene, potassium permanganate, hair, clothing | Tie back hair. Avoid wearing loose clothing. Avoid open flames when using flammable chemicals. Be aware of locations of fire safety equipment. | Notify your teacher immediately. Use fire safety equipment if applicable. |

**Eye Safety**
Proper eye protection should be worn at all times by anyone performing or observing science activities.

**Clothing Protection**
This symbol appears when substances could stain or burn clothing.

**Animal Safety**
This symbol appears when safety of animals and students must be ensured.

**Radioactivity**
This symbol appears when radioactive materials are used.

## LAB 1.1 LABORATORY MANUAL

# Laboratory Techniques and Lab Safety

**C**hemistry has been developed largely through experimentation. Chemistry courses use laboratory experiences to demonstrate, clarify, and develop principles of chemistry.

Behavior in the laboratory is more structured than in the classroom. Certain rules of conduct pertaining to safety and keeping a clean work environment must be followed at all times. You must also adopt correct procedures for using glassware and other pieces of equipment. General safety rules are summarized at the beginning of this lab manual. However, there often will be more specific safety rules or special procedures to follow when performing an experiment. Your teacher will provide these added instructions before you perform any lab activity. If you are unsure of any procedure, always ask your teacher before proceeding.

In this activity, you will practice some laboratory techniques and apply laboratory safety rules. You will determine the mass of different solid materials, measure the volume of a liquid, and separate mixtures of chemicals. You will also review specific safety rules.

## Problem

How can the mass of an object be measured? How can the volume of a liquid be measured? How can a mixture be separated?

## Objectives

- **Measure** the mass of solid substances.
- **Measure** a volume of water.
- **Separate** components of a mixture through filtration.

## Materials

table salt
sand
distilled water
100-mL graduated
  cylinder
250-mL beakers (2)
50-mL beakers (2)
balance
ring stand

ring
funnel
scoops (2)
stirring rod
filter paper
weighing paper
water bottle
watch glass

## Safety Precautions

- **Always wear safety goggles and a lab apron.**
- **Never eat or taste any substance used in the lab.**

## Pre-Lab

1. What is the safety rule concerning working alone in the laboratory?

2. What is the safety rule concerning the handling of excess chemicals?

3. What should you do if you spill a chemical?

4. Read the entire laboratory activity. Hypothesize what safety precautions will be needed to handle the different chemicals and lab equipment in this experiment. Record your hypothesis on page 3.

## Procedure

**Figure A**

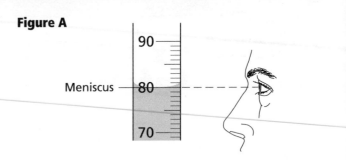

1. Using a scoop, transfer a small amount of table salt to a 50-mL beaker.

2. Measure the mass of a piece of weighing paper to 0.1 g using a laboratory balance. Record this mass in **Data Table 1.**

3. Add about 5.0 g of table salt from the 50-mL beaker to the weighing paper. Record the mass of the weighing paper and table salt to 0.1 g in **Data Table 1.**

4. Transfer the table salt to the 250-mL beaker and place all excess table salt into an appropriate waste container, as indicated by your teacher.

5. Using another scoop, transfer a small amount of sand to the second 50-mL beaker. Using the techniques described in steps 2 and 3, measure out about 5.0 g of sand. Then transfer the sand to the 250-mL beaker containing the table salt.

6. Using a 100-mL graduated cylinder, measure out 80 mL of distilled water. Measure the volume of the water to 0.1 mL by reading at the bottom of the meniscus, as illustrated in **Figure A.** Record the volume of water measured in **Data Table 1.**

7. Pour the water into the 250-mL beaker containing the table salt and sand. Using the stirring rod, gently stir the mixture for 1 minute. Record your observations in **Data Table 2.**

8. Place a clean 250-mL beaker on the base of the ring stand. Attach the ring to the ring stand and set the funnel in the ring so that the stem of the funnel is in the beaker. Adjust the height of the ring so that the bottom of the funnel stem is approximately halfway up the beaker. Fold a piece of filter paper as illustrated in **Figure B.** Place the folded filter cone in the funnel.

9. To avoid splashing and to maintain control, you will pour the liquid down a stirring rod. Place the stirring rod across the top of the 250-mL beaker that contains the mixture, as shown in **Figure B.** The stirring rod should rest in the spout and extend several inches beyond the spout. Grasp the beaker with your hand and place your index finger over the stirring rod to keep it in place. Slowly pour the contents of the beaker into the filter cone, allowing the liquid to pass through the filter paper and collect in the beaker.

10. While holding the beaker at an angle, use the water bottle to rinse the beaker and wash any remaining solid from the beaker into the filter cone. Record your observations in **Data Table 2.**

11. Allow the filter cone to drain. Then remove the filter cone and carefully unfold the filter paper. Place the filter paper on a watch glass and record your observations in **Data Table 2.**

**Figure B**

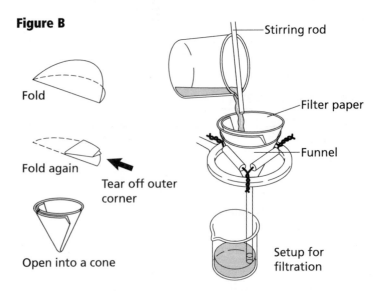

## Hypothesis

_____

_____

_____

_____

## Cleanup and Disposal

1. Place all chemicals in the appropriately labeled waste container.
2. Return all lab equipment to its proper place.
3. Clean up your work area

## Data and Observations

| Data Table 1 | |
| --- | --- |
| Mass of table salt + weighing paper (g) | |
| Mass of weighing paper (g) | |
| Mass of table salt (g) | |
| Mass of sand + weighing paper (g) | |
| Mass of weighing paper (g) | |
| Mass of sand (g) | |
| Volume of water (mL) | |

- To find the "Mass of table salt," subtract the "Mass of weighing paper" from the "Mass of table salt + weighing paper."
- To find the "Mass of sand," subtract the "Mass of weighing paper" from the "Mass of sand + weighing paper."

| Data Table 2 | |
| --- | --- |
| **Step** | **Observations** |
| Step 7 | |
| Step 10 | |
| Step 11 | |

**LAB 1.1**

## Analyze and Conclude

1. **Observing and Inferring** Why were the excess reagents not put back into the original reagent bottle?

_____

_____

2. **Comparing and Contrasting** What differences were observed between the mixture of salt and sand in the 250-mL beaker and the same materials after the water was added?

_____

_____

3. **Drawing a Conclusion** Why were the samples of table salt and sand placed into 50-mL beakers prior to weighing?

_____

_____

4. **Thinking Critically**

   **a.** If one of the pieces of glassware is dropped and breaks, why is it necessary to clean up the broken glass immediately?

   _____

   _____

   **b.** If one of the pieces of broken glass is dropped and breaks, why is it necessary to tell the teacher immediately?

   _____

   _____

5. **Thinking Critically** Why is it necessary to wear safety goggles and a lab apron while performing experiments in the lab?

_____

_____

6. **Error Analysis** What are some possible sources of error in this activity?

_____

_____

### Real-World Chemistry

**1.** Why is eating, drinking, or chewing gum not allowed in a laboratory?

**2.** Why must you always wash your hands after working in a laboratory?

**3.** Why do you never work alone in a chemical laboratory?

**LAB 2.2 LABORATORY MANUAL**

# Making a Graph

Use with
Section 2.4

**D**ifferent types of graphs may be drawn to illustrate the data measured during an experiment. The most common type of graph used in science is the line graph. A line graph shows the relationship between two sets of values. These value pairs are often collected in a lab activity and organized in a data table.

The results of an experiment are often shown on a graph that displays the data that has been collected. Graphs can make known facts easier to understand and analyze. With a line graph, it is possible to estimate values for points that fall between those actually measured. This process is called interpolation. Graphs can also be used to estimate data points beyond the measured points through a process called extrapolation.

The dependent variable is plotted on the vertical axis of a line graph, which is called the *y*-axis. The quantities displayed on this axis reflect the changes that take place or depend upon the way the experiment is performed. The independent variable is plotted on the horizontal axis of a graph, which is the *x*-axis.

In this activity, you will collect data and draw a line graph. Be certain that your graph is neat and easy to read. Use a sharp pencil to establish points and draw a fine line.

## Problem

How can data be displayed on a graph? How can this graph provide information beyond the initial data plotted?

## Objectives

- **Measure** the temperature changes that occur when a mixture of ice and water is heated to its boiling point.
- **Graph** experimental data.
- **Interpolate** data between measured quantities.

## Materials

| | |
|---|---|
| hot plate | 250-mL beaker |
| ring stand | beaker tongs |
| thermometer clamp | crushed ice |
| Celsius thermometer | graph paper |
| stirring rod | distilled water |

## Safety Precautions

- Always wear safety goggles, a lab apron, and gloves.
- Hot objects may not appear to be hot.
- Open flames may ignite hair or loose clothing.

## Pre-Lab

**1.** State the difference between a data table and a graph.

**2.** Distinguish between an independent variable and a dependent variable.

**3.** Differentiate between extrapolation and interpolation.

**4.** Read the entire laboratory activity. Form a hypothesis about the shape of your graph. Record your hypothesis on page 15.

**5.** Predict the anticipated boiling temperature of water.

## Procedure

### Part A: Gathering Data

**1.** Pack crushed ice into the beaker until the beaker is about three-fourths full of ice.

**2.** Add enough distilled water to bring the ice–water mixture up to the 200-mL line.

**3.** Stir the ice–water mixture well with the stirring rod.

**4.** Place the beaker on the hot plate, and insert the thermometer into the ice–water mixture. Clamp the thermometer to the ring stand so that the thermometer does not touch the side or bottom of the beaker.

**5.** Wait 1 minute, then measure the temperature and start the timer. Record this temperature in **Data Table 1.**

**6.** Turn on the hot plate, and begin heating the ice–water mixture. Stir the ice–water mixture continuously.

**7.** Measure and record the temperature at 1-minute intervals. When no further temperature changes occur, take five additional readings. You might not use all the available space in **Data Table 1,** or you might need to add additional rows.

**8.** In **Data Table 2,** record the temperature at which the ice is completely melted and the temperature at which the water boils.

**9.** Turn off the hot plate.

### Part B: Making the Graph

**1.** On graph paper, draw and label the axes of the graph. Label the y-axis "Temperature (°C)." Label the x-axis "Time (min)."

**2.** Establish a scale for the y-axis, beginning at −10°C and continuing to 110°C. Count the number of squares along the axis. Divide the number of squares by 12, which is the number of 10-degree units in the temperature range. If the quotient is not a whole number, round the value to the next highest integer. This integer tells you how many squares along the y-axis of the graph represent 10°C. Number the y-axis at 10-degree intervals. Be sure to number the lines, not the spaces, just to the outside of the graph.

**3.** Establish a scale for the x-axis, beginning at 0 min and continuing to the number of minutes that data was recorded. Count the number of squares along the axis. Divide the number of squares by the total number of minutes that data was collected. If the quotient is not a whole number, round the value to the next highest integer. Assign this value to each square along the x-axis of the graph. Number the x-axis at 5-minute intervals. Place the numbers outside the axis.

**4.** Plot each pair of values that are shown in the data table. Show each set of data as a point with a small circle drawn around it.

**5.** Draw a line that represents the best fit of the data. If the points do not fall in a straight line, draw a smooth curve to represent the "best fit." In cases where the points do not fall exactly on the line, attempt to have as many data entries represented above the line as below the line.

**6.** As an option, you can use a computer or a graphing calculator connected to a printer to graph the data. You can use the following instructions or use those that specifically apply to your computer program or graphing calculator.

### Part C: Computer Graphing (optional)

**1.** Enter all data onto a computer spreadsheet.

**2.** Highlight the two columns of numerical data.

**3.** Click the graph icon.

**4.** Select *X-Y* GRAPH.

**5.** Check gridlines.

**6.** Title the graph "Heating Water."

**7.** Select OK

**8.** Go to EDIT
   - Select TITLES
   - Title the X axis "Time (Min.)."
   - Title the Y axis "Celsius Temp."
   - Select OK.

**9.** Go to FORMAT
   - Select SHADING AND COLOR
   - Select color choice (if a color printer is being used). Black is the default color.

- Select SOLID as the pattern choice.
- Select HOLLOW CIRCLE as the marker choice.
- Select FORMAT.
- Select CLOSE.

**10.** Go to EDIT.

- Select COPY.
- Select PASTE.
- Paste graph into a word processing document to submit with the lab report.

**11.** As an option to step 10, go to FILE.

- Select PRINT PREVIEW.
- If graph is complete, print the document to submit with the lab report.

## Hypothesis

_____

_____

_____

_____

## Cleanup and Disposal

**1.** Be sure the heat source is turned off.

**2.** Return all lab equipment to its proper place.

**3.** Report any broken or damaged equipment.

## Data and Observations

| Time (min) | Temp. (°C) | Time (min) | Temp. (°C) | Time (min) | Temp. (°C) |
|:---:|:---:|:---:|:---:|:---:|:---:|
| **Data Table 1** | | | | | |
| 1 | | 10 | | 19 | |
| 2 | | 11 | | 20 | |
| 3 | | 12 | | 21 | |
| 4 | | 13 | | 22 | |
| 5 | | 14 | | 23 | |
| 6 | | 15 | | 24 | |
| 7 | | 16 | | 25 | |
| 8 | | 17 | | 26 | |
| 9 | | 18 | | 27 | |

| Data Table 2 | |
|:---|:---|
| **Condition** | **Temperature (°C)** |
| Ice completely melts | |
| Water boils | |

**LAB**  **2.2**

## Analyze and Conclude

1. **Using Numbers** Calculate the Celsius temperature change between the melting point of the ice and the boiling point of the water. Fahrenheit is another commonly used temperature scale. The interval between the melting point of the ice and the boiling point of the water is 180°F. How many Fahrenheit degrees are equal to one Celsius degree?

_____

2. **Observing and Inferring** Why were you instructed to wait 1 minute after inserting the thermometer into the ice water before starting to record data?

_____

_____

3. **Making a Prediction** What do you think would happen to the temperature of the water if heating at the boiling point continued for an additional 5 minutes?

_____

_____

4. **Interpreting Data** Using your graph, interpolate how much time would elapse before a temperature of 50°C would be reached.

_____

5. **Drawing Conclusion** What purpose does a graph serve?

_____

_____

6. **Making Predictions** Predict which data would change and which data would stay the same if a less intense source of heat was used.

_____

_____

7. **Error Analysis** Why might the recorded boiling temperature of water be greater or less than 100°C?

_____

_____

### Real-World Chemistry

1. Hypothesize about why the Celsius temperature scale was previously called the Centigrade scale.

2. Graphs of ongoing data, such as temperature changes in a 24-hour period, are often recorded mechanically. Describe how this process might be done automatically.

3. Explain why a line graph might not be appropriate to show the chemical composition of Earth's crust.

**LAB 3.1 LABORATORY MANUAL**

# The Density of Wood

**W**ood is prized for its physical properties, such as strength, compressibility, hardness, density, color, or grain pattern. Chemists classify physical and chemical properties as either intensive or extensive. All chemical properties are intensive, but physical properties can be either. Density is an important physical property of matter that is often used for identifying substances. By determining the density of a piece of wood, you can identify the specific sample.

## Problem

By measuring the mass and volume of blocks of wood, can the identity of the wood be determined?

## Objectives

- **Measure** the mass and volume of several blocks of wood.
- **Calculate** the density of wood from these measurements.
- **Make and use graphs** of mass versus volume to illustrate the mathematical relationship.

## Materials

wood samples of oak, white pine, balsa, and cedar
balance

metric ruler
CRC Handbook of Chemistry and Physics (optional)

## Safety Precautions

- Always wear safety goggles and a lab apron.
- Be aware of possible splintering on the wooden blocks.

## Pre-Lab

1. Compare and contrast intensive and extensive properties.

2. Give two examples each of intensive and extensive properties.

3. Read the entire laboratory activity. Form a hypothesis as to whether or not you expect the densities to be different for different sized blocks of the same type wood. Explain why or why not. Record your hypothesis on page 18.

4. Review the equations for calculating
   **a.** volume of a rectangular block.
   **b.** density from mass and volume.
   **c.** slope for a straight line.

## Procedure

1. Select a block from the materials table. Although three different blocks of the same letter (for example, A-1, A-2, A-3) will eventually be measured, choose only one sample to measure at a time.

2. Measure the blocks carefully. In the data table, record their lengths to the nearest 0.01 cm and their masses to the nearest 0.01 g. When calculating volumes and densities, apply the rules of significant figures.

3. Repeat your observations with two other block samples of the same type wood (having the same letter codes) and record the information in the data table.

## Hypothesis

_____

_____

## Cleanup and Disposal

1. Return the wood blocks to the materials table.
2. Make sure your balance is left in the same condition as you found it.

## Data and Observations

| Sample ID | Observations | Length (cm) | Height (cm) | Width (cm) | Volume (cm³) | Mass (g) | Density (g/cm³) | Average Density (g/cm³) |
|---|---|---|---|---|---|---|---|---|
| | | | | | | | | |
| | | | | | | | | |
| | | | | | | | | |

1. Calculate the densities for each of the blocks and then the average density for all three blocks.
2. Using the *CRC Handbook* or another table of densities, find the densities for each of the four woods: oak, white pine, balsa, and cedar. Record these ranges. Decide which of the woods your sample might represent. Your answer should be based on both your calculated averaged density and your qualitative observations about the sample. For example, find out if any of the wood types emit a distinct odor or are known as a light-colored or dark-colored wood.

_____

_____

3. Classify each of the following as an intensive or extensive property of the wood samples: **a.** color; **b.** smell; **c.** grain pattern of the wood; **d.** mass; **e.** volume; and **f.** density. Provide justification for your classification.

_____

_____

_____

## Analyze and Conclude

1. **Graphing Data** Make a graph of volume versus mass for each of the blocks. Be sure to label both axes with units and give your graph a title.
2. **Using Numbers** Using the three points, draw the best-fit straight line through the points. Find the slope of the line. What are the units for the slope? The value of the slope should look like another value you have previously calculated. Which one is it?

_____

_____

3. **Drawing a Conclusion** The slope of a straight line is constant. No matter where you measure the slope on the line, the slope is the same. You should find that the slope is equal to the change in mass divided by the change in volume. Use this information to explain why you think density is an intensive or extensive property.

_____

_____

_____

4. **Error Analysis** Find out from your teacher whether you correctly identified your wood samples. Compare your average density for the three samples with the density range given in the *CRC Handbook of Chemistry and Physics* or by your teacher. Calculate the percent error, if any. List at least two possible sources of error in the lab.

## Real-World Chemistry

1. In the *CRC Handbook of Chemistry and Physics*, the densities are recorded as ranges, rather than single values for the different types of wood. In terms of environmental conditions such as temperature, humidity, amount of rainfall, and disease, explain why samples of the same type of wood might vary slightly in their densities.

2. Different types of woods are generally classified as softwood if they come from conifers or hardwood if they were lumbered from deciduous trees. Look up the densities of some softwood trees, such as spruce or juniper, and compare these with hardwoods, such as elm or poplar. Explain whether or not you see a connection between the hardness of wood and its density.

3. Wood has many valuable physical properties. An important physical property of wood is toughness, a measure of strength against sudden and repeated stress. Hickory and ash are so tough that they are used for making baseball bats. Another physical property of wood is elasticity and resonance. Because spruce has high elasticity, it is a wood used in making the soundboards of pianos. Would you categorize these properties as intensive or extensive? Why?

**LAB** (3.2) **LABORATORY MANUAL**

# Properties of Water

**L**iquid water is difficult to find in the universe. Scientists have found frozen ice in places such as Mars and gaseous water vapor in atmospheres such as that on Venus. However, no one has been able to find liquid water anywhere other than on Earth. Water is the only natural substance that is found in all three states of matter (solid, liquid, and gas) at the temperatures normally found on Earth. By exploring a few of the properties of water, you will discover what makes water unique.

## Problem

What is unique about these three properties of water: boiling point, specific heat capacity, and density change over phase change?

## Objectives

- **Graph** the estimated boiling point of water.
- **Collect, graph,** and **interpret** temperature versus time data.
- **Compare** the heat capacity of sand with that of water.
- **Calculate** and **compare** the densities of liquid water and ice.

## Materials

| | |
|---|---|
| 2 beakers (400-mL) | timer or stopwatch |
| ring stand and clamp | balance |
| wire gauze | 50-mL graduated cylinder |
| Bunsen burner | graph paper |
| sand | water |
| thermometer | |

## Safety Precautions

- **Always wear safety goggles and a lab apron.**
- **Hair and loose clothing must be tied back.**
- **Hot objects will not appear to be hot. Be careful when handling the sand and water after heating.**

## Pre-Lab

1. The following is a partial list of the properties of water. Classify the properties as chemical or physical: acts as a universal solvent, has high boiling point, exhibits high specific heat capacity, has density of about 1g/mL, has a pH that is neutral, has no odor, is colorless.

2. Describe hydrogen bonding and boiling point.

3. Define the following terms: **a.** temperature; **b.** heat; and **c.** specific heat capacity.

4. Review the equation for calculating density.

5. Read the entire laboratory activity. Form a

hypothesis as to whether the density of ice will be higher or lower density than the density of water. Record your hypothesis on page 24.

## Part A: Boiling Point

## Procedure

Look at the table on the next page, which compares the boiling point of the hydrides (compounds with hydrogen in them) of the carbon (IVA) and oxygen (VA) families. Note that the boiling point of $H_2O$ is missing. Plot on a graph the boiling point temperatures of the compounds versus their molecular weights.

| The Carbon Family, Group IVA Elements | | The Oxygen Family, Group VA Elements | |
| --- | --- | --- | --- |
| Compound | Boiling point °C | Compound | Boiling point °C |
| $CH_4$ | $-164$ | $H_2O$ | Predict |
| $SiH_4$ | $-112$ | $H_2S$ | $-61$ |
| $GeH_4$ | $-90$ | $H_2Se$ | $-41$ |
| $SnH_4$ | $-52$ | $H_2Te$ | $-2$ |

## Data and Observations

From the data, predict and plot the *expected* boiling point of water.

## Analyze and Conclude

1. **Interpreting Data** From the graphed data, what is your predicted boiling point for water? How many degrees different is this from the actual boiling point of water?

_____

_____

2. **Making and Using Graphs** According to your predicted boiling point, in what state (solid, liquid, or gas) would water exist at room temperature (25°C) without hydrogen bonding?

_____

3. **Drawing Conclusions** What does this exercise tell you about the power of hydrogen bonding?

_____

## Part B: Specific Heat Capacity

## Procedure

1. In one 400-mL beaker, put 300 g of water. In another beaker, put 300 g of sand.

2. Place a thermometer in the sand and allow it to equilibrate for approximately 1 min. Record the temperature in your data table, then remove the thermometer.

3. While waiting for the temperature to equilibrate, set up an apparatus similar to the one in Figure A.

4. Light the Bunsen burner and adjust the flame so that it is medium hot with a large light blue cone.

5. Slide the burner under the sand and begin timing.

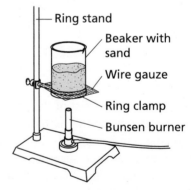

Ring stand

Beaker with sand

Wire gauze

Ring clamp

Bunsen burner

**Figure A**

6. Heat the sand for 1 min. Then, shut off the burner and immediately place the thermometer in the sand so that the bulb is in the center of the sand. Wait until the highest temperature has been reached and then record this as the "After heating 1 min" temperature in **Data Table 1.**

7. After recording the temperature, immediately start timing and recording the temperature every 30 s for a total of 120 s.

8. Set aside the beaker of sand.

9. Place the thermometer in the water and allow it to equilibrate for about 1 min.

10. Turn the Bunsen burner on, but DO NOT make any adjustments. The burner should be identical to its previous settings for the beaker of sand.

11. Slide the burner under the water and begin timing. Repeat steps 5–8 using the beaker of water.

## Cleanup and Disposal

1. Do not allow the sand to go down the drain.

2. Carefully return the warm sand to the designated container.

## Data and Observations

| Data Table 1 | | |
|---|---|---|
| | **Sand temperature (°C)** | **Water temperature (°C)** |
| Initial temperature | | |
| After heating 1 min | | |
| Turn burner off | | |
| After cooling 30 s | | |
| After cooling 60 s | | |
| After cooling 90 s | | |
| After cooling 120 s | | |

1. On a sheet of graph paper, make a graph of time versus temperature for your after cooling data. You should have four points each for sand and water. This graph is called a cooling curve. Make sure you place the independent variable on the x-axis.

2. Which substance, sand or water, required less heat to raise its temperature?

_____

3. Which substance, sand or water, lost its heat more rapidly?

_____

## Analyze and Conclude

1. **Interpreting Data** Discuss the differences in the cooling curves for sand and water. Explain their significance.

_____

_____

2. **Applying Concepts** Of all known substances, water has one of the highest heat capacities. In light of this, explain how and why water is used as a coolant in car radiators.

_____

_____

## Part C: Density
### Procedure

1. Obtain the mass of a clean, dry, 50-L graduated cylinder.
2. Pour exactly 49.0 mL of tap water in a plastic graduated cylinder.
3. In **Data Table 2,** record the mass of the cylinder and the 49.0 mL of water.
4. Place the graduated cylinder in the freezer overnight.
5. On the following day, record the mass and volume of the ice as soon as it is removed from the freezer.
6. Calculate the density for both water and ice.

## Hypothesis

_____

_____

## Cleanup and Disposal
Loosen the ice in the graduated cylinder by running hot water over the outside.

## Data and Observations

| Data Table 2 | |
| --- | --- |
| Mass of the graduated cylinder | |
| Mass of the cylinder + water | |
| Mass of water | |
| Volume of water | |
| Density of water | |
| Mass of the cylinder + ice | |
| Mass of ice | |
| Volume of ice | |
| Density of ice | |

## Analyze and Conclude

1. **Recognizing Cause and Effect** If the mass remains constant for the water and ice but the volume changes, explain how this will affect the density.

_____

_____

2. **Error Analysis** Was your hypothesis supported? Explain. What could be done to improve the precision and accuracy of your measurements?

_____

_____

### Real-World Chemistry

1. Wine grapes must be grown in temperate climates because the grapes and their vines cannot tolerate weather too hot or too cold. Usually, grapes are grown near bodies of water, such as rivers or lakes. Why do you think grapes are grown near water?

2. Moisture and changing temperatures are the major contributors to the formation of potholes. Explain how one of water's properties can deteriorate highways so viciously.

# LAB 4.1 LABORATORY MANUAL

# Simulation of Rutherford's Gold Foil Experiment

Use with Section 4.2

In 1910, Rutherford's collaborator Hans Geiger was investigating the structure of the atom by observing how a beam of alpha particles scattered after hitting a thin sheet of gold foil. Expecting little or no deflection of the alpha particles, Geiger and Rutherford were startled when some of the alpha particles were deflected at very large angles. They concluded that there must be a small region in the center of the atom, now known as the nucleus, that contains all of the atom's positive charge and most of its mass. In this lab, you will calculate the trajectory of an alpha particle ($\alpha$-particle) as it passes near a gold atom's nucleus. Using this trajectory and some of Geiger's original data, you will estimate the size of a gold atom's nucleus.

## Problem

What is the size of an atomic nucleus?

## Objectives

- **Calculate** the trajectory of an $\alpha$-particle as it passes near the nucleus of a gold atom.
- **Estimate** the size of a gold atom's nucleus using Geiger's data.

## Materials

calculator
pencil
graph paper

## Pre-Lab

1. Read about the gold foil experiment in your textbook. Describe the plum-pudding atomic model. How did the gold foil experiment show the plum-pudding model to be in error? Describe the nuclear atomic model that replaced the plum-pudding model.

2. Read the entire laboratory activity. Is it correct to say that when an $\alpha$-particle passes near a gold atom's nucleus, the angle through which it deflects depends on the $\alpha$-particle's distance from the nucleus?

## Procedure

1. Look at **Figure A.** The positions of the $\alpha$-particle and the gold atom nucleus are shown on a standard $x$-$y$ grid. The gold atom nucleus is located at the origin (0, 0). Assume that the gold atom nucleus is much more massive than the $\alpha$-particle

and that the position of the nucleus does not change. The initial position of the $\alpha$-particle is $x = -6.000 \times 10^{-13}$ m and $y = 2.000 \times 10^{-13}$ m. The $\alpha$-particle is initially traveling parallel to the $x$-axis with an $x$-velocity ($v_x$) of $1.500 \times 10^7$ m/s and a $y$-velocity ($v_y$) of zero. **Data Table 1** contains initial values for $x$, $y$, $v_x$, and $v_y$. The unknown value to be determined is the final angle ($\theta$) of the $\alpha$-particle. The value of $\theta$ will be determined by advancing the $\alpha$-particle along its path at $1.33 \times 10^{-20}$ s intervals. Plot the initial positions of the gold atom nucleus and the $\alpha$-particle on **Figure B.**

2. Calculate the distance ($r$) between the gold atom nucleus and the $\alpha$-particle by using the relationship $r = \sqrt{(x^2 + y^2)}$. Record the result in **Data Table 1.** Use a precision of at least four significant figures for all calculations in the lab.

**Figure A**

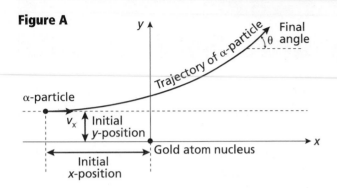

5. Calculate the next $y$-position ($y_{new}$) of the $\alpha$-particle by using the equation in step 4 and substituting $y$ for $x$ throughout.

6. Calculate the new distance between the $\alpha$-particle and the nucleus ($r_{new}$) by using the equation in step 2 and substituting $x_{new}$ and $y_{new}$ for $x$ and $y$, respectively.

7. Calculate the new $y$-velocity (new $v_y$) by adding $\Delta v_y$, calculated in step 3, to the previous value of $v_y$ found in **Data Table 1.**

8. Calculate the new $x$-velocity (new $v_x$) using the equation shown below.

$$\text{new } v_x = \sqrt{(v_\alpha^2 - v_y^2)}$$

In this equation, $v_\alpha$ is the speed of the $\alpha$-particle and has a value of $1.5 \times 10^7$ m/s. It is assumed that the $\alpha$-particle maintains a constant speed throughout its trajectory.

9. Calculate $\Delta v_y$ as done in step 3.

10. Plot the new location of the $\alpha$-particle in **Figure B.**

11. Repeat steps 4–10 until **Data Table 1** is complete.

12. Determine the final angle ($\theta$) of the $\alpha$-particle using the last two points of the $\alpha$-particle's trajectory and the equation shown below.

$$\theta = 1/\tan((y_{last} - y_{next\text{-}to\text{-}last})/(x_{last} - x_{next\text{-}to\text{-}last}))$$

3. Calculate the change in $y$-velocity ($\Delta v_y$) of the $\alpha$-particle using the equation shown below. The change in velocity is proportional to the force on the $\alpha$-particle.

$$\Delta v_y = (7.311 \times 10^{-20} \text{ m}^3/\text{s})(1/r^2)(y/r)$$

In this equation, the ($1/r^2$) term represents the electrostatic repulsion force on the $\alpha$-particle by the gold atom nucleus. The ($y/r$) term converts the total velocity change ($\Delta v$) into the $y$-component of the velocity change ($\Delta v_y$). The proportionality constant $7.311 \times 10^{-20}$ m$^3$/s accounts for the charges of the particles and the time interval used.

4. Calculate the next $x$-position ($x_{new}$) of the $\alpha$-particle using the equation shown below.

$$x_{new} = x_{old} + (v_x)(\Delta t)$$

Remember that the time step ($\Delta t$) is $1.33 \times 10^{-20}$ s. Use the initial value of $v_x$ for the $\alpha$-particle found in **Data Table 1.**

**Figure B**

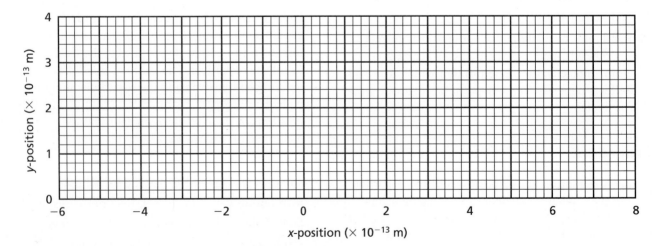

## Data and Observations

| Data Table 1 | | | | | |
|---|---|---|---|---|---|
| x-position x (m) | y-position y (m) | Distance between particles r (m) | x-velocity $v_x$ (m/s) | y-velocity $v_y$ (m/s) | Change in y-velocity $\Delta v_y$ (m/s) |
| $-6.000 \times 10^{-13}$ | $2.000 \times 10^{-13}$ | | $1.500 \times 10^7$ | 0.000 | |
| | | | | | |
| | | | | | |
| | | | | | |
| | | | | | |
| | | | | | |
| | | | | | |
| | | — | — | — | — |

| Data Table 2 | | | | | | | | | | | | |
|---|---|---|---|---|---|---|---|---|---|---|---|---|
| Initial y-position ($10^{-13}$ m) | 1.5 | 2.0 | 2.5 | 3.0 | 3.5 | 4.0 | 4.5 | 5.0 | 5.5 | 6.0 | 6.5 | 7.0 |
| θ (°) | 19.3 | 13.3 | 10.2 | 8.2 | 6.7 | 5.7 | 4.9 | 4.2 | 3.7 | 3.3 | 2.9 | 2.6 |

| Data Table 3 | | |
|---|---|---|
| Angle θ (°) | Initial y-position y ($10^{-13}$ m) | Detected α-particles per minute |
| 2.8 | | 247 |
| 5.6 | | 330 |
| 9.0 | | 316 |
| 12.4 | | 212 |
| 15.6 | | 98 |

**1.** What was the initial y-position of the α-particle? How is this position related to the y-direction distance between the α-particle and the nucleus?

_____

**2.** What value of θ did you obtain in step 12?

_____

**3. Data Table 2** shows values of θ that are obtained for initial y-position values of $1.5 \times 10^{-13}$ m to $7.0 \times 10^{-13}$ m. (You may like to perform these calculations on a spreadsheet.) Graph the initial y-position versus θ and draw a smooth curve through the data points. Label this graph **Figure C.**

4. **Data Table 3** shows the original data from the gold foil experiment performed in 1910. This data is from a scientific paper written by Hans Geiger. Use **Figure C** to estimate the initial *y*-position for each value of the θ given in Geiger's data. Record each estimate in **Data Table 3.** Plot the initial *y*-position values against the number of detected α-particles per minute given in **Data Table 3.** Label this graph **Figure D.**

## Analyze and Conclude

1. **Collecting and Interpreting Data**  Draw a smooth line through the data points in **Figure D.** Extend a straight dashed line that passes through the first two data points back until it intersects the *x*-axis. The value for initial *y*-position where the dashed line intersects the *x*-axis is an *upper bound* for the size of a gold atom nucleus. That is, the radius of a gold atom nucleus must be smaller than this value. Determine the upper bound on the radius of a gold atom nucleus from **Figure D** and record the value below.

_____

2. **Error Analysis**  Compare your experimentally determined value for the radius of a gold atom nucleus with the currently accepted radius of approximately $6 \times 10^{-15}$ m. What sources of error might account for the difference in the values?

_____

_____

_____

### Real-World Chemistry

1. A computer disk drive is composed of many layers. The primary layer is made of aluminum and is 1.0 mm thick. If the diameter of an aluminum atom is 2.5 angstroms, how many aluminum atoms thick is the primary layer?

2. If the diameter of the aluminum nucleus was $4 \times 10^{-15}$ m, how much of the 1.0 mm thickness is actually occupied by the nuclei of the Al atoms?

3. Explain what occupies the remaining space in the thickness of the computer disk primary layer.

**LAB 4.2  LABORATORY MANUAL**

# Half-life of Barium-137$^m$

**Use with
Section 4.4**

**N**uclear decay is a random process, yet it proceeds in a predictable fashion. To resolve this paradox, consider an everyday analogy. An unstable nucleus in a sample of radioactive material is like a popcorn kernel in a batch of popcorn that is being heated. When a kernel pops, it changes form. Similarly, an unstable nucleus changes form when it decays.

It is practically impossible to predict which particular kernel will pop at any given instant, and in this way the popping of corn is a random process, much like radioactive decay. However, the corn-popping process is predictable in the sense that you can say how much time it will take to prepare a batch of popcorn. Similarly, a sample of radioactive material decays within a known time period. This period is called a half-life.

The half-life of a radioactive species is defined as the time it takes for the activity of the sample to drop by 50%. In this activity, you will investigate the decay of $^{137}Ba^m$, a *metastable* isotope of barium that undergoes gamma decay with a half-life of several minutes.

## Problem
What is the half-life of $^{137}Ba^m$?

## Objectives
- **Verify** the random behavior of radioactive decay.
- **Determine** the half-life of $^{137}Ba^m$.

## Materials
gamma ray
    detector
counter or timer
sample of $^{137}Ba^m$

## Safety Precautions

- Always wear safety goggles, gloves, and a lab apron.
- Skin or clothing that comes into contact with the barium should be washed thoroughly with soap and water.
- The *depleted* sample may be washed down the sink drain.

## Pre-Lab

**1.** A nuclide that undergoes a gamma decay event emits a gamma ray. A gamma ray detector counts the rate at which gamma rays are emitted. The decay rate of a radioisotope is often expressed in counts per min (cpm). Consider $^{87}Sr^m$, a metastable isomer of strontium that undergoes gamma decay with a half-life of 2.8 hours. A particular sample of $^{87}Sr^m$ has an initial decay rate of 1280 cpm. After 2.8 hours, the rate drops 50% to 640 cpm. Complete the table on the next page.

| Decay Rate of $^{87}Sr^m$ | | | | | | |
|---|---|---|---|---|---|---|
| Time (h) | 0 | 2.8 | 5.6 | 8.4 | 11.2 | 14.0 | 16.8 |
| Decay rate (cpm) | 1280 | 640 | 320 | 160 | | | |

2. Plot a graph of decay rate versus time and draw a smooth line through the data points. This curve is an example of an exponential decay curve. Label the graph **Figure A.**

3. Read over the entire laboratory activity. Hypothesize how the activity of the $^{137}Ba^m$ sample will behave. Record your hypothesis in the next column.

## Procedure

1. Connect the detector-counter apparatus by following the directions given by your teacher. Switch the apparatus on.

2. There is always some level of ambient radioactivity in an environment. This radiation is known as background radiation. Measure and record the background activity by recording the counts registered by the gamma ray detector in 30-s intervals for 5 min. Record the data in **Data Table 1.**

3. **CAUTION: Wear gloves, a lab apron, and safety goggles.** Ask your teacher to bring a sample of $^{137}Ba^m$ to your workstation.

4. Place the sample near the detector. The precise location of the sample is not critical, provided that the detector is registering a good signal. However, the sample should not be moved once it has been placed in a satisfactory location. Record the number of counts registered by the detector in 30-s intervals in **Data Table 2** until the count rate becomes indistinguishable from the background radiation count rate recorded in step 2.

## Hypothesis

_____

_____

_____

## Cleanup and Disposal

1. Wash the depleted sample down the drain.

2. Clean up your work area.

## Data and Observations

1. Convert the background radiation readings in **Data Table 1** to a count rate in cpm by multiplying them by 2.

| Data Table 1 | | | | | | | | | |
|---|---|---|---|---|---|---|---|---|---|
| Time (s) | 0 | 30 | 60 | 90 | 120 | 150 | 180 | 210 | 240 | 300 |
| Counts | | | | | | | | | | |
| Count rate (cpm) | | | | | | | | | | |

**LAB 4.2**

**2.** Calculate the average background count rate in cpm.

_____

**3.** Convert the readings in **Data Table 2** to a count rate in cpm by multiplying them by 2. Subtract the background radiation rate obtained in step 2 from each count rate to obtain the corrected count rate.

| | | | | Data Table 2 | | | | |
|---|---|---|---|---|---|---|---|---|
| Time (min) | Counts | Count rate (cpm) | Corrected count rate (cpm) | Time (min) | Counts | Count rate (cpm) | Corrected count rate (cpm) |
| | | | | | | | |
| | | | | | | | |
| | | | | | | | |
| | | | | | | | |
| | | | | | | | |
| | | | | | | | |
| | | | | | | | |
| | | | | | | | |
| | | | | | | | |
| | | | | | | | |
| | | | | | | | |
| | | | | | | | |
| | | | | | | | |
| | | | | | | | |
| | | | | | | | |
| | | | | | | | |
| | | | | | | | |
| | | | | | | | |
| | | | | | | | |
| | | | | | | | |

## Analyze and Conclude

1. **Making and Using Graphs** Plot a graph of corrected count rate versus time using data from **Data Table 2.** Choose suitable scales for each axis. Draw a smooth curve through the plotted points. Label the graph **Figure B.**

2. **Measuring and Using Numbers** Calculate the half-life of $^{137}Ba^m$. Choose a count rate ($r$) within the range of corrected count rate values in **Data Table 2.** Use this count rate and the graph in **Figure B** to determine the time related to this rate, t($r$). Repeat this process for half the chosen count rate ($r/2$). Record all values in **Data Table 3.** Estimate the half-life of $^{137}Ba^m$ by subtracting t($r$) from t($r/2$). Repeat this procedure for several values of $r$.

| | | Data Table 3 | | |
|---|---|---|---|---|
| $r$ | t($r$) | $r/2$ | t($r/2$) | t($r/2$) − t($r$) |
| | | | | |
| | | | | |
| | | | | |
| | | | | |

3. **Measuring and Using Numbers** Calculate the average value of the half-life from your estimated values in **Data Table 3.**

_____

_____

4. **Error Analysis**

   **a.** Over what range did the background count rate fluctuate?

   _____

   **b.** Based on the range of values in **Data Table 3,** estimate the uncertainty in your determination of the half-life of $^{137}Ba^m$.

   _____

### Real-World Chemistry

**1.** Radioactive liquids are sometimes used medically to trace blood flow. Do you think the radioactive isotopes used for this purpose should have a long or a short half-life? Why?

**2.** Some waste fuel rods from the nuclear power industry contain radioactive nuclei with very long half-lives. Explain why this is a problem.

**LAB 5.1 LABORATORY MANUAL**

# The Photoelectric Effect

**Use with Section 5.2**

**E**lectric current, which is the flow of electrons, is in many ways directly analogous to the flow of water. Think of a river flowing over a waterfall. The volume of water flowing past a point in the river each second is analogous to electrical current, and the height of the waterfall is analogous to a voltage drop.

Consider the photoelectric effect in this activity in the following way. Imagine a pond being bombarded by a shower of hailstones. Above the pond is a funnel. Some of the splashes from the pond are high enough to enter the funnel, where they flow back down to the pond's surface. The hailstones are like photons, ejecting water droplets from the surface of the pond. The more energetic the hailstones are, the more energetic the splashing. The flow of water through the funnel is a current that can be measured.

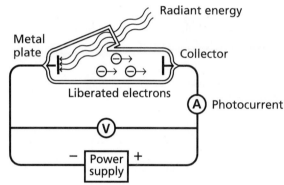

When a photon of light hits the surface of a piece of metal, it may, if there is sufficient energy, eject an electron from the metal. Such an electron is called a photoelectron, and the mechanism is known as the photoelectric effect. The diagram at the right shows a setup for measuring the photoelectric effect.

Albert Einstein's 1905 work on the photoelectric effect paved the way for one of the greatest advances of twentieth-century science, the theory of quantum mechanics. Light had always been regarded as a wave. Quantum mechanics introduced the concept of light being transmitted in wave *packets*, or photons, that have particle-like qualities as well as wave-like qualities.

The energy of a photon is now recognized as being proportional to the frequency of the photon. The constant of proportionality relating the photon's frequency and energy is known as Planck's constant. It has a value of $6.626 \times 10^{-34}$ J·s, and is denoted by the letter *h*. In this activity, you will measure the value of Planck's constant by observing the photoelectric effect.

**Problem**

What is the value of Planck's constant?

**Objectives**

- **Observe** the photoelectric effect.
- **Determine** the value of Planck's constant.

**Materials**

phototube
ammeter
voltmeter
power supply
mercury arc lamp
and power supply

set of mercury line
filters
connecting wires
graph paper
(2 sheets)

**LAB 5.1**

## Safety Precautions

- Always wear safety goggles and an apron.
- Do not touch the mercury lamp as it may become hot.
- Use caution when handling the mercury lamp. Mercury is toxic.

## Pre-Lab

1. Describe what happens when a photon of light, with sufficient energy, hits a metal plate.

2. Define *photoelectron*.

3. Explain what is meant by photoelectric effect.

4. Explain the quantum mechanical concept of light.

5. Read the entire laboratory activity. Form a hypothesis about how a photon's frequency and energy are related and may be used to calculate Planck's constant. Record your hypothesis in the next column.

## Procedure

1. Referring to **Figure A,** assemble the laboratory equipment. Have your teacher check that the apparatus is set up correctly before switching on the power.

2. Plug in the mercury lamp and allow it to warm up for 10 minutes before taking data.

3. Set the ammeter on the least sensitive scale.

4. Place the 404.7-nm filter over the phototube entrance. Position the mercury lamp so that it illuminates the phototube through the filter. The ammeter should register a current.

5. Adjust the voltage of the power supply until the ammeter shows zero current. Record this voltage as the last entry in **Data Table 1** for 404.7 nm.

6. Reduce the voltage of the power supply until the current nears the maximum value (for the given range) on the ammeter. Record the voltage and current as the first entry in **Data Table 1** for 404.7 nm.

7. Note the range in voltage values between step 5 and step 6 and divide the difference by five.

**Figure A**

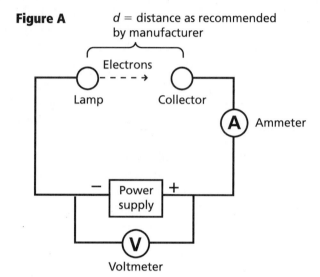

8. Increase the voltage of the power supply by the calculated value from step 7. Record the new voltage and current readings in **Data Table 1.**

9. Repeat step 8 three more times.

10. Repeat steps 4 through 9 for each of the other filters: 435.6 nm, 546.1 nm, 577.0 nm, and 690.7 nm.

## Hypothesis

_____

_____

_____

_____

## Cleanup and Disposal

1. Return all lab equipment to its proper place.

2. Clean up your workstation.

Name _____ Date _____ Class _____

## Data and Observations

| Data Table 1 | | | | | | | | | |
|---|---|---|---|---|---|---|---|---|---|
| 404.7 nm | | 435.6 nm | | 546.1 nm | | 577.0 nm | | 690.7 nm | |
| Voltage (V) | Current (A) | Voltage (V) | Current (A) | Voltage (V) | Current (A) | Voltage (V) | Current (A) | Voltage (V) | Current (A) |
| | | | | | | | | | |
| | | | | | | | | | |
| | | | | | | | | | |
| | | | | | | | | | |
| | 0 | | 0 | | 0 | | 0 | | 0 |

**1.** For each of the filters, plot voltage (V) versus current (A) on a graph. The data for each filter should describe two regions, an initial falling of current with increasing voltage and a final region where the current is zero whatever the voltage. Draw a smooth curve through the data points for each filter. Record the voltage at which the current falls to zero as the stopping voltage in **Data Table 2.**

| Data Table 2 | | | |
|---|---|---|---|
| Wavelength (nm) | Frequency (Hz) | Stopping voltage (V) | Energy (J) |
| 404.7 nm | | | |
| 435.6 nm | | | |
| 546.1 nm | | | |
| 577.0 nm | | | |
| 690.7 nm | | | |

**2.** Calculate the frequency of each wavelength of light given in **Data Table 2.** Recall that $v = c/\lambda$, that $c = 3 \times 10^8$ ms$^{-1}$, and that a nanometer is $10^{-9}$ m.

**3.** Calculate the energy corresponding to each frequency in **Data Table 2** by multiplying each stopping voltage by the charge of an electron, e. Recall that the charge of an electron is $1.6 \times 10^{-19}$ coulombs. Because a volt is equivalent to a joule of energy per coulomb of charge, the product eV has units of joules.

**4.** Plot frequency (Hz) versus energy (J) on graph paper for the values in **Data Table 2.** Draw a best-fit straight line through the data points. Make sure that the range of the energy axis reaches a sufficiently negative value to allow the best-fit line to intercept the energy axis. A preliminary sketch may be helpful for this.

**5.** Find the slope and y-intercept of the best-fit line on the frequency versus energy graph. To calculate the slope, choose two points $(v_1, E_1)$ and $(v_2, E_2)$ that are well separated on the best-fit line and use the following equation.

$$\text{slope} = (E_2 - E_1)/(v_2 - v_1)$$

The value of the intercept is the value of the best-fit line where it crosses the vertical energy axis at $v = 0$.

## Analyze and Conclude

1. **Measuring and Using Numbers**  The slope calculated in step 5 on page 35 is an estimate of Planck's constant ($h$), one of the fundamental constants of nature. Recalling that one hertz is one cycle per second, or 1/s, the slope has units of J $\times$ s. Record your experimentally determined value of Planck's constant below and compare it to the accepted value of $6.626 \times 10^{-34}$ J·s.

_____

_____

2. **Measuring and Using Numbers**  Multiply the $y$-intercept by $-1$. This is your estimate for the *work function* $\Phi$ of the metal from which the emitter in the phototube is made. It is the energy required for an electron to escape the surface of the metal. Record your value for the work function below. If the documentation for the phototube used in the lab is available, compare your value for the work function to the value given in the documentation.

_____

_____

3. **Thinking Critically**  The form of your second graph is completely determined by two values: the work function $\Phi$, which is a property of the emitter material, and Planck's constant $h$, which is a fundamental constant of nature. The graph would look precisely the same if the lamp had been twice as bright. Explain why this observation leads to the conclusion that light has a particle-like aspect.

_____

_____

_____

_____

4. **Error Analysis**  What was the percent error in your value of Planck's constant? List possible sources of error from the experiment.

_____

_____

**Real-World Chemistry**

Which are more energetic, photons of blue light or red light? Explain.

# Electron Charge to Mass Ratio

**Use with Section 5.3**

**T**he charge and mass of an electron are often denoted by the letters e and m, respectively. In 1897, J. J. Thomson calculated the e/m ratio for an electron, and for this he was awarded a Nobel prize in 1905. In this activity, you will follow in Thomson's footsteps and determine the charge to mass ratio of an electron.

In an electromagnetic tube, electrons are produced by a hot filament. Electrons are emitted from the surface of the filament in a process known as thermionic emission. As shown in **Figure A,** the filament is surrounded by a small, can-shaped enclosure with a high voltage applied to it. Emitted filament electrons accelerate towards the can. Electrons passing through the slit escape at high speed and produce an electron beam. This setup is often called an electron gun.

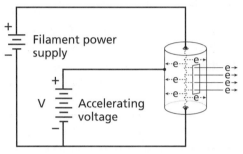

**Figure A**

Normally an electron beam is invisible to the human eye. However, when the electromagnetic tube contains a low-pressure gas that ionizes upon collision with an electron (emitting light when the ion recombines), the path of the electron beam can be seen.

Large coils, known as Helmholtz coils, are mounted around the electromagnetic tube and produce a uniform magnetic field throughout the tube. As the electron beam moves through this magnetic field, it is forced into a circular path. The radius of the circle depends on the speed of the electrons, the strength of the magnetic field, and the mass and charge of the electrons.

The velocity, v, of an electron with mass, m, that has been accelerated by a voltage, V, is given by the following equation.

$$1/2mv^2 = eV$$

The radius of the circular path of an electron with velocity v in a magnetic field of strength B is given by the following equation.

$$mv^2/r = Bev$$

Eliminating v in the two equations, and solving for (e/m) yields the following.

$$(e/m) = 2V/(B^2r^2)$$

This is called the e/m ratio equation. On the right hand side, V is the voltage of the electron gun, which is known, and r is the radius of the circular path of the electron beam, which is measurable. Thus, if B (the strength of the magnetic field) is known, e/m can be calculated. Fortunately, the magnetic field due to a pair of Helmholtz coils is known. In fact, the magnetic field B, in Teslas, is proportional to the current I, in amps, going through the coils.

$$B = kI$$

Here, k is a constant that depends on the particular coils being used. For a coil of radius R and N number of turns in each coil, k is given by the following equation.

$$k = (9.0 \times 10^{-7})(N/R)$$

**LAB 5.2**

### Problem

What is the charge to mass ratio (e/m ratio) of an electron?

### Objective

**Determine** the ratio of charge $e$ to mass $m$ for an electron.

### Materials

electromagnetic tube and power supply
Helmholtz coils and power supply
ammeter
voltmeter
connecting leads

## Safety Precautions

- Always wear safety goggles and a lab apron.
- Hot objects may not appear to be hot.

## Pre-Lab

1. What is the equation for the charge to mass ratio (e/m) in terms of the voltage ($V$), current ($I$), constant (k), electron travel radius ($r$), coil radius ($R$), and number of coil turns ($N$)? Use this equation and the fact that the e/m ratio will be a constant to answer questions 2–4.

2. If the voltage ($V$) of the electron gun is increased, will the radius of the electron beam increase, decrease, or remain unchanged?

3. If the number of turns in the Helmholtz coil ($R$) is doubled, how will the radius of the electron beam ($r$) change?

4. If the current through the Helmholtz coil ($I$) is increased, will the radius of the electron beam increase, decrease, or remain unchanged?

## Procedure

1. Measure the diameter of one of the Helmholtz coils. Divide the diameter by 2 to get the radius. Record the radius ($R$), in meters, in **Data Table 1.** The number of turns $N$ should be written on the coil. Record $N$ in **Data Table 1.** Calculate the constant k using the equation given in the introduction, and record the value in **Data Table 1.**

2. Assemble the electromagnetic tube apparatus. **Figure A** provides a sketch of the general setup, but details vary depending on the particular hardware being used. Your teacher will provide specific details. Do not switch the apparatus on.

3. Assemble the Helmholtz coils apparatus around the electromagnetic tube. The entire arrangement is shown in **Figure B.** Ask your teacher to inspect

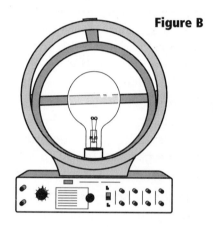

**Figure B**

your experimental arrangement before switching the apparatus on.

4. Adjust the filament current and voltage to their recommended values (as provided by your teacher) and allow the filament to warm up for several minutes. When the electron beam is strong and steady, darken the room.

5. Set the accelerating potential ($V$) to about 70 volts. Some models of electromagnetic tubes may use different operating values than those given here, but the principle of the procedure will be the same. Adjust the current in the Helmholtz coils such that the electron beam turns in a circle of radius 0.04 m (4 cm). Different Helmholtz coils are optimized to produce different size circles. Choose a radius suitable for your equipment. Methods for setting the radius of the electron beam vary depending on the equipment. Refer to your teacher for information. Record the accelerating voltage, Helmholtz current, and electron beam radius in **Data Table 2.**

**6.** Repeat step 5 for accelerating voltages at 5-volt intervals up to 100 V. Keep the electron beam circle radius fixed and adjust the coil current accordingly.

## Cleanup and Disposal

**1.** Return all lab equipment to its proper place.

**2.** Clean up your workstation.

## Data and Observations

| Data Table 1 | | |
|---|---|---|
| *R* Radius of Helmholtz coil (m) | *N* Number of turns in coil | k |
| | | |

| Data Table 2 | | |
|---|---|---|
| *V* Accelerating voltage (*V*) | *I* Current in Helmholtz coils (A) | *r* Radius of electron beam path (m) |
| | | |
| | | |
| | | |
| | | |
| | | |
| | | |
| | | |
| | | |
| | | |

## Analyze and Conclude

**1. Measuring and Using Numbers** Enter the accelerating voltage values from **Data Table 2** into **Data Table 3.** Using the values for the radius of the electron beam path (*r*) from **Data Table 2,** calculate the corresponding $r^2$ values and enter them into **Data Table 3.**

**2. Measuring and Using Numbers** Using the values for the current in Helmholtz coils (*I*) from **Data Table 2,** the value for k from **Data Table 1,** and the equation $B = kI$, calculate the values for magnetic field strength (*B*) and enter them in **Data Table 3.** Then calculate the square of the field strength ($B^2$) and enter the values in **Data Table 3.**

**3. Measuring and Using Numbers** Using the values in **Data Table 3** and the equation $e/m = 2V/(B^2 r^2)$, calculate the e/m ratios needed to complete **Data Table 3.**

| Data Table 3 | | | | |
|---|---|---|---|---|
| *V*<br>**Accelerating voltage**<br>**(V)** | *B*<br>**Magnetic field**<br>**strength (Tesla)** | *B²*<br>**Square of magnetic**<br>**field strength (Tesla²)** | *r²*<br>**Square of electron**<br>**beam path radius (m²)** | **e/m ratio**<br>**(c/kg)** |
|  |  |  |  |  |
|  |  |  |  |  |
|  |  |  |  |  |
|  |  |  |  |  |
|  |  |  |  |  |
|  |  |  |  |  |
|  |  |  |  |  |
|  |  |  |  |  |
|  |  |  |  |  |

4. **Measuring and Using Numbers** Calculate the average value of the e/m ratio from the results in **Data Table 3.** Note that the units of the e/m ratio are Coulombs per kilogram (C/kg).

_____

5. **Thinking Critically** Compare the e/m ratio value you obtained with the accepted value of $1.76 \times 10^{11}$ C/kg. Account for any differences between the two values.

_____

_____

6. **Error Analysis** Use the variation in the e/m ratio values in **Data Table 3** to estimate the *statistical* uncertainty associated with your average value for the e/m ratio.

_____

_____

**Real-World Chemistry**

1. Another name for a beam of electrons is a cathode ray. Cathode ray tubes, or CRT for short, are used extensively in video monitors and televisions. The electrons are ejected from the electron gun and directed at a screen coated with substances that glow different colors when struck with the electrons. The electron beam must strike different regions of the screen at different times and frequencies to create a clear image. With the experience gained in this lab, what force do you think is used to deflect the beam of electrons?

2. The electron gun used in a CRT is located centered behind the screen. The beam is precisely deflected to reach specific spots on the screen. Why are large-screen CRT displays longer (deeper) than small-screen CRT displays?

# LAB 6.1 LABORATORY MANUAL

# Properties of the Periodic Table

**Use with Section 6.3**

**T**he periodic table organizes a remarkable amount of information about the chemical and physical properties of the elements. The information is organized in such a manner that trends in properties and important relationships can be readily identified. In this activity, you will identify several elements based on their properties and the properties of the surrounding elements in the periodic table.

## Problem

What relationships and trends exist in the periodic table?

## Objectives

- **Construct** a simplified version of the periodic table.
- **Identify** trends and relationships among elements in the same group.
- **Identify** trends and relationships among elements in the same period.
- **Draw conclusions** about the predictability of chemical properties of the elements.

## Materials

index cards (18)
outline of the periodic table showing chemical symbols only

## Pre-Lab

1. Which property—the atomic mass or atomic number—uniquely identifies a chemical element? Explain how the property uniquely identifies each atom.

2. Describe the general characteristics of metals, nonmetals, and metalloids.

3. Read over the entire laboratory activity. Develop a hypothesis about which properties are the most useful for identifying the group to which an unknown element belongs. Develop a hypothesis about which properties are the most useful for determining the sequence of the elements within a group. Develop a hypothesis about which properties are the most useful for identifying the period to which an element belongs. Record all of your hypotheses on page 43.

## Procedure

1. For each unknown element listed in **Data Table 1,** copy its chemical and physical properties onto separate index cards. Be sure to record the letter of the unknown element on each index card. The following abbreviations are used in **Data Table 1:** IP = ionization potential, BP = boiling point, MP = melting point.

2. Begin by grouping cards that have common chemical properties. You should have eight groups.

3. Within each group of cards, arrange the cards into a column based on their physical properties.

4. Arrange the groups from left to right, based on trends in physical and chemical properties.

5. Based on the arrangement of the cards from step 4, record the letter of each index card in its corresponding location in **Data Table 2.**

| **Unknown element** | **Physical properties** | **Chemical properties** |
|---|---|---|
| A | colorless monatomic gas; density less than atmosphere; IP = 24.6 eV; BP = −272°C; MP = −269°C | not reactive |
| B | colorless monatomic gas; density similar to that of the atmosphere; IP = 21.6 eV; BP = −249°C; MP = −246°C | not reactive |
| C | colorless monatomic gas; density greater than that of the atmosphere; IP = 15.8 eV; MP = −189°C; BP = −186°C | not reactive |
| D | IP = 10.5 eV; MP = 44°C; BP = 280°C | forms many different oxides |
| E | conducts electricity and heat in its brittle, black, solid form; not conductive in its very hard, crystalline form; IP = 11.3 eV; MP = 3652°C | reacts with oxygen to form monoxides and dioxides, forms tetrahalides |
| F | pale yellow diatomic gas; IP = 17.4 eV; MP = −220°C; BP = −188°C | forms binary compounds with most metals and all semiconductors |
| G | colorless diatomic gas; density less than that of the atmosphere; IP = 13.6 eV; MP = −259°C; BP = −253°C | reacts violently with oxygen |
| H | greenish colored diatomic gas; IP = 13.0 eV; MP = −101°C; BP = −35°C | forms binary compounds with most metals and all semiconductors |
| I | colorless diatomic gas; not attracted to magnet in its liquid or solid form; similar in density to the atmosphere; IP = 14.5 eV; MP = −210°C; BP = −196°C | causes glowing splint to go out, forms many different oxides |
| J | IP = 9.3 eV; MP = 1278°C; BP = 2970°C | forms a monoxide when reacted with oxygen |
| K | IP = 6.0 eV; MP = 660°C; BP = 2467°C | forms trihalides |
| L | yellow solid; poor conductor of heat and electricity; IP = 10.4 eV; MP = 113°C; BP = 445°C | reacts with oxygen, forms a dihydrogen compound |
| M | colorless gas; attracted to a magnet in its liquid and solid form; density similar to that of the atmosphere; IP = 13.6 eV; MP = −218°C; BP = −183°C | causes glowing splint to burst into flame, causes glowing steel wool to burst into flame, forms an orange compound when reacted with iron, forms a dihydrogen compound |
| N | IP = 8.2 eV; MP = 1410°C; BP = 2355°C; semiconductor | forms tetrahalides, forms dioxides |
| O | metallic finish; malleable; conducts electricity; conducts heat; IP = 7.7 eV; MP = 650°C; BP = 1090°C | burns brightly in presence of oxygen to form a white powder, reacts with acid to form hydrogen gas, forms a monoxide when burned with oxygen |
| P | metallic finish; malleable; IP = 5.1 eV; MP = 98°C; BP = 883°C | reacts quickly with the atmosphere, readily forms ions in water |
| Q | metallic finish; malleable; IP = 5.4 eV; MP = 181°C; BP = 1342°C | reacts quickly with the atmosphere, readily forms ions in water |
| R | IP = 8.3 eV; MP = 2079°C; BP = 2550°C; semiconductor | forms trihalides |

**Data Table 1**

**LAB 6.1**

## Hypothesis

_____

_____

## Data and Observations

| Data Table 2 | | | | | | | |
|------|------|------|------|------|------|------|------|
| 1A | 2A | 3A | 4A | 5A | 6A | 7A | 8A |
|  |  |  |  |  |  |  |  |
|  |  |  |  |  |  |  |  |
|  |  |  |  |  |  |  |  |
|  |  |  |  |  |  |  |  |
|  |  |  |  |  |  |  |  |

## Analyze and Conclude

**1.** Write a description of the properties used to classify elements into each group.

_____

_____

_____

**2. Analyzing Information** Which properties tend to increase as you move down through a group? Which decrease?

_____

_____

**3. Analyzing Information** Are there any groups that are an exception to the group trends identified in question 2? Describe possible reasons for these exceptions.

_____

_____

_____

**4. Thinking Critically** What other element properties would be helpful in creating a periodic table?

_____

_____

5. **Drawing a Conclusion** Summarize what you have learned about the organization of the periodic table. How accurate were your hypotheses?

_____

_____

_____

6. **Error Analysis** Using an element identity key provided by your teacher, convert the unknown element letters (A through R) used in **Data Table 2** to their actual chemical symbols. List your arrangement of the actual chemical identities in **Data Table 3.** Compare the arrangement of elements in **Data Table 3** with an actual periodic table. How accurately does your periodic table match the actual periodic table? Complete **Data Table 4.**

| Data Table 3 | | | | | | | |
|---|---|---|---|---|---|---|---|
| 1A | 2A | 3A | 4A | 5A | 6A | 7A | 8A |
|  |  |  |  |  |  |  |  |
|  |  |  |  |  |  |  |  |
|  |  |  |  |  |  |  |  |
|  |  |  |  |  |  |  |  |
|  |  |  |  |  |  |  |  |

| Data Table 4 | |
|---|---|
| Number of elements in correct group |  |
| Number of elements in incorrect group |  |
| Percentage of elements in correct groups (Divide the number of elements in correct group by 18 and multiply by 100.) |  |
| Number of elements in correct position |  |
| Number of elements in incorrect position |  |
| Percentage of elements in correct position (Divide the number of elements in correct position by 18 and multiply by 100.) |  |

## Real-World Chemistry

1. Using chemical separation processes can require significant amounts of energy. What makes aluminum so ideal for recycling?

2. Oxygen is a vital element for many processes. The space shuttle, for example, relies on engines powered by liquid oxygen to reach an orbit around Earth. The atmosphere contains oxygen ($O_2$), nitrogen ($N_2$), and many other gases. Can elemental oxygen be extracted from the atmosphere using processes that rely on physical properties only? Describe how the differing boiling points of oxygen and nitrogen can be used to help separate the two gases.

**LAB 6.2 LABORATORY MANUAL**

# Periodic Trends in the Periodic Table

Use with
Section 6.3

The periodic table organizes elements into related groups. Within these groups, trends in common properties occur. These trends may be used to predict unknown property values for other elements in the same group. In this activity, you will predict properties of elements in the periodic table based on periodic trends.

**Problem**

How accurately can properties be predicted using trend information in the periodic table?

**Objectives**

- **Identify** trends among elements in the same group
- **Draw conclusions** about the accuracy of predicting chemical properties using group trends.

**Materials**

20 index cards, each with property information for one of the first 20 elements. The property information, at a minimum, should include melting point, ionization energy, and electronegativity.

Reference material with experimental values for melting point, ionization energy, and electronegativity for elements 31–36.

---

**Pre-Lab**

1. What periodic trends exist for ionization energy?

2. What periodic trends exist for electronegativity?

3. Read over the entire laboratory activity. Hypothesize which method you expect to be the best in confirming the known properties of Ca and K. The worst? Hypothesize which method you expect to be the best in predicting the properties of elements 31–36. Record your hypothesis on page 46.

**Procedure**

1. Arrange the index cards for the elements in each group in order of increasing period.

2. Predict the properties of K and Ca using Method 1. Record your results in **Data Table 1**.

3. Predict the properties of K and Ca using Method 2. Record your results in **Data Table 2**.

4. Using a suitable reference, such as your textbook, record the known values for K and Ca in **Data Table 3**. Also record the predicted values for K and Ca from **Data Table 1** and **Data Table 2** in **Data Table 3**. Compare the accuracy of Method 1 and Method 2 for predicting the properties of K and Ca. Identify the best method to use for predicting each property.

5. Use the best predictive method (1 or 2) for each property to predict the properties of elements 31–36 in groups 3A–7A. Record the predicted values in **Data Table 4**.

6. Using a suitable reference, such as your textbook, locate the known value for the indicated property and record it in **Data Table 4**.

**Method 1: Using element row in the periodic table**

Complete the following steps using elements in the same group as potassium. The term *property value* refers to the melting point, ionization energy, or electronegativity of the element. Record your results in **Data Table 1**.

1a. Scale the value of the property of the element in row 3 of the periodic table by multiplying the value by 1.35.

1b. Scale the value of the property of the element in row 2 of the periodic table by multiplying the value by 0.35.

1c. Predict the value of the property of the element in row 4 by subtracting the scaled value of the element in row 2 from the scaled value of the element in row 3. (1c = 1a − 1b) (This is the predicted property value using the atomic mass proportions method.)

**1d.** Repeat steps 1a through 1e until you have predicted values for the melting point, ionization energy, and electronegativity.

**1e.** Repeat steps 1a through 1f using elements in the same group as calcium.

### Method 2: Using atomic number proportions

Complete the following steps using elements in the same group as potassium. The term *property value* refers to the melting point, ionization energy, or electronegativity of the element. Record your results in **Data Table 2.**

**2a.** Subtract the atomic number of the element in period 2 from the element in period 3.

**2b.** Subtract the property value of the element in period 2 from the element in period 3

**2c.** Subtract the atomic number of the element in period 3 from the element in period 4.

**2d.** Multiply the value found in step 2b by the value in step 2c and divide by the value in step 2a.

**2e.** Add the value derived in step 2d to the property value of the element in period 3. (This is the predicted property value using the atomic number method.)

**2f.** Repeat steps 2a through 2e until you have predicted values for the melting point, ionization energy, and electronegativity.

**2g.** Repeat steps 2a through 2f using elements in the same group as calcium.

## Hypothesis

_____

_____

_____

## Data and Observations

| Data Table 1 (Method 1) | | | | | | |
|---|---|---|---|---|---|---|
| | Melting point | Ionization energy | Electro-negativity | Melting point | Ionization energy | Electro-negativity |
| | Potassium (K) | | | Calcium (Ca) | | |
| **1a.** property value$_{period\ 3\ element}$ × 1.35 | | | | | | |
| **1b.** property value$_{period\ 2\ element}$ × 0.35 | | | | | | |
| **1c.** predicted property value = property value$_{step\ 1a}$ − property value$_{step\ 1b}$ | | | | | | |

| Data Table 2 (Method 2) | | | | | | |
|---|---|---|---|---|---|---|
| | Melting point | Ionization energy | Electro-negativity | Melting point | Ionization energy | Electro-negativity |
| | Potassium (K) | | | Calcium (Ca) | | |
| **2a.** atomic number$_{period\ 3\ element}$ − atomic number$_{period\ 2\ element}$ | | | | | | |
| **2b.** property value$_{period\ 3\ element}$ − property value$_{period\ 2\ element}$ | | | | | | |
| **2c.** atomic number$_{period\ 4\ element}$ − atomic number$_{period\ 3\ element}$ | | | | | | |
| **2d.** (value$_{step\ 2b}$ × value$_{step\ 2c}$)/value$_{step\ 2a}$ | | | | | | |
| **2e.** predicted property value = property value$_{period\ 3\ element}$ + value$_{step\ 2d}$ | | | | | | |

**LAB 6.2**                                                      LABORATORY MANUAL

| Data Table 3: Identifying the Best Method for Each Property | | | | | | |
|---|---|---|---|---|---|---|
| | Melting point (°C) | | Ionization energy (kcal/mol) | | Electronegativity | |
| | K | Ca | K | Ca | K | Ca |
| Method 1 value | | | | | | |
| Method 2 value | | | | | | |
| Known value | | | | | | |
| Best method | | | | | | |

| Data Table 4: Predicting Property Values for Period 4 Group 3A–7A Elements | | | | |
|---|---|---|---|---|
| Atomic number | Property | Best method used | Calculated value | Known value |
| 31 | Ionization energy | | | |
| | Electronegativity | | | |
| | Melting point | | | |
| 32 | Ionization energy | | | |
| | Electronegativity | | | |
| | Melting point | | | |
| 33 | Ionization energy | | | |
| | Electronegativity | | | |
| | Melting point | | | |
| 34 | Ionization energy | | | |
| | Electronegativity | | | |
| | Melting point | | | |
| 35 | Ionization energy | | | |
| | Electronegativity | | | |
| | Melting point | | | |
| 36 | Ionization energy | | | |
| | Electronegativity | | | |
| | Melting point | | | |

**LAB 6.2**                                                    **LABORATORY MANUAL**

## Analyze and Conclude

1. **Comparing and Contrasting** Which method is best for predicting melting point for groups 1 and 2?

_____

2. **Comparing and Contrasting** Which method appears to be best for predicting ionization potential for groups 1 and 2?

_____

3. **Comparing and Contrasting** Which method appears to be best for predicting electronegativity for groups 1 and 2?

_____

4. **Thinking Critically** What may be the cause of the inaccuracies observed?

_____

_____

5. **Thinking Critically** After completing the predictions for elements 31 through 36, which method do you believe is better over multiple groups? Explain.

_____

_____

_____

6. **Thinking Critically** Do you think simple models can be used to accurately predict unknown element properties?

_____

7. **Error Analysis** In the Pre-Lab hypothesis, did you select the best method for predicting the properties of Ca and K? Did you select the best method for predicting the properties of elements 31 to 36? Did a single method work best for all cases?

_____

_____

_____

**Real-World Chemistry**

1. In 1960, there were 102 known elements in the periodic table. Since 1960, a significant amount of nuclear research has been done. As of 1997, there were 112 elements in the periodic table. What do you suspect caused the increase in the number of elements?

2. What unique property of elements 103 and greater would be most useful in placing them in the correct position in the periodic table?

**LAB** **7.1** **LABORATORY MANUAL**

# Is there potassium in coffee?

Use with
Section 7.3

Potassium is a chemically active element in Group 1 of the periodic table, an alkali metal. Potassium reacts easily with oxygen and with water, producing the flammable gas oxygen. Because air contains both oxygen and water vapor, potassium is stored under an oily liquid such as kerosene, which does not react with potassium. Potassium is essential for the growth and maintenance of organisms. Potassium compounds are one of the three main ingredients in fertilizers, along with compounds containing nitrogen and phosphorus. Potassium compounds are used in photography and in medicine. Matches and fireworks also contain potassium compounds.

When a test confirms the presence of a substance without determining the amount of substance present, the process is called qualitative analysis. In this activity, you will detect the presence of potassium in coffee by the characteristic yellow color that appears when potassium ions react with sodium hexanitrocobaltate. To make it easier to detect the yellow color, the coffee solution will be decolorized with charcoal, an allotropic form of solid carbon.

## Problem

Can the presence of potassium in coffee be confirmed with a chemical test?

## Objective

**Detect** the presence of potassium in coffee.

## Materials

coffee
decolorizing
  charcoal
dry charcoal
nitric acid ($HNO_3$)
potassium nitrate
  ($KNO_3$)
sodium hexanitro-
  cobaltate
  ($Na_3CO_3(NO_2)_6$)
250-mL beaker
10-mL graduated
  cylinder
test tubes (4)

funnel
Bunsen burner
balance
solid stopper to fit
  test tube
test-tube rack
test-tube clamp
labels or grease
  pencil
weighing paper
filter paper
striker or matches
stirring rods (3)

## Safety Precautions

- Always wear safety goggles, a lab apron, and gloves.
- Dispose of chemical wastes as directed by your teacher.
- Broken glassware can easily puncture skin.
- Nitric acid is toxic and corrosive to skin.
- Potassium nitrate should not come into contact with skin.
- Sodium hexanitrocobaltate is an irritant, slightly toxic, and a possible sensitizer.
- Open flames might ignite hair or loose clothing.

## Pre-Lab

1. State three uses of potassium.
2. Describe the function of carbon in this activity.
3. What is the significance of the test tube containing distilled water?
4. Read the entire laboratory activity. Form a hypothesis about why coffee is likely to contain potassium. Record your hypothesis in the next column.

## Procedure

1. Label three test tubes *1, 2,* and *3*. Place all four test tubes in a test-tube rack.
2. Place about 8 mL of coffee in the unlabeled test tube and add 0.2 g of decolorizing charcoal to the coffee. Put a stopper in the test tube and shake its contents for 2 min.
3. Use a dry 10-mL graduated cylinder to measure about 6 mL of dry charcoal.
4. Use the filter paper and funnel to construct a filter. With the stem of the funnel inserted in test tube 1, place the dry charcoal into the filter and pour the coffee-charcoal mixture into the filter.
5. If the collected filtrate in test tube 1 is not colorless or pale yellow, filter the filtrate again and record the final color in **Data Table 1.**
6. Fill a 250-mL beaker half full with cool water.
7. Using a striker, light the Bunsen burner and gently warm the filtrate. **CAUTION: Do not point the test tube at anyone during the heating process.** Using a test-tube clamp, continuously move the test tube in and out of the flame while gently shaking the contents.

8. Slowly boil the solution until there is about 2 mL left in the test tube.
9. Cool the contents of the test tube by placing the test tube in the beaker containing cool water.
10. Clean and dry the graduated cylinder. Use it to measure about 2 mL of potassium nitrate into test tube 2. Clean the cylinder and measure about 2 mL distilled water into test tube 3.
11. To each of the three labeled test tubes, add 5 or 6 drops of nitric acid and 1 mL of sodium hexanitrocobaltate. Record the color of these solutions in **Data Table 1.**
12. Mix each solution with a clean stirring rod.
13. Let the solutions stand for 5 minutes.
14. Note and record in **Data Table 1** any color changes observed in each test tube.

## Hypothesis

_____

_____

_____

_____

## Cleanup and Disposal

1. Dispose of all chemicals as instructed by your teacher.
2. Return all equipment to its proper place.
3. Clean up your workstation.
4. Wash your hands before leaving the lab.

## Data and Observations

| Data Table 1 | | |
|---|---|---|
| Test-tube number | Initial color | Color after 5 min |
| 1 | | |
| 2 | | |
| 3 | | |

**LAB 7.1**                                                    **LABORATORY MANUAL**

## Analyze and Conclude

**1. Observing and Inferring** What color changes did you observe after 5 minutes?

_____

_____

_____

**2. Observing and Inferring** Cite the experimental evidence used to establish that coffee contains potassium.

_____

_____

_____

_____

_____

**3. Predicting** What results might you expect if a plant material, other than coffee, was tested?

_____

_____

_____

_____

_____

**4. Predicting** What additional test might be done to confirm that the color change is due to the presence of potassium?

_____

_____

_____

_____

**5. Predicting** If a sample of a potassium compound was heated in a Bunsen burner flame, would the flame color be yellow? Explain.

_____

_____

_____

_____

**6. Thinking Critically** Suggest a method to show that the charcoal decolorized the coffee and did not add potassium to the solution.

_____

_____

_____

_____

_____

**7. Error Analysis** What are some possible sources of error in this activity?

_____

_____

_____

## Real-World Chemistry

**1.** Potassium chromate is a carcinogen, potassium permanganate is used as a germicide, and potassium hydrogen tartrate, commonly known as cream of tartar, is a white solid found in baking powder. Explain how potassium can have such diverse uses.

**2.** Each year in the United States, about 30 million prescriptions for potassium supplements are written for people with hypertension (high blood pressure). These supplements are often prescribed with diuretics. Diuretics cause increased urination and reduce the volume of retained fluids in the body, thus reducing blood pressure. Explain why potassium supplements are prescribed.

## LAB 7.2 LABORATORY MANUAL

# The Periodic Puzzle

**Use with Section 7.3**

Imagine the following scenario. You are the new lab assistant for a professor in a highly underbudgeted chemistry department. Your first task is to finish a project started by the former assistant, who suffered an accident while failing to observe proper safety procedures. The accident occurred while he was in the process of labeling and storing example specimens of each element in identical containers.

Unfortunately, the labels on 36 containers were either damaged or burned beyond recognition during the incident. To further complicate matters, much of the information contained in the assistant's notebook was damaged as well. This notebook contained practical facts about the elements' uses and traits, and data collected by other students. What did survive, however, were the etched serial numbers on each of the containers, which the assistant often referenced in notes.

The professor and some of the students have assigned an alphabetic label (from **a** to **jj**) to each of the mystery elements, and they've combined the remaining information with some of their own preliminary observations. Using this data and your deductive reasoning skills, can you determine the identities of the 36 elements?

## Problem

How can you place elements in a periodic table based on their characteristics?

## Objective

**Identify** various elements by using your understanding of periodic properties and relationships.

## Materials

a computer with access to the Internet

## Pre-Lab

Read the entire laboratory activity. Decide upon the best strategy for solving the puzzle.

## Procedure

The professor provided you with a list of notes and observations based on data from the damaged notebook. **Figure A** is a periodic table with the unknown elements omitted.

1. Element **c** has the highest melting point of the metals.

2. Element **ff** started to turn white when its container was opened.

3. The assistants were reluctant to burn some of the elements after element **e** produced a violet vapor with an extremely unpleasant odor.

4. Compounds of element **y** combined with element **u** can be found in "hard water."

5. As useful as element **h** can be, it can also be quite poisonous if ingested. That is why other metals are used in its place to perform its previous functions.

6. Clearly, the person who ordered element **q** was not a chemist, because the unstable element would have decayed long before its arrival.

7. Element **j** is used to make permanent magnets.

8. If a patient drinks a compound of elements **u** and **p,** doctors can view the patient's digestive tract.

| Scandium 21 Sc 44.956 | | Vanadium 23 V 50.942 | Manganese 25 Mn 54.938 | Iron 26 Fe 55.845 | Cobalt 27 Co 58.933 | | | Cadmium 48 Cd 112.41 | Aluminum 13 Al 26.982 | Silicon 14 Si 28.086 | | Oxygen 8 O 15.999 | | Helium 2 He 4.0026 |

Noble gases:
- Neon 10 Ne 20.180
- Argon 18 Ar 39.948
- Krypton 36 Kr 83.80
- Xenon 54 Xe 131.29
- Radon 86 Rn (222.02)
- Ununoctium 118 Uuo (293)

Other main-group elements:
- Bromine 35 Br 79.904
- Astatine 85 At (209.99)
- Tellurium 52 Te 127.60
- Polonium 84 Po (208.98)
- Ununhexium 116 Uuh (289)
- Antimony 51 Sb 121.76
- Bismuth 83 Bi 208.98
- Germanium 32 Ge 72.61
- Ununquadium 114 Uuq (289)
- Gallium 31 Ga 69.723
- Indium 49 In 114.82
- Thallium 81 Tl 204.38

Transition elements:
- Yttrium 39 Y 88.906
- Lutetium 71 Lu 174.97
- Lawrencium 103 Lr (262.11)
- Rutherfordium 104 Rf (263.11)
- Niobium 41 Nb 92.906
- Molybdenum 42 Mo 95.94
- Dubnium 105 Db (262.11)
- Seaborgium 106 Sg (266.12)
- Technetium 43 Tc (97.907)
- Rhenium 75 Re 186.21
- Bohrium 107 Bh (264.12)
- Ruthenium 44 Ru 101.07
- Osmium 76 Os 190.23
- Hassium 108 Hs (269.13)
- Rhodium 45 Rh 102.91
- Iridium 77 Ir 192.22
- Meitnerium 109 Mt (268.14)
- Ununnilium 110 Uun (272.15)
- Unununium 111 Uuu (272.15)
- Ununbium 112 Uub (277)
- Zirconium 40 Zr 91.224
- Hafnium 72 Hf 178.49

Lanthanides:
- Lanthanum 57 La 138.91
- Cerium 58 Ce 140.115
- Praseodymium 59 Pr 140.908
- Neodymium 60 Nd 144.24
- Promethium 61 Pm 144.913
- Samarium 62 Sm 150.36
- Europium 63 Eu 151.965
- Gadolinium 64 Gd 157.25
- Terbium 65 Tb 158.925
- Dysprosium 66 Dy 162.50
- Holmium 67 Ho 164.930
- Erbium 68 Er 167.26
- Thulium 69 Tm 168.934
- Ytterbium 70 Yb 173.04

Actinides:
- Actinium 89 Ac (227.03)
- Thorium 90 Th 232.04
- Protactinium 91 Pa 231.04
- Neptunium 93 Np (237.05)
- Plutonium 94 Pu (244.06)
- Americium 95 Am (243.06)
- Curium 96 Cm (247.07)
- Berkelium 97 Bk (247.07)
- Einsteinium 99 Es (252.08)
- Fermium 100 Fm (257.10)
- Mendelevium 101 Md (258.10)
- Nobelium 102 No (259.101)

Alkali / alkaline earth metals:
- Rubidium 37 Rb 85.468
- Strontium 38 Sr 87.62
- Cesium 55 Cs 132.905

9. Element **b** is a silvery metal that was submerged in some sort of oil.

10. Of the known metals, element **d** is an essential nutrient for plant growth and is found in most soils. It is also essential in the human diet.

11. Element **t** is the lightest element.

12. Element **f** is a significant part of stainless steel. It has an atomic number that is six times greater than that of element **x.**

13. Element **z** is most commonly found as part of a compound with element **l.**

14. Element **gg** plays a key role in photography, among other things.

15. Most often, when someone thinks of element **a,** the person immediately thinks of nuclear power. This is probably because all the isotopes of **a** are radioactive.

16. In the early 1800s, element **w** had been thought to be identical to the element directly above it in the periodic table.

17. The common names for the allotropes of element **v** are based upon their colors.

18. Thankfully, the container holding element **l** was not destroyed in the accident because this element can be quite poisonous when inhaled.

19. Most solar cells rely upon the natural properties of element **bb.**

20. Element **k** is synthetic.

21. Element **ee** is the most malleable metal.

22. Element **i** is a shiny, silver liquid.

23. It has been hypothesized that element **dd,** the most reactive nonmetal, can be substituted for element **t** in organic compounds.

24. Neither element **gg** nor element **ii** are ferromagnetic, but their magnetic properties change when they are combined with each other chemically or physically, in alloys.

25. Element **n** is the heaviest alkaline-earth metal.

26. Element **x** is a lightweight metal through which x rays pass easily.

27. Elements **g** and **aa** share similar physical properties, but the allotropes of element **aa** are much more widely known. Element **aa** is found in organic compounds.

28. Although every compound of element **o** is poisonous, it had once been used to treat medical conditions.

29. Element **hh** is a shiny, reddish metal.

30. Hydrochloric acid had a considerably more dramatic effect on element **jj** than it did on the other metals in element **jj**'s group, elements **s** and **j.**

31. Element **m** was used to plate steel to make cans.

## Data and Observations

| Table 1: The Mystery Elements | | | | | | | | | | | |
|------|--|---|--|---|--|---|--|----|--|----|--|
| a | | g | | m | | s | | y | | ee | |
| b | | h | | n | | t | | z | | ff | |
| c | | i | | o | | u | | aa | | gg | |
| d | | j | | p | | v | | bb | | hh | |
| e | | k | | q | | w | | cc | | ii | |
| f | | l | | r | | x | | dd | | jj | |

## Analyze and Conclude

1. **Acquiring and Analyzing Information** Which element was the most difficult to identify? How did you identify it?

_____

_____

_____

2. **Thinking Critically** What are some of the reasons that this scenario is unlikely to take place in real life?

_____

_____

_____

_____

3. **Using the Internet** Was there a particular web site or type of web site that you found most useful for solving the puzzle? If so, which web site, and why?

_____

_____

_____

### Real-World Chemistry

1. The computer has added a new dimension to chemistry. Databases of chemical information are maintained not only for elements, but also for molecules. The database of substances at Chemical Abstracts Service reports more than 23 million registered substances. How can so many different substances and molecules be created from just over 100 different elements?

2. Each registered substance in the database is given a unique number or key. For example, the element argon (Ar) has a key number of 7440-37-1. What would you expect to happen if you searched the Internet with this unique key? What is the benefit of having a unique number for each substance?

3. Many substances must have Material Safety Data Sheets (MSDS) to describe their hazards and methods to correctly handle the substance. Using an internet search engine, find the primary health risk associated with argon, a noble gas.

## LAB 8.1 LABORATORY MANUAL

# Properties of Ionic Compounds

Use with
Section 8.2

**W**hat parts of your body are ionic compounds? Those that compose your skin? Your hair? Actually, most of the human body is composed of nonionic compounds. But, you could not live without sodium chloride and other ionic compounds found inside you. How can you distinguish ionic compounds from other types of compounds? By investigating sodium chloride, you will explore some of the common properties of ionic compounds.

## Problem

What are some of the properties of ionic compounds?

## Objectives

- **Observe** the crystal shape of NaCl.
- **Compare and contrast** ionic compounds with a nonionic compound.
- **Explain** the differences in the conductivity of ionic compounds in different forms.

## Materials

NaCl, coarse grain
NaCl, fine grain
LiCl
sugar (sucrose)
hammer
stereoscope, micro-
  scope, or hand
  lens
crucible
Bunsen burner

ring stand and
  clamp
wire gauze
conductivity
  indicator
100-mL beaker
crucible
clay triangle
distilled water

## Safety Precautions

- **Always wear safety goggles and a lab apron.**
- **Hot objects will not appear to be hot. Be careful when handling any material that has been heated.**
- **Do not touch or taste any chemicals used or formed in the laboratory.**
- **Do not touch both electrodes on the conductivity indicator at the same time—a small electrical jolt could result.**

## Pre-Lab

1. Define crystal lattice energy.
2. Explain what forces must be overcome for a substance to melt.
3. Describe what is necessary for a substance to be a conductor of electricity.
4. Read the entire laboratory activity. Form a hypothesis as to whether distilled water is a conductor of electricity. Record your hypothesis on page 58.
5. Define and give an example of an electrolyte.

## Procedure

### Part A: Crystal Lattice Structure

1. Use a stereoscope, a microscope, or a hand lens to observe both coarse and fine salt. Record your observations in the data table.
2. With a hammer, gently tap on a coarse grain until it breaks. Note the shapes of the broken pieces and record your observations.

## Part B: Melting Point

**1.** Set up the apparatus as shown in **Figure A**.

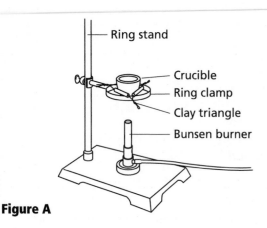

- Ring stand
- Crucible
- Ring clamp
- Clay triangle
- Bunsen burner

**Figure A**

**2.** Sprinkle a pea-sized pile of NaCl in the crucible and heat it with a low flame until the NaCl melts, or for 2 minutes, whichever comes first. If the salt melts within the 2-minute period, record the melting point as low. If the salt does not melt within 2 minutes, record the melting point as high.

**3.** In the fume hood, and using the same apparatus shown in **Figure A,** repeat step 2 for sugar. (Note: Like most compounds in living organisms, sugar is nonionic.) Make sure the flame is the same setting as your burner in step 2.

## Part C: Conductivity

### Solid

**1.** On a piece of paper, make a small pile of NaCl, about the size of three peas. Place the contacts of the conductivity indicator in the pile. Record the results.

### Solution

**2.** Pour about 50 mL of distilled water into a clean 100-mL beaker. Notice that like most ionic substances, NaCl dissolves easily in water.

**3.** Making sure that you have wiped off the contact wires, place the conductivity indicator in the distilled water. Record the results in the data table.

**4.** Transfer and dissolve the pile of NaCl into the distilled water. Dissolving in water is another property shown by many ionic compounds. Place the conductivity indicator in the salt solution. Record the results.

**5.** Repeat step 3 with an equal amount of sugar. (Note: Some nonionic compounds dissolve in water, but many do not.)

### Molten

**6.** Set up the apparatus as shown in **Figure A.**

**7.** In a clean, dry crucible, mass out approximately 1 g of lithium chloride, LiCl, another typical ionic compound. (The melting point of sodium chloride, NaCl, is too high to observe using classroom laboratory equipment.)

**8.** Before heating it, place the conductivity indicator in the solid LiCl. Record the results.

**9.** Place the crucible in the clay triangle and heat the crucible until the LiCl melts. This may take several minutes.

**10.** Quickly turn off the burner and plunge the clean contact wires of the conductivity indicator into the molten LiCl. Record your observations.

**11.** Remove the conductivity indicator, allow the wires to cool, and then carefully clean the contact wires.

**12.** **CAUTION: Do NOT touch the crucible until after it has cooled for about 10 minutes.**

## Hypothesis

_____

_____

## Cleanup and Disposal

**1.** Follow your teacher's directions for disposing of the LiCl.

**2.** Make sure your balance is left in the same condition as you found it.

**3.** Be careful that your burner and clamp are cooled before putting them away.

**4.** Carefully return all laboratory equipment to the proper place and dispose of all waste in the designated containers.

**LAB 8.1**                                                    **LABORATORY MANUAL**

## Data and Observations

### Part A: Crystal Lattice

| Observations about the coarse and fine NaCl | |
|---|---|
| Observations about the pieces of NaCl after breaking the coarse salt | |

### Part B: Melting Point

| Observations about the melting point of NaCl (high or low melting point) | |
|---|---|
| Observations about the melting of sugar (high or low melting point) | |

### Part C: Conductivity

| Test Substance | Conductivity Indicator (Record light as off, dull, bright, or blinking) | Conductor Rating (good, poor, or none) |
|---|---|---|
| Solid NaCl | | |
| Distilled water | | |
| NaCl dissolved in distilled water | | |
| Sugar dissolved in distilled water | | |
| Solid LiCl | | |
| Molten LiCl | | |

**1.** From the results of Part A, and using words like *soft*, *ductile*, *malleable*, *brittle*, *hard*, or *pliable*, how would you describe sodium chloride?

_____

**2.** Sodium chloride and lithium chloride are typical ionic compounds, while sugar represents a typical nonionic compound. In general, how do these two types of compounds compare in their melting points?

_____

_____

**3.** In Part C, why was it important to use distilled water instead of tap water for the conductivity measure?

_____

_____

**LAB 8.1**

## Analyze and Conclude

1. **Recognizing Cause and Effect** In a crystal lattice structure, the electrons are held tightly by the ions, which are rigidly held in place by electrostatic attraction. Discuss how this characteristic explains why ionic compounds generally (a) have high melting points and (b) do not conduct electricity in the solid state.

_____

_____

_____

_____

2. **Comparing and Contrasting** Nonionic compounds do not exist in crystal lattice structures but rather as individual particles, which are affected by other particles. In other words, nonionic compounds experience forces between particles. Based on what you learned in Part B about the melting points of ionic versus nonionic compounds, how do you think the attractive energy between particles compares with the energy of the crystal lattice?

_____

_____

3. **Thinking Critically** Explain how ionic compounds, which do not conduct electricity in the solid form, can conduct electricity when they are in the molten state or dissolved in water.

_____

_____

_____

4. **Drawing a Conclusion** All ionic compounds exist in only one state at room temperature. From what you learned in this investigation, what is that state and why do you think they do not exist in the other states at room temperature?

_____

_____

5. **Error Analysis** What could be done to improve the precision and accuracy of your investigation?

### Real-World Chemistry

1. The human body is mainly composed of non-ionic compounds, such as water, carbohydrates, lipids, and proteins. Why then are people such good conductors of electricity?

2. Magnesium carbonate, an ionic compound, is sometimes used as a thermal insulator in buildings. Why would you expect ionic compounds to be good thermal insulators?

3. Ionic compounds often have higher melting points than metals. Using at least two properties of ionic compounds, explain why cookware is not made from ionic compounds.

**LAB 8.2 LABORATORY MANUAL**

# Formation of a Salt

**Use with Section 8.2**

**P**lease pass the sodium chloride! It is amazing that food is seasoned with an ionic compound that is composed of two deadly elements—sodium and chlorine. The gain or loss of electrons can make a big difference in properties. Reacting sodium hydrogen carbonate, which is baking soda, with hydrochloric acid (HCl), the acid found in your stomach, produces salt, carbon dioxide, and water, according to the following equation:

$$NaHCO_3(cr) + HCl(aq) \rightarrow NaCl(cr) + CO_2(g) + H_2O(l)$$

If we evaporate the water, then all that should remain is the salt, NaCl.

## Problem

How can we form a salt?

## Objectives

- **Observe** the reaction of $NaHCO_3$ with HCl.
- **Draw** the Lewis electron-dot diagrams for $Na^+$ and $Cl^-$.
- **Give examples** of how to identify an ionic compound such as NaCl.

## Materials

6*M* HCl
$NaHCO_3$
100-mL beaker
10-mL graduated cylinder
dropper
phenol red indicator

distilled water
Bunsen burner
ring stand
ring clamp
wire gauze
microscope or hand lens
balance

## Safety Precautions

- Always wear safety goggles and a lab apron.
- Hot objects will not appear to be hot. Be careful when handling the cooling beaker.
- Do not touch or taste any chemicals used or formed in the laboratory.
- 6*M* HCl is toxic by ingestion or inhalation and corrosive to the skin and eyes.

## Pre-Lab

1. Define ionic bond.
2. Write the electron configuration for each of the following: Na, $Na^+$, Cl, and $Cl^-$.
3. Identify the noble gases that $Na^+$ and $Cl^-$ resemble in their electron configurations.
4. Draw the Lewis electron-dot diagrams for $Na^+$ and $Cl^-$.

## Procedure

1. Mass a clean, dry 100-mL beaker.
2. Place 0.50 g of sodium hydrogen carbonate ($NaHCO_3$) into the beaker.
3. Add about 15 mL of distilled water to the beaker and swirl the solution gently to dissolve the sodium hydrogen carbonate. Add more water if necessary to dissolve the powder completely.

**4.** Add 2–3 drops of phenol red indicator. The solution should be red in color. Place a piece of white paper under the beaker to view the color of the solution better.

**5.** While gently swirling the beaker, add the hydrochloric acid by single drops until the color of the solution changes to a definite yellow.

**6.** Set up the apparatus as shown in **Figure A.** Gently heat the contents of the beaker to evaporate the water. **CAUTION: Do not heat the solution too much or it will spatter out of the beaker.** When only about 5 mL of water is left in the beaker, shut off the flame and allow the heat of the beaker to evaporate the rest of the water.

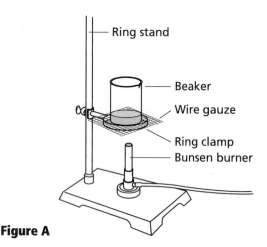
Ring stand
Beaker
Wire gauze
Ring clamp
Bunsen burner

**Figure A**

**7.** Allow the beaker to cool for at least 5 minutes. **CAUTION: The beaker will appear cool before it is ready to be handled.**

**8.** Mass the cooled beaker with the white powder.

**9.** Examine the contents of the beaker. Examine the contents under a microscope or hand lens to see if the powder has the characteristic cubic shape of sodium chloride.

**10.** Record your data in the data table.

## Cleanup and Disposal

**1.** Place unused chemicals in the waste can.

**2.** Rinse out the contents of your cooled beakers in the sink.

**3.** Make sure your balance is left in the same condition as you found it.

**4.** Be careful that your burner and clamp are cooled before putting them away.

## Data and Observations

| Mass of the empty beaker | g |
|---|---|
| Mass of the beaker + NaHCO₃ | g |
| Mass of the NaHCO₃ | g |
| Mass of the beaker + NaCl | g |
| Mass of the NaCl | g |

**1.** As you added the hydrochloric acid, what did you observe?

_____

**2.** What gas was released during the chemical reaction?

_____

**3.** The sodium hydrogen carbonate underwent a chemical change. What evidence do you have of this change?

_____

**4.** Describe the resulting white powder in the cooled beaker.

_____

## Analyze and Conclude

**1. Thinking Critically** How can you identify the product as being different from the reactant? **CAUTION: Remember never to taste anything in the laboratory.**

_____

_____

**2. Recognizing Cause and Effect** To make sure that the white powder was all sodium chloride and not mixed with sodium hydrogen carbonate, would you need to add a little less or a little more hydrochloric acid to the reaction? Explain your decision.

_____

_____

**3. Drawing a Conclusion** Knowing that this was a chemical reaction, explain why the mass of the product was different from the mass of the original sodium hydrogen carbonate.

_____

_____

**4. Error Analysis** What might have affected the accuracy of this investigation?

_____

_____

### Real-World Chemistry

**1.** Sodium hydrogen carbonate is a common ingredient in antacid remedies. Using information from the equation for the reaction, explain how this chemical could relieve a stomach that contains excess acid.

**2.** Studies have proven conclusively that fluoride is an effective tooth decay preventative. As a result, in the late 1960s and 1970s, many communities in the United States began adding trace quantities of fluoride to their drinking water supplies. However, strong opposition arose against this "tampering" with the water supply. One of the common arguments was that fluorine was known to be a deadly gas. What would be your response to this argument?

# Covalent Bonding in Medicines

**Use with
Section 9.4**

**A**spirin, acetaminophen, and ibuprofen are all commonly sold
nonprescription pain relief medicines. Aspirin, the most widely
used drug, acts a pain reliever (analgesic), a fever reducer (antipyretic),
and an anti-inflammatory agent. Aspirin tablets are manufactured by
combining about 0.3 grams of aspirin with a binding agent such as
starch. Aspirin inhibits the production of an enzyme that is responsible
for the activation of pain sensors in the body. Ibuprofen acts in much
the same way as aspirin. The chemical formula for ibuprofen is $C_{13}H_{18}O_2$.
Acetaminophen also acts as a pain reliever and fever reducer.
Acetaminophen is not an anti-inflammatory. The chemical formula for
aspirin is $C_9H_8O_4$. Acetaminophen has the formula $C_8H_9NO_2$.

The atoms in the molecules of these pain relievers are covalently
bonded. Electrons are shared between atoms in a series of single and
double covalent bonds. The covalent bonds in aspirin, acetaminophen,
and ibuprofen are similar to those found in methane and carbon dioxide.

To study covalent molecules, chemists find the use of models and
drawings of structures helpful. In models, colored wooden or plastic
balls are used to represent atoms. These balls have holes drilled in them
according to the number of covalent bonds they will form. The holes are
bored at angles that approximate the accepted bond angles.

Element representations are:

| Sphere Color | Element |
|--------------|----------|
| Black | Carbon |
| Yellow | Hydrogen |
| Blue | Nitrogen |
| Red | Oxygen |

Sticks and springs are used to represent bonds. Single bonds are
shown with sticks, while double bonds are shown with two springs. A
pair of dots (:) or a dash (—) is used to represent a single bond in a
drawn structure. A double bond is shown as two pair of dots (::) or two
dashes (=).

**LAB** (9.1)                                                    **LABORATORY MANUAL**

## Problem

How can molecules such as aspirin, acetaminophen, and ibuprofen be represented by models and drawn structures?

## Objectives

- **Construct models** to show the single and double bonds in some covalent compounds.
- **Draw** a representation of the structure of these molecules.
- **Examine** models of covalent compounds in medicines and draw their structural formulas.

## Materials

wooden or plastic molecular model set (ball and stick)
pliers

## Safety Precautions

**Always wear safety goggles and a lab apron.**

## Pre-Lab

1. Define covalent bond.
2. Distinguish between a single covalent bond and a double covalent bond.
3. Explain how a single bond is represented in a drawn structure.
4. Explain how a double bond is represented in a drawn structure.
5. Read the entire laboratory activity. Form a hypothesis about how your drawn structures will compare to the models. Record your hypothesis in the next column.

## Procedure

### Part A

1. Construct models for the substances methane ($CH_4$) and carbon dioxide ($CO_2$).
2. Identify the bonds as single covalent bonds or double covalent bonds.
3. In **Data Table 1,** draw the Lewis structure for each substance, first using dots and then using dashes to represent the bonding electrons.
4. After your teacher has checked your work, disassemble the models.

### Part B

1. Examine the models of aspirin, acetaminophen, and ibuprofen.
2. In **Data Table 2,** draw the structures for each substance using dashes (—) to represent the bonds.
3. Ask your teacher to check your work.

## Hypothesis

_____

_____

_____

## Cleanup and Disposal

1. Be sure all sticks and springs have been removed from the spheres.
2. Neatly reassemble the model kit.

## Data and Observations

| Data Table 1 | |
| --- | --- |
| Dot structure of $CH_4$ | Structure of $CH_4$ using dashes |
| | |
| Dot structure of $CO_2$ | Structure of $CO_2$ using dashes |
| | |

| Data Table 2 |
| --- |
| Aspirin |
| |
| Acetaminophen |
| |
| Ibuprofen |
| |

## Analyze and Conclude

1. **Observing and Inferring** What structural shape do aspirin, acetaminophen, and ibuprofen have in common?

_____

_____

2. **Comparing and Contrasting** Compare the complexity of the bonds in all of the diagrams.

_____

_____

3. **Collecting and Interpreting Data** Compare the appearance of the drawn structure of aspirin with the model.

_____

_____

4. **Predicting** Predict the possibility of other medicines that might have the same common structural shape as aspirin, acetaminophen, and ibuprofen.

_____

_____

5. **Drawing a Conclusion** Explain why different pain relievers are manufactured and sold.

_____

_____

6. **Error Analysis** Compare your structures for aspirin, acetaminophen, and ibuprofen to those of other students. What could have caused any differences?

_____

_____

### Real-World Chemistry

1. Aspirin is known to inhibit blood clotting. Explain why surgeons recommend that no aspirin be taken immediately before or after surgery.

2. Aspirin is associated with Reyes syndrome, a disease of the brain that may arise in children recovering from chicken pox. What alternatives to aspirin might be used to relieve pain and fever in children recovering from this virus?

# Covalent Compounds

**Use with
Section 9.5**

**E**lectronegativity is a scale used to determine an atom's attraction for an electron in the bonding process. Differences in electronegativities are used to predict whether the bond is pure covalent, polar covalent, or ionic. Molecules in which the electronegativity difference is zero are considered to be pure covalent. Those molecules that exhibit an electronegativity difference of more than zero but less than 1.7 are classified as polar covalent. Ionic crystals exist in those systems that have an electronegativity difference of more than 1.7.

The structures used to show the bonding in covalent molecules are called Lewis structures. When bonding, atoms tend to achieve a noble gas configuration. By sharing electrons, individual atoms can complete the outer energy level. In a covalent bond, an octet of electrons is formed around each atom (except hydrogen.)

To study covalent molecules, chemists find the use of models helpful. Colored wooden or plastic balls are used to represent atoms. These balls have holes drilled in them according to the number of covalent bonds they will form. The holes are bored at angles that approximate the accepted bond angles.

Sticks and springs are used to represent bonds. Single bonds are shown with sticks, while double and triple bonds are shown with two springs and three springs, respectively. While the sizes of the atoms are not proportionately correct, the models are useful to represent the arrangement of the atoms according to their bond angles.

## Problem

How can we determine the type of bonds in a compound and draw and construct models of molecules?

## Objectives

- **Construct models** to show the shapes of some covalent compounds.
- **Draw** a Lewis representation of the structure of some molecules.
- **Compare** models and Lewis structures of molecules.

## Materials

wooden or plastic molecular model set (ball and stick)
pliers
electronegativity tables

## Safety Precautions

**Always wear safety goggles and a lab apron.**

## Pre-Lab

1. Define covalent bond.

2. Give the electron configuration of oxygen, hydrogen, nitrogen, and carbon.

3. How many covalent bonds will each of oxygen, hydrogen, nitrogen, and carbon form?

4. Describe how electronegativity differences are used to predict whether a bond is pure covalent, polar covalent, or ionic.

5. Read the entire laboratory activity. Form a hypothesis about how to show sharing of electrons in a covalent bond in an illustration and in a model and how the type of bond is determined. Record your hypothesis on page 71.

## Procedure

### Part A

1. Look at your ball-and-stick model sets. Identify the different pieces that represent atoms, single bonds, double bonds, and triple bonds

2. Select one of every different color of ball. Each hole that has been bored into the sphere represents a single chemical bond. Count the number of holes present in the different colored balls. Record your observations in **Data Table 1.**

### Part B

1. Use an electronegativity table (see page 169 in your textbook) to determine the electronegativity difference between the two elements in the compounds in **Data Table 2.**

2. Use the tables on the right to determine the percentage of ionic character and bond type of each of the compounds. Record your answers on **Data Table 2.**

### Part C

1. Construct a model for $H_2$.

2. Compute the electronegativity difference for the atoms in the molecule and identify the type of bond. Record your answer on **Data Table 3.**

3. Draw the Lewis structure for the molecule in the space provided on **Data Table 3.**

4. After your teacher has checked your work, disassemble the model.

5. Repeat steps 1–4 for each of the compounds listed in **Data Table 3.**

**Table 1**

| Electronegativity and Bond Type | |
|---|---|
| **Electronegativity difference** | **Bond type** |
| 0 | pure covalent |
| Greater than zero but less than 1.7 | polar covalent |
| Greater than 1.7 | ionic |

**Table 2**

| Relationship Between Electronegativity Difference and Ionic Character | | |
|---|---|---|
| **Electronegativity difference** | **Type of bond** | **Percent ionic character** |
| 0 | pure covalent | 0 |
| 0.2 | polar covalent | 1 |
| 0.4 | polar covalent | 4 |
| 0.6 | polar covalent | 9 |
| 0.8 | polar covalent | 15 |
| 1.0 | polar covalent | 22 |
| 1.2 | polar covalent | 30 |
| 1.4 | polar covalent | 39 |
| 1.6 | polar covalent | 48 |
| 1.8 | ionic | 56 |
| 2.0 | ionic | 63 |
| 2.2 | ionic | 70 |
| 2.4 | ionic | 76 |
| 2.6 | ionic | 82 |
| 2.8 | ionic | 86 |
| 3.0 | ionic | 89 |
| 3.2 | ionic | 92 |

**LAB 9.2**

## Hypothesis

_____

_____

_____

## Cleanup and Disposal

1. Be sure all sticks and springs have been removed from the spheres.
2. Neatly reassemble the model kit.

## Data and Observations

| Data Table 1 | | |
|---|---|---|
| **Ball color** | **Number of holes** | **Identity of element** |
| Red | | oxygen |
| Orange | | bromine |
| Yellow | | hydrogen |
| Green | | chlorine |
| Blue | | nitrogen |
| Purple | | iodine |
| Black | | carbon |

| Data Table 2 | | | |
|---|---|---|---|
| **Formula** | **Electronegativity difference** | **Percent ionic character** | **Type of bond** |
| KCl | | | |
| $K_2O$ | | | |
| $Br_2$ | | | |
| $MgI_2$ | | | |
| HBr | | | |
| $CaCl_2$ | | | |
| NaBr | | | |
| MgS | | | |
| $Al_2S_3$ | | | |
| NaCl | | | |
| $F_2$ | | | |
| $SO_2$ | | | |
| HCl | | | |
| CO | | | |

**LAB 9.2**

| Data Table 3 | | | | | | | | |
|---|---|---|---|---|---|---|---|---|
| Molecule | $H_2$ | $Cl_2$ | $N_2$ | $O_2$ | HCl | $H_2O$ | $CO_2$ | $NH_3$ | $CH_4$ |
| Electronegativity difference | | | | | | | | |
| Type of bond | | | | | | | | |
| Lewis formula | | | | | | | | |

## Analyze and Conclude

1. **Observing and Inferring** Both water and carbon dioxide are triatomic molecules. Explain the meaning of *triatomic*.

_____

_____

2. **Collecting and Interpreting Data** Compare the appearance of the Lewis structure for a compound with a ball and stick model of the compound.

_____

_____

3. **Predicting** Predict the shape and Lewis structure for $CBr_4$.

_____

4. **Drawing a Conclusion** Explain why a formula without electronegativity data or a Lewis structure cannot be used to predict bond type.

_____

_____

5. **Error Analysis** Compare the ball and stick models you constructed with your Lewis structures. Do any of them differ in the number of bonds? What could be some causes for the errors?

_____

_____

## Real-World Chemistry

**1.** Explain why water is a liquid at room temperature and carbon dioxide is a gas.

**2.** Naphthalene ($C_{10}H_8$), a common ingredient in moth balls, melts at 80.2°C. Sodium chloride (NaCl), common table salt, melts at 800.7°C. What do these melting points indicate about the bonding pattern of each compound?

**LAB 10.1 LABORATORY MANUAL**

# Single-Replacement Reactions

**A** single-replacement chemical reaction is one in which one substance from a compound is replaced by another substance. A generic equation for such a reaction is as follows.

$$A + BC \rightarrow AC + B$$

The reactivity of a substance depends on its ability to gain or lose electrons. It is possible to arrange the elements into a series based upon their reactivity. Such a list is called an activity series.

While there are many types of replacement reactions, we will concern ourselves with two different kinds. In one type, a more active metal replaces a less active metal from solution. Consider the reaction between zinc and copper(II) sulfate.

$$Zn(s) + CuSO_4(aq) \rightarrow ZnSO_4(aq) + Cu(s)$$

In this reaction, the more active zinc replaces the less active copper from solution. The reaction is evident because the blue color of the copper sulfate solution slowly turns colorless and a deposit of copper can be seen to form on the strip of zinc.

A second type of replacement reaction involves the replacement of hydrogen from acid by a metal. Consider the reaction between zinc and hydrochloric acid.

$$Zn(s) + 2HCl(aq) \rightarrow ZnCl_2(aq) + H_2(g)$$

The zinc metal is active enough to replace the hydrogen from the acid. Bubbles of hydrogen gas can be seen rising to the surface, and the piece of zinc is consumed. On the other hand, if the less active metal, copper, is placed into a hydrochloric acid solution, no reaction will take place.

In this activity, you will use a few metals, their compounds, and dilute hydrochloric acid to show single-replacement reactions and construct an activity series.

## Problem

What elements will replace other elements in single-replacement reactions? How can the results of these reactions be used to form an activity series?

## Objectives

- **Classify** reactions as single-replacement chemical reactions.
- **Use numbers** to write balanced equations for single-replacement reactions.
- **Sequence** metals into an activity series.

## Materials

zinc (1-cm × 3-cm strips) (3)
copper (1-cm × 3-cm strips) (2)
lead (1-cm × 3-cm strip)
sandpaper
0.2M lead (II) nitrate (Pb(NO$_3$)$_2$)
0.2M copper (II) sulfate (CuSO$_4$)

0.2M magnesium sulfate (MgSO$_4$)
0.2M silver nitrate (AgNO$_3$)
3M hydrochloric acid (HCl)
test tubes (6)
test-tube rack

**LAB (10.1)**

# LABORATORY MANUAL

## Safety Precautions

- **Always wear safety goggles, a lab apron, and gloves.**
- **Dispose of chemical wastes as directed by your teacher.**
- **Lead nitrate and copper(II) sulfate are moderately toxic by ingestion or inhalation.**
- **Magnesium sulfate may irritate the eyes.**
- **Silver nitrate solution is highly toxic and will stain skin or clothing.**
- **Hydrochloric acid is corrosive to skin, is toxic, and reacts with metals.**

## Pre-Lab

1. What is a single-replacement reaction?
2. Explain what determines the reactivity of a metal.
3. Distinguish between a more active metal and a less active metal.
4. Read the entire laboratory activity. Form a hypothesis about how an activity series can be formulated. Record your hypothesis in the next column.

## Procedure

1. Number six clean test tubes 1 through 6.
2. Use sandpaper to thoroughly clean one piece of lead, two pieces of copper, and three pieces of zinc.
3. For steps 4–9, observe and record any indication of a chemical reaction in **Data Table 1.** If no sign is noticeable immediately, wait about 10 minutes and then reexamine the test tube.
4. Place the lead strip into test tube #1 and add 10 mL of 0.2$M$ copper(II) sulfate solution.
5. Place a strip of copper into test tube #2 and add 10 mL of 0.2$M$ silver nitrate.
6. Place a strip of copper into test tube #3 and add 10 mL of 3$M$ hydrochloric acid.
7. Place a strip of zinc into test tube #4 and add 10 mL of 0.2$M$ lead(II) nitrate solution.

8. Place a strip of zinc into test tube #5 and add 10 mL of 0.2$M$ magnesium sulfate solution.
9. Place a strip of zinc into test tube #6 and add 10 mL of 3$M$ hydrochloric acid.

## Hypothesis

_____

_____

_____

_____

_____

## Cleanup and Disposal

1. Dispose of materials as directed by your teacher.
2. Return all lab equipment to its proper place.
3. Report any broken or damaged equipment.
4. Wash your hands thoroughly before leaving the lab.

**LAB 10.1**

## Data and Observations

| Data Table 1 | |
|---|---|
| Test-tube number | Indication of a chemical reaction |
| 1 | |
| 2 | |
| 3 | |
| 4 | |
| 5 | |
| 6 | |

## Analyze and Conclude

1. **Measuring and Using Numbers** Complete and balance each of the equations in **Data Table 2.** If no reaction was observed, write *no reaction*.

| Data Table 2 | |
|---|---|
| Test-tube number | Chemical equation |
| 1 | $Pb + CuSO_4 \rightarrow$ |
| 2 | $Cu + AgNO_3 \rightarrow$ |
| 3 | $Cu + HCl \rightarrow$ |
| 4 | $Zn + Pb(NO_3)_2 \rightarrow$ |
| 5 | $Zn + MgSO_4 \rightarrow$ |
| 6 | $Zn + HCl \rightarrow$ |

2. **Observing and Inferring** Identify which element was more active and which element was less active in each of the six tests conducted. Summarize the information in **Data Table 3** by writing the symbol of the element in the appropriate space.

| Data Table 3 | | |
|---|---|---|
| Test-tube number | Symbol of more active element | Symbol of less active element |
| 1 | | |
| 2 | | |
| 3 | | |
| 4 | | |
| 5 | | |
| 6 | | |

3. **Collecting and Interpreting Data** Of the three metals, Pb, Cu, Zn, which is the most active?

_____

4. **Collecting and Interpreting Data** Of the three metals, Pb, Cu, Zn, which is the least active?

_____

5. **Drawing a Conclusion** Cite the experimental evidence that indicated which of the three metals, PH, Cu, Zn, was most active and which metal was least active.

_____

_____

_____

6. **Sequencing** Arrange the metals Pb, Cu, Zn, Ag, and Mg in order of activity, from least active to most active.

_____

7. **Sequencing** Is hydrogen more active or less active than Cu, Zn, Ag, and Mg?

_____

_____

8. **Drawing a Conclusion** Cite the experimental evidence used to establish the location of hydrogen in this activity series.

_____

_____

_____

9. **Predicting** What additional test would be necessary to establish the exact position of hydrogen in this activity series?

_____

_____

10. **Error Analysis** Compare your activity series to one in a textbook or reference book. Explain any differences.

_____

_____

### Real-World Chemistry

1. Explain why acids are not stored in steel containers.

2. Sodium is a very active metal. Explain why sodium is only found in compounds in nature.

3. Explain why magnesium metal, rather than copper metal, might be used to study the effect of concentration of hydrochloric acid on rates of reactions.

**LAB 10.2** **LABORATORY MANUAL**

# Double-Replacement Reactions

**W**hen ionic compounds dissolve in water, the ions in the crystal separate and move throughout the solution. When two such solutions are mixed, all types of positive ions in the new solution are attracted to all types of negative ions in the solution. Sometimes a reaction takes place. This reaction is called a double-replacement reaction. Double-replacement reactions are sometimes called ionic reactions.

In this type of reaction, the ions of two compounds change places. Such a reaction is usually generically shown as

$$AB + CD \rightarrow AD + CB$$

As the solutions are mixed, positive A and C ions exist in solution, as do negative B and D ions, and these oppositely charged ions attract each other. A reaction takes place if a compound forms that removes ions from solution. Products that remove ions from solution in a double-replacement reaction are a precipitate, a gas, or a slightly ionized material, such as water.

## Problem

How can double-replacement reactions be identified?

## Objectives

- **Identify** double-replacement chemical reactions.
- **Write** balanced chemical equations for double-replacement reactions.

## Materials

3$M$ hydrochloric acid (HCl)
6$M$ hydrochloric acid (HCl)
2$M$ sodium hydroxide (NaOH)
0.2$M$ barium chloride ($BaCl_2$)
0.2$M$ ammonium chloride ($NH_4Cl$)
0.2$M$ copper(II) sulfate ($CuSO_4$)
0.2$M$ iron(III) chloride ($FeCl_3$)
0.2$M$ potassium nitrate ($KNO_3$)
0.2$M$ potassium iodide (KI)
0.2$M$ sodium carbonate ($Na_2CO_3$)

0.2$M$ sodium chloride (NaCl)
0.2$M$ sodium sulfate ($Na_2SO_4$)
0.2$M$ sodium sulfite ($Na_2SO_3$)
0.2$M$ lead(II) nitrate ($Pb(NO_3)_2$)
0.2$M$ zinc nitrate ($Zn(NO_3)_2$)
test tubes (10)
test-tube racks (2)
thermometer
10-mL graduated cylinder

## Safety Precautions

- **Always wear safety glasses, a lab apron, and gloves.**
- **Dispose of chemical wastes as directed by your teacher.**
- **Hydrochloric acid and sulfuric acid are toxic and corrosive to skin and react with metals.**
- **Sodium hydroxide is corrosive.**
- **Ammonium chloride is slightly toxic.**
- **Barium chloride is highly toxic.**
- **Copper(II) sulfate is moderately toxic by ingestion or inhalation.**
- **Iron(III) chloride and zinc nitrate are tissue irritants and are slightly toxic.**
- **Lead(II) nitrate and sodium sulfite are moderately toxic.**
- **Magnesium sulfate may irritate the eyes.**
- **Potassium nitrate is a skin irritant.**

**LAB 10.2**

## Pre-Lab

1. Explain the mechanism of a double-replacement reaction.

2. Define *precipitate*.

3. Read the entire laboratory activity. Form a hypothesis about what observable products will indicate that a double-replacement reaction has gone to completion. Record your hypothesis in the next column.

4. Summarize the procedures you will follow to test your hypothesis.

## Procedure

For each of the following, note if a precipitate or a gas forms. The formation of water will not be obvious. When water forms, energy is usually given off. Therefore, if no product is immediately visible, insert a thermometer into the contents of the test tube to determine if heat is released. Use the increase in temperature as evidence for formation of water. If no evidence of a chemical reaction is evident, record "No Reaction" in the "Evidence of Reaction" column of **Data Table 1**.

1. Pour 3 mL of 2*M* sodium hydroxide into a clean test tube. Slowly add 3 mL of 0.2*M* copper(II) sulfate.

2. Pour 3 mL of 0.2*M* sodium chloride into a clean test tube. Slowly add 3 mL of 0.2*M* potassium nitrate.

3. Pour 3 mL of 0.2*M* sodium carbonate into a clean test tube. Slowly add 3 mL of 6*M* hydrochloric acid.

4. Pour 3 mL of 0.2*M* barium chloride into a clean test tube. Slowly add 3 mL of 0.2*M* sodium sulfate.

5. Pour 3 mL of 3*M* hydrochloric acid into a clean test tube. Slowly add 3 mL of 2*M* sodium hydroxide.

6. Pour 3 mL of 0.2*M* zinc nitrate into a clean test tube. Slowly add 3 mL of 0.2*M* copper(II) sulfate.

7. Pour 3 mL of 2*M* sodium hydroxide into a clean test tube. Slowly add 3 mL of 0.2*M* iron(III) chloride.

8. **CAUTION: Perform this reaction in the fume hood.** Pour 3 mL of 0.2*M* sodium sulfite into a clean test tube. Slowly add 1 mL of 3*M* hydrochloric acid.

9. Pour 3 mL of 0.2*M* ammonium chloride into a clean test tube. Slowly add 3 mL of 0.2*M* copper(II) sulfate.

10. Pour 3 mL of 0.2*M* lead(II) nitrate into a clean test tube. Slowly add 3 mL of 0.2*M* potassium iodide.

## Hypothesis

_____

_____

## Cleanup and Disposal

1. Dispose of materials as directed by your teacher.

2. Return all lab equipment to its proper place.

3. Report any broken or damaged equipment.

4. Wash your hands thoroughly before leaving the lab.

## Data and Observations

| Data Table 1 | |
|---|---|
| **Test-tube number** | **Evidence of reaction** |
| 1 | |
| 2 | |
| 3 | |
| 4 | |
| 5 | |
| 6 | |
| 7 | |
| 8 | |
| 9 | |
| 10 | |

## Analyze and Conclude

1. **Interpreting Data** Write balanced chemical equations for each of the reactions performed. If no reaction was observed write "No Reaction." Be sure to show the state for each reactant and product.

_____

_____

_____

_____

_____

_____

_____

_____

_____

_____

_____

2. **Making Predictions** Predict the result of mixing sulfuric acid and potassium hydroxide solutions.

_____

_____

_____

_____

_____

3. **Error Analysis** Compare your data table with others in your class. What could have caused any differences?

_____

_____

_____

_____

_____

**Real-World Chemistry**

1. Explain why barium sulfate is used in X-ray diagnosis of the gastrointestinal system.

2. Explain why using a base such as baking soda is effective in cleaning up a spill of an acid, such as vinegar, in the kitchen.

# Estimating the Size of a Mole

**Use with Section 11.3**

**A**vogadro's number is the number of particles (atoms, molecules, or formula units) that are in a mole of a substance. In this lab, you will relate a common object to the concept of Avogadro's number by finding the mass and volume of one mole of the object.

## Problem

How much is a mole? Why is Avogadro's number used when counting atoms but not in counting everyday amounts?

## Objectives

- **Measure** the average mass of a split pea and **calculate** its volume.
- **Calculate** the mass and volume of a mole of split peas.
- **Compare** the mass and volume of a mole of split peas to the masses and volumes of atoms and compounds.

## Materials

balance
split peas
100-mL graduated cylinder
sheet of notebook paper

## Safety Precautions

- **Always wear safety goggles and a lab apron.**
- **Never eat or taste any substances used in the lab.**
- **Do not spill split peas down the sink drain.**
- **Pick up any split peas that spill on the floor.**

## Pre-Lab

1. What is the value of Avogadro's number?
2. Determine the mass of 1 mol of gold (Au), of aluminum chloride ($AlCl_3$), and of glucose ($C_6H_{12}O_6$).
3. If you had 24.65 g of aluminum chloride, how many moles would that be?
4. Read the entire laboratory activity. Form a hypothesis as to the mass and volume of a mole of split peas. Record your hypothesis on page 82.

## Procedure

1. Using a balance or electronic scale, determine the mass of the empty graduated cylinder. Record this mass in **Data Table 1.**
2. Count out exactly 25 split peas. Place them in the graduated cylinder.
3. Obtain the mass of the graduated cylinder and the 25 split peas, and record this mass in **Data Table 1.**
4. Using the notebook paper as a funnel, fill the graduated cylinder to the 100-mL line with split peas.
5. Measure the mass of the graduated cylinder and the 100 mL of split peas. Record this mass in **Data Table 1.**

## Hypothesis

_____

_____

## Cleanup and Disposal

**1.** Empty all of the split peas from the graduated cylinder into the storage container.

**2.** Return all lab equipment to its proper place.

## Data and Observations

| Data Table 1 | |
|---|---|
| **Find the mass of one split pea:** | |
| Mass of empty graduated cylinder | g |
| Mass of 25 split peas and graduated cylinder | g |
| Mass of 25 split peas | g |
| Mass of one split pea | g |
| **Find the volume of one split pea:** | |
| Mass of 100 mL split peas and graduated cylinder | g |
| Mass of 100 mL ($cm^3$) split peas | g |
| Number of split peas in 100 mL ($cm^3$) | |
| Volume of one split pea | mL |
| **Find the mass and volume of a mole of split peas:** | |
| Mass of one mole of split peas | kg |
| Volume of one mole of split peas | mL |

Record the results of each of the following calculations in **Data Table 1.**

**1.** From the masses you measured, calculate the mass of 25 split peas.

_____

**2.** Calculate the mass of one split pea.

_____

**3.** Calculate the mass of 100 mL of split peas.

_____

**4.** From the mass of 100 mL of split peas and the mass of one split pea, calculate the number of split peas in 100 mL.

_____

**5.** From the number of split peas in 100 mL, calculate the volume of one split pea.

_____

**6.** Using Avogadro's number ($6.02 \times 10^{23}$) and the mass of one split pea, calculate the mass of 1 mol of split peas.

_____

**7.** In a similar manner, calculate the volume of 1 mol of split peas.

_____

## Analyze and Conclude

**1. Observing and Inferring** Why was the mass of 25 split peas determined rather than the mass of just one split pea?

_____

**2. Comparing** How does the mass of a mole of split peas compare with the masses of gold, aluminum chloride, and glucose you calculated in the pre-lab?

_____

_____

**3. Drawing Conclusions** Why is Avogadro's number useful when discussing atoms?

_____

_____

_____

**4. Error Analysis** How did your hypothesis as to the mass and volume of a mole of split peas compare to the actual values you calculated during the lab?

_____

_____

### Real-World Chemistry

**1.** Different units are used to count objects in daily life. What is a common unit you use to measure the number of eggs? The number of shoes? Why aren't moles used to measure these amounts?

**2.** In the lab, you changed units of mass and volume to moles. Think of the world's monetary systems. Why is it important to be able to change from one unit to another if you are traveling in a foreign country?

# LAB 11.2 LABORATORY MANUAL

# Mole Ratios

Use with
Section 11.4

**T**he mole ratio of cations to anions in an ionic compound consists of small, whole numbers. For example, the mole ratio of $Mg^{2+}$ ions to $Br^-$ ions in $MgBr_2$ is 1:2. For every 1 mol of $Mg^{2+}$ ions present, there are 2 mol of $Br^-$ ions. The mole ratio of ions in KBr is 1:1. In water solution, one mole of KBr will produce 1 mol $Br^-$ ions, but 1 mol $MgBr_2$ will produce 2 mol $Br^-$ ions.

Suppose you have different compounds that contain $Cl^-$ ions. How could you determine the mole ratios in these compounds? Most chloride compounds dissolve in water, but some do not. Reacting dissolved chloride ions with a cation that forms an insoluble chloride compound can be used to determine the amount of chloride ions present. One such cation is silver. Reacting a chloride-containing solution with sufficient silver nitrate ($AgNO_3$) solution will precipitate any dissolved chloride ions. A solution of KCl will react with a certain amount of $AgNO_3$. The same volume of $BaCl_2$ solution of the same concentration will require twice as much $AgNO_3$ to precipitate all the $Cl^-$ ions.

## Problem

What is the ratio of cations to anions in an ionic compound? How can this ratio be determined?

## Objectives

- **Measure** the reacting ratios of silver nitrate solution with solutions of various chloride compounds.
- **Calculate** the ratio of positive ion to chloride ion in four chloride compounds.
- **Determine** the ratio of positive ion to chloride ion in an unknown compound.

## Materials

0.10*M* silver nitrate ($AgNO_3$)
0.10*M* potassium chloride (KCl)
0.10*M* sodium chloride (NaCl)
0.10*M* barium chloride ($BaCl_2$)

0.10*M* aluminum chloride ($AlCl_3$)
dichlorofluorescein
test tubes (10)
10-mL graduated cylinder
dropper

## Safety Precautions

- **Always wear safety goggles, a lab apron, and gloves.**
- **Silver nitrate is corrosive and will stain skin and clothing.**
- **Silver nitrate and barium chloride are toxic. Potassium chloride and aluminum chloride are slightly toxic.**

# Pre-Lab

**1.** What is meant by the term *mole*?

**2.** What do you need to know to calculate the number of moles of a substance?

**3.** Read the entire laboratory activity. Form a hypothesis about the expected ratios of reacting volumes. Form a second hypothesis about how these ratios can be used to determine the cation to anion ratio in an unknown substance. Record your hypotheses in the next column.

**4.** Summarize the procedures you will follow to test your hypotheses.

**5.** What is the net ionic equation for the reaction between $AgNO_3(aq)$ and $KCl(aq)$?

## Procedure

### Part A: Testing known solutions

**1.** Pour 1.00 mL of the KCl solution into a clean, dry test tube.

**2.** Add 2 drops of dichlorofluoroscein indicator solution to the test tube.

**3.** Add silver nitrate drop by drop to the solution until the dichlorofluoroscein turns from white to pink. Hold the dropper vertically as you add the drops. Carefully shake the tube from side to side as the drops are being added. Do not spill any solution.

**4.** Count and record in **Data Table 1** the number of drops needed to turn the solution from white to pink.

**5.** Repeat the procedure for a second 1-mL sample of KCl.

**6.** Repeat steps 1–5, using solutions of NaCl, $BaCl_2$, and $AlCl_3$, in turn, instead of KCl.

### Part B: Testing a solution of unknown concentration

**7.** Obtain an unknown sample from your teacher. Record the number of the sample.

**8.** Repeat steps 1–5, using the unknown solution instead of KCl.

## Hypotheses

_____

_____

_____

_____

## Cleanup and Disposal

**1.** Pour any materials containing silver into a container provided by your teacher.

**2.** Return all lab equipment to its proper place.

**3.** Report any broken or damaged equipment.

**4.** Wash your hands thoroughly before leaving the lab.

## Data and Observations

| Data Table 1 | | | | |
|---|---|---|---|---|
| Sample | Trial 1 drops of $AgNO_3$ | Trial 2 drops of $AgNO_3$ | Average drops of $AgNO_3$ | Cation/anion ratio |
| KCl | | | | |
| NaCl | | | | |
| $BaCl_2$ | | | | |
| $AlCl_3$ | | | | |
| Unknown | | | | |

## Analyze and Conclude

1. **Using Numbers** Calculate the average number of drops of $AgNO_3$ used for each solution. Record these numbers in **Data Table 1.**

_____

2. **Using Numbers** Assume that the cation-anion ratio is 1:1 for KCl. All the solutions are the same concentration, which means that they all contain the same number of moles of ionic compound per liter of solution. Using this information and your results, calculate the cation to anion ratio for each of the known solutions. Record these ratios in **Data Table 1.**

_____

3. **Comparing** How do your answers in question 2 compare with the ratios you predicted in your hypothesis using the formulas for the compounds?

_____

4. **Inferring** Why must all the solutions being tested be the same concentration?

_____

_____

5. **Making Predictions** Assume you did not know the concentration of the silver nitrate solution. How would this unknown concentration compare with the concentration of the KCl solution if half as much $AgNO_3$ solution as KCl solution was used?

_____

_____

6. **Drawing Conclusions** Summarize how the results of this laboratory activity relate to the formulas of the compounds tested.

_____

_____

_____

7. **Error Analysis** What could you have done to improve the precision of the measurements?

_____

_____

### Real-World Chemistry

1. Body fluids are often tested in medical facilities to determine the concentrations of certain substances. How could the techniques used in this lab activity be applied to such testing?

2. Silver is a valuable metal. Explain how you could separate any dissolved $Ag^+$ ions from the solutions you disposed of in the discard beaker.

## LAB 12.1 LABORATORY MANUAL

# Observing a Limiting Reactant

**Use with Section 12.3**

When two substances react, they react in exact amounts. You can determine what amounts of the two reactants are needed to react completely with each other by means of mole ratios based on the balanced chemical equation for the reaction. In the laboratory, precise amounts of the reactants are rarely used in a reaction. Usually, there is an excess of one of the reactants. As soon as the other reactant is used up, the reaction stops. The reactant that is used up is called the *limiting reactant*. Based on the quantities of each reactant and the balanced chemical equation, you can predict which substance in a reaction is the limiting reactant.

**Problem**

How can the mole concept be used to predict the limiting reactant in a chemical reaction?

**Objectives**

- **Calculate** the number of moles of each reactant.
- **Write** a balanced chemical equation for the reaction of hydrochloric acid and magnesium.
- **Predict**, using the balanced chemical equation, which substance will be the limiting reactant.
- **Compare** the actual results with your predicted results.

**Materials**

dropper bottle containing 6*M* HCl
magnesium ribbon (2 pieces, 3–5 cm each)
test-tube rack
20 × 150-mm test tube
test-tube holder

## Safety Precautions

- Always wear safety goggles, a lab apron, and gloves.
- Point open end of test tube away from your face and away from others.
- Do not inhale released vapors.
- Handle acids carefully.
- Do not use open flames in the lab. Hydrogen gas is flammable.

## Pre-Lab

1. Magnesium and hydrochloric acid react to form magnesium chloride and hydrogen gas. Write the balanced chemical reaction for the reaction.

2. Calculate
   **a.** the number of moles of magnesium in 5.0 g of magnesium.
   **b.** the number of moles of hydrochloric acid in 10 mL of 6.0*M* HCl; 6.0*M* HCl contains 6 moles of HCl per liter of solution.

3. Based on the chemical equation and your calculations, what would be left over if these amounts of magnesium and hydrochloric acid were combined? What would be used up?

4. Describe the term *limiting reactant* in your own words.

5. Read the entire laboratory activity. Form a hypothesis about which reactant will be the limiting reactant at steps 5, 6, and 7 in the experiment. Record your hypothesis on page 90.

**LAB 12.1**

## Procedure

**1.** Obtain two pieces of magnesium ribbon that are 3–5 cm long.

**2.** Determine and record the mass of the first piece of magnesium. Set the second piece aside to use in step 8.

**3.** In the data table, record your observations of the color, length, and texture of your piece of magnesium.

**4.** Bend the piece of magnesium several times and put it into the test tube.

**5.** Place the test tube containing the magnesium in a test-tube rack and add ten drops of 6*M* HCl. Record in **Data Table 1** any observations during and immediately following the reaction. **CAUTION: Do not inhale vapors or look down into test tube. Observe the reaction from the side of the test tube.**

**6.** After the reaction has stopped, add another ten drops of 6*M* HCl to the test tube. Record any observations during and immediately following the reaction.

**7.** Now begin adding 6*M* HCl one drop of at a time, watching the reaction and recording observations after each drop has stopped reacting. Stop adding drops of hydrochloric acid when all of the magnesium ribbon in the test tube has reacted.

**8.** Place the second piece of magnesium ribbon into the test tube and record your observations.

## Hypothesis

_____

_____

## Cleanup and Disposal

**1.** Dispose of the waste material in a waste container in the fume hood as instructed by your teacher. **CAUTION: Use a test-tube holder to move the test tube.**

**2.** Clean up your lab area and wash your hands before leaving the lab.

## Data and Observations

Mass of Mg (g) _____

| Data Table 1 | |
|---|---|
| **Substance(s)** | **Observations** |
| Mg | |
| Mg + 10 drops HCl | |
| Mg + 20 drops HCl | |
| Mg + 21 drops HCl (if needed) | |
| Mg + 22 drops HCl (if needed) | |

**Data Table 1,** *continued*

| Substance(s) | Observations |
|---|---|
| Mg + 23 drops HCl (if needed) | |
| Mg + 24 drops HCl (if needed) | |
| Mg + 25 drops HCl (if needed) | |
| HCl + second piece of magnesium | |

## Analyze and Conclude

1. **Observing and Inferring** What was the total number of drops of HCl needed to react with all of the magnesium?

_____

_____

2. **Observing and Inferring** Explain what happened when the second piece of magnesium was added to the test tube. Did it react? Why or why not?

_____

_____

_____

_____

3. **Collecting and Interpreting Data** Based on your observations, describe which substance was the limiting reactant at the end of step 5, step 6, and step 7. How were you able to determine this?

_____

_____

_____

4. **Measuring and Using Numbers** What volume of $6M$ HCl would be necessary to completely react with the first strip of magnesium?

_____

_____

**5. Thinking Critically** What steps would need to be added to this lab to accurately determine the stoichiometric ratio of Mg to HCl at each step in this lab?

_____

_____

_____

**6. Error Analysis** Compare your data with that of your classmates. Did others use more drops or fewer drops of HCl while using a similar size piece of magnesium? What could be the sources of error?

_____

_____

_____

## Real-World Chemistry

**1.** Why is it important for a chemical manufacturer to be able to determine which reactant is the limiting reactant?

**2.** How would the idea of limiting reactants be used when discussing automobiles?

**LAB 12.2 LABORATORY MANUAL**

# Determining Reaction Ratios

Use with
Section 12.3

**M**ole ratios can be used to determine the amount of one substance needed to react with a given amount of another substance. In this experiment, you will react a substance called an acid with another substance called a base. Acids can be defined as substances that dissociate and produce hydrogen ($H^+$) ions when dissolved in water. Bases are substances that ionize to produce hydroxide ($OH^-$) ions when they dissolve in water. When acids and bases react with each other, the $H^+$ ions and $OH^-$ ions join to form water ($H_2O$). The resulting solution no longer has an excess of either $H^+$ ions or $OH^-$ ions. The solution has become *neutral*. This process is called neutralization. By using the mole ratio of hydrogen ions and hydroxide ions in the balanced chemical equation, you can predict the point at which a solution becomes neutral.

## Problem
What volume of $1M$ hydrochloric acid will be needed to neutralize three different bases?

## Objectives
- **Classify** substances as acids or bases.
- **Determine** the types and numbers of ions that are released upon dissociation of the acid and the bases.
- **Measure** the amount of base needed to neutralize a given amount of hydrochloric acid.
- **Calculate** the mole ratios of the acid and bases used in this activity.

## Materials
1.0$M$ hydrochloric acid (HCl)
1.0$M$ sodium hydroxide (NaOH)
1.0$M$ barium hydroxide ($Ba(OH)_2$)
1.0$M$ ammonium hydroxide ($NH_4OH$)
125-mL Erlenmeyer flask
50-mL graduated cylinder

150-mL beakers (3)
50-mL burette (3)
glass funnel
ring stands (3)
wash bottle with distilled water
phenolphthalein indicator
burette clamps (3)
waste beaker or other container

## Safety Precautions

- Always wear safety goggles and a lab apron.
- Use caution when working with acids and bases.
- Fill the burette carefully with base.
- Read all labels before mixing chemicals.

## Pre-Lab

1. Determine how each substance used in this lab forms ions when placed in water and write the equations for the reactions. Which are acids? Which are bases?

2. Write a balanced chemical reaction for each of the following double replacement reactions:
   **a.** hydrochloric acid reacts with sodium hydroxide
   **b.** hydrochloric acid reacts with barium hydroxide
   **c.** hydrochloric acid reacts with ammonium hydroxide

3. Read the entire laboratory activity. How will you know when the solution is neutral? Formulate a hypothesis that predicts which substance you will have to use the most of to neutralize the acid and which substance you will have to use the least of. Record your hypothesis in the next column.

4. What color is phenolphthalein in an acidic solution? What color is phenolphthalein in a basic solution? Why is a solution of phenolphthalein used in this activity?

5. What safety precautions should you follow when performing this activity?

## Procedure

Note: If your instructor has set up the burettes, you may begin at step 7.

1. Set up each of the three burettes as shown in **Figure A.**

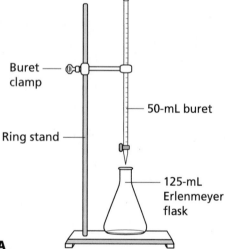

Buret clamp

50-mL buret

Ring stand

125-mL Erlenmeyer flask

**Figure A**

2. Label your 150-mL beakers *sodium hydroxide, barium hydroxide,* and *ammonium hydroxide.*

3. Using the appropriate beaker, obtain about 75 mL of each of the solutions listed in step 2.

4. Using the glass funnel, add about 5 mL of NaOH to the first burette. Take the burette out of the clamp and swirl the 5 mL of NaOH around the burette to coat the entire inside with solution. Empty this 5 mL of NaOH rinse into a waste beaker.

5. Fill this burette to the zero (0 mL) line with NaOH.

6. Rinse the funnel with distilled water. Repeat steps 4 and 5 using $Ba(OH)_2$ and $NH_4OH$ and the other two burettes. Be sure to rinse the funnel with distilled water each time.

7. Using your 50-mL graduated cylinder, measure 25 mL of HCl.

8. Pour the 25-mL of HCl into the Erlenmeyer flask and add 2–3 drops of phenolphthalein indicator. Swirl the mixture.

9. In **Data Table 1,** observe and record the initial volume of solution in the burette containing the NaOH. The initial reading does not have to be zero.

10. Place the Erlenmeyer flask under the burette containing the NaOH. While swirling the flask, open the stopcock and begin to run some of the sodium hydroxide solution into the hydrochloric acid. **CAUTION: Do not touch the tip of the burette to the side of the flask, as illustrated in Figure A.**

11. When you begin to see pink swirls in the flask, stop the flow of sodium hydroxide. Swirl the flask until the color disappears.

12. Continue to alternate adding sodium hydroxide and swirling. Stop adding sodium hydroxide when the light pink color does not disappear.

13. In **Data Table 1,** record the final volume of the solution in your burette.

14. Check your color with your teacher and dispose of the solution according to your teacher's directions.

15. Rinse your Erlenmeyer flask with generous amounts of distilled water. Repeat steps 7–14 using the $Ba(OH)_2$ and the $NH_4OH$. Be sure to rinse the flask after each trial.

## Hypothesis

_____

_____

_____

_____

## Cleanup and Disposal

**1.** Clean up your lab area including any spills on the lab table.

**2.** Return all lab equipment to its proper place.

**3.** Wash your hands with soap and water before leaving the lab area.

## Data and Observations

| Data Table 1 | | | | | |
|---|---|---|---|---|---|
| Trial # | mL of HCl in flask | Substance in burette | Burette initial volume (mL) | Burette final volume (mL) | mL base used |
| 1 | | NaOH | | | |
| 2 | | Ba(OH)$_2$ | | | |
| 3 | | NH$_4$OH | | | |

## Analyze and Conclude

**1. Collecting and Interpreting Data** Rank the volumes of the bases used in order from the least amount used to the greatest amount.

_____

_____

_____

**2. Collecting and Interpreting Data** For each neutralization, give the ratio of volume of acid to volume of base.

_____

_____

_____

**3. Drawing a Conclusion** How do the ratios from question 2 compare with the equations that you wrote in the pre-lab?

_____

_____

_____

_____

4. **Predicting**  In this activity, the concentration of each of the reactants was 1.0*M*, which means that each solution contains 1 mol of dissolved substance per liter of solution. What do you think would happen if these concentrations were different?

_____

_____

_____

5. **Error Analysis**  How did your volumetric ratios compare with the mole ratios in the equations? Discuss any error that may have occurred in the activity that made these quantities differ.

_____

_____

_____

## Real-World Chemistry

1. Muriatic acid can be sold as part of a powder containing hydrochloric acid. Why might it be necessary for a gardener to use this product?

2. Why would it be necessary for manufacturers to be able to identify and quantify waste products that are being released into the environment? What are some of the waste products of the industries in your area?

# Freezing Bacteria

**Use with Section 13.4**

**W**hen liquid water freezes, the water molecules form a crystal lattice. At standard pressure, the freezing point of water is 0°C. The temperature at which water begins to freeze can be altered if ice-nucleating particles are present. These particles attract water molecules and assist in the freezing process. Ice-nucleating proteins (INP) can be extracted from *Pseudomonas syringae*, a bacteria that is found on grasses, trees, and other plants. In this activity, you will study the effect of INP on the temperature at which water begins to freeze.

## Problem

How does the presence of ice-nucleating protein affect the freezing point of water?

## Objectives

- **Compare** the freezing points of distilled water and distilled water containing ice-nucleating bacteria.
- **Graph** the relationship between time and temperature for distilled water and distilled water containing ice-nucleating bacteria.

## Materials

4*M* CaCl₂ solution
ice-nucleating protein
4-mL graduated pipettes (2)
10-mL graduated cylinder
600-mL beaker
small-tip dropping pipettes (2)
test tubes (7)
test-tube rack
solid rubber stoppers to fit test tubes (3)

labels
distilled water
crushed ice
ring stand
test-tube utility clamps (2)
thermometer clamps (2)
stirring rod
spatula
graph paper

## Safety Precautions

- **Always wear safety goggles, a lab apron, and gloves.**
- **Dispose of wastes as directed by your teacher.**
- **Organisms or substances extracted from organisms should always be treated as if they were hazardous.**
- **Observe proper hygiene when handling bacterial protein. Be sure to wear gloves and wash your hands with antibacterial soap after handling the protein.**

## Pre-Lab

1. Read over the entire laboratory activity. What role do the test tubes containing distilled water play in the experimental design?

2. Why is it important to have equivalent volumes in the test tubes used in Part B?

3. Form a hypothesis about the effect an ice-nucleating protein will have on the freezing temperature of water. Record your hypothesis on page 98.

## Procedure

### Part A

1. Label a test tube *stock INP*.

2. Pour 10 mL of distilled water into the test tube and then use a spatula to add 4 or 5 granules of ice-nucleating protein to the water.

3. Stopper the test tube and shake the test tube a few times until the protein and water are well mixed.

4. Put about 400 mL of crushed ice into a 600-mL beaker.

5. Add enough $4M$ $CaCl_2$ solution to cover the ice. Stir the mixture with a stirring rod and then insert a thermometer. Record this temperature in Data and Observations.

6. Label two test tubes *INP* and a second set of two test tubes $H_2O$.

7. Using a clean dropping pipette, decant some of the stock INP solution.

8. Place 1 small drop of the solution into each of the two test tubes labeled *INP*. Save the remaining solution for Part B.

9. Using a clean dropping pipette, decant some distilled water.

10. Place 1 small drop of the distilled water into each of the two test tubes labeled $H_2O$.

11. Place all four test tubes into the beaker containing the ice and the $CaCl_2$ solution.

12. Observe the test tubes to determine in which test tubes ice crystals form sooner.

13. Remove the test tubes and save the cooling bath for Part B.

### Part B

1. Label one clean test tube *INP* and a second clean test tube $H_2O$.

2. Using a graduated pipette, add 4 mL of the stock INP mixture prepared in Part A to the test tube marked *INP*.

3. Using a graduated pipette, add 4 mL distilled water to the test tube marked $H_2O$.

4. Clamp the test tubes and the thermometers in the beaker containing the ice and the $CaCl_2$, as shown in **Figure A.** Make sure that the bulbs of

**Figure A**

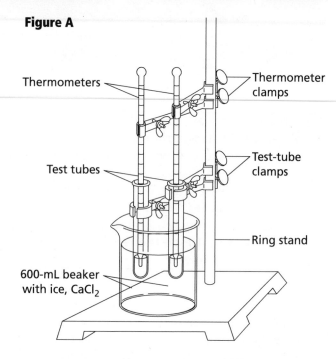

Thermometers

Thermometer clamps

Test-tube clamps

Test tubes

Ring stand

600-mL beaker with ice, $CaCl_2$

the thermometers are suspended in the liquid and not touching the bottom or the sides of the test tube. Once the test tubes and thermometers are in position, do not move them.

5. Record the temperature of the *INP* test tube in **Data Table 1** in the row marked *0 min* and the temperature of the $H_2O$ test tube in **Data Table 2** in the row marked *0 min*. Then record the temperature every 4 min for 60 min in the respective data tables. Also record the phase of the test tube contents: *liquid, solid*, or a *mixture* of liquid and solid.

## Hypothesis

_____

_____

_____

## Cleanup and Disposal

1. Dispose of materials as instructed by your teacher.

2. Return all lab equipment to its proper place.

3. Wash your hands thoroughly with antibacterial soap before leaving the lab.

## Data and Observations

Initial temperature of $CaCl_2$ solution and water (°C) = _____

| Time (min) | Temperature (°C) | Change of temperature (°C) | Phase | Time (min) | Temperature (°C) | Change of temperature (°C) | Phase |
|---|---|---|---|---|---|---|---|
| | | | Data Table 1: INP | | | | |
| 0 | | | | 32 | | | |
| 4 | | | | 36 | | | |
| 8 | | | | 40 | | | |
| 12 | | | | 44 | | | |
| 16 | | | | 48 | | | |
| 20 | | | | 52 | | | |
| 24 | | | | 56 | | | |
| 28 | | | | 60 | | | |

| Time (min) | Temperature (°C) | Change of temperature (°C) | Phase | Time (min) | Temperature (°C) | Change of temperature (°C) | Phase |
|---|---|---|---|---|---|---|---|
| | | | Data Table 2: Water | | | | |
| 0 | | | | 32 | | | |
| 4 | | | | 36 | | | |
| 8 | | | | 40 | | | |
| 12 | | | | 44 | | | |
| 16 | | | | 48 | | | |
| 20 | | | | 52 | | | |
| 24 | | | | 56 | | | |
| 28 | | | | 60 | | | |

# LABORATORY MANUAL

## Analyze and Conclude

### Part A

**1. Observing and Inferring** What was the temperature of the ice and the $CaCl_2$ mixture?

**2. Thinking Critically** What was the purpose of the $CaCl_2$ in the ice? (Hint: What would be the temperature of an ice-water mixture?

### Part B

**3. Making and Using Graphs** Plot time versus temperature for both INP and water on the same graph.

**4. Acquiring and Analyzing Information** At which temperature did ice begin forming in each test tube? How does INP affect the temperature at which water begins to freeze?

**5. Drawing a Conclusion** Why did the water droplets in one set of test tubes begin to solidify before the water droplets in the other set of test tubes?

**6. Error Analysis** What sources of error might have been introduced in this lab?

## Real-World Chemistry

**1.** When crops freeze, the ice crystals that form damage the cell walls of the plants, which ultimately destroys the cells. Explain how removal of INP from plant surfaces could help the plants.

**2.** Modern snowmaking equipment utilizes ice-nucleating proteins derived from bacteria. The protein causes more droplets of water to freeze before reaching the ground, even if the air temperature is slightly above water's normal freezing point. Ice-nucleating protein for snowmaking is freeze-dried before it is shipped to the ski slopes. Explain the process of freeze-drying.

# Boiling Points

**W**hen the kinetic-molecular theory is applied to liquids, the
forces of attraction between molecules become important.
Molecular polarity and molecular size cause the boiling points of
substances to differ. The boiling point occurs when the vapor
pressure of a liquid equals the external atmospheric pressure. At the
boiling point, molecules throughout the liquid have enough energy
to vaporize. By measuring temperature at a constant pressure, you
can determine the boiling point of a substance.

## Problem

Can the boiling point of
a substance be used to
distinguish substances?

## Objectives

- **Record** temperature data
  to determine the boiling
  points of two liquids.
- **Draw conclusions** about
  using boiling points to
  distinguish unknowns.

## Materials

250-mL beakers (2)
ice (150 mL)
boiling chips
hot plate
ring stand and
  clamp
test tubes (2)

unknown liquids
thermometer
2-hole rubber
  stopper
plastic or rubber
  tubing (60-cm
  length)

## Safety Precautions

     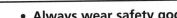

- **Always wear safety goggles and a lab apron.**
- **Apparatus must be open to the atmosphere so that there is no buildup
  of gas pressure.**
- **Vapors given off must be condensed and collected into the test tube in
  the ice bath.**
- **Assume the liquids are flammable. Use hot plates; do not use around
  flames.**
- **Perform this experiment only in a well-ventilated room.**

## Pre-Lab

1. Read the entire laboratory activity. Form a
   hypothesis about whether the boiling point of a
   substance can be used to distinguish substances.
   Record your hypothesis and the basis for your
   prediction on page 102.

2. Predict whether the boiling points of the liquids
   tested will be greater or less than the boiling
   point of water. Give a reason for your prediction.

3. What effect does the addition of heat have on the
   kinetic energy of a liquid?

4. Define *boiling point*.

5. What two variables cause the boiling points of
   substances to be different?

## Procedure

1. Obtain a test tube containing an unknown liquid from your teacher and add one or two boiling chips to it.

2. Assemble the apparatus shown in **Figure A.**

3. Fill one 250-mL beaker half full with tap water and place the beaker on the hot plate.

4. Insert the thermometer and tubing into the stopper. Lubricate the stopper with glycerol if needed. Place the stopper in the test tube. Adjust the thermometer so that the bulb is submerged in the liquid, but not touching the bottom of the test tube.

5. Clamp the test tube to the ring stand in the water bath.

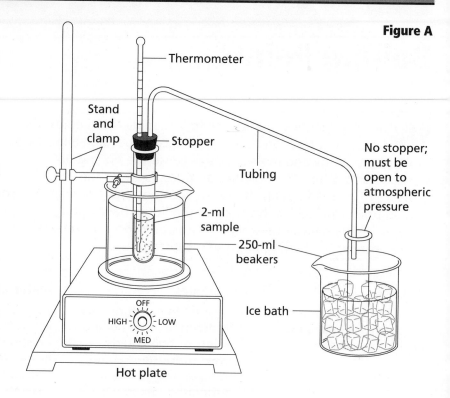

6. Assemble the ice bath. The vapors will condense and collect in the second test tube. Place enough ice in a 250-mL beaker to fill it half full. Place the second test tube in the ice bath. Insert the loose end of the tubing into the test tube. Make sure that this end of the tubing is open to the atmosphere. **CAUTION: Do not use a rubber stopper.**

7. Turn on the hot plate and heat the water bath slowly. Record the boiling point when the liquid begins to boil in **Data Table 1.** There should be a steady stream of bubbles. Record the temperatures to one place after the decimal point.

8. Turn off the hot plate. Allow the equipment to cool before handling.

## Hypothesis

_____

_____

_____

## Cleanup and Disposal

1. Return both test tubes to your teacher.

2. Clean and return all lab equipment to its proper place.

## Data and Observations

1. Record the boiling point of your unknown liquid in **Data Table 1.**

2. Your teacher will make a table with the data collected by all the groups for unknowns A and B.

**LAB 13.2**

| Data Table 1 | | | |
|---|---|---|---|
| **Unknown A** | **Boiling point (°C)** | **Unknown B** | **Boiling point (°C)** |
| Group 1 | | Group 1 | |
| Group 2 | | Group 2 | |
| Group 3 | | Group 3 | |
| Group 4 | | Group 4 | |
| Group 5 | | Group 5 | |
| Average | | Average | |

## Analyze and Conclude

1. **Observing and Inferring** Explain the pathway of heat transfer from the hot plate to the unknown liquid.

   _____

   _____

2. **Applying Concepts** What is the external pressure in this experiment?

   _____

3. **Acquiring and Analyzing Data** Calculate the average boiling points for unknown A and unknown B. Use at least three temperatures in your calculations. If any data points differ from the average by more than 2 degrees, discard that data and recalculate the average.

   _____

   _____

   _____

4. **Comparing and Contrasting** Compare your average boiling point for unknowns A and B with the reference data provided by your teacher. Identify the unknown liquids. What is the difference between the accepted boiling points of the liquids?

   _____

   _____

5. **Error Analysis** The error for a measurement is the difference between the accepted value and the experimental value for a measurement. Calculate the error for the average boiling point for each substance. Were the measurements accurate enough to confirm your hypotheses? List possible sources of errors.

   _____

   _____

   _____

## Real-World Chemistry

1. How would the boiling point change if this experiment was performed at the Dead Sea (394 m below sea level) or Mt. Everest (8848 m high)?

2. Explain what happens in a pressure cooker. What is the advantage in using a pressure cooker? What are the potential dangers?

**LAB 14.1  LABORATORY MANUAL**

# Charles's Law

Use with
Section 14.1

Jacques Charles first showed the relationship between temperature and volume of a gas in 1787. His work showed that gases expand in a linear manner as the temperature is increased and contract linearly as the temperature is decreased, provided the pressure is kept constant.

The graphical plot of the temperature versus volume of a gas produces a straight line. If several different gases are studied and the temperature-volume data is plotted, the extrapolations of these graphs all intersect at the same temperature, $-273°C$. The Kelvin equivalent of this temperature is expressed as 0 K, or absolute zero. The mathematical expression to change Celsius temperature to Kelvin is: $K = C° + 273°$.

The relationship between Kelvin temperature and the volume of a gas is expressed as Charles's law: The volume of a confined gas, at a constant pressure, is directly proportional to its Kelvin temperature. Mathematically, Charles's law is:

$$\frac{V_1}{T_1} = \frac{V_2}{T_2}$$

In this expression, $V$ is the volume, $T$ is Kelvin temperature, *1* indicates initial conditions, and *2* indicates final conditions.

In this activity, you will measure the volume of a gas (air) at two different temperatures.

## Problem

What is the change in the volume of a gas if the temperature is changed?

## Objectives

- **Predict** how the volume of a gas will change when the temperature is raised or lowered.
- **Calculate** what the change in volume of a gas should be when the temperature is changed.
- **Make** and **use graphs** to predict the volume of the gas at different temperatures.

## Materials

125-mL dropping bottle with hinged dispenser caps (2)
250-mL graduated cylinder
1000-mL beakers (2)

hot plate
thermometer
ring stand
clamp
ice

## Safety Precautions

- **Always wear safety goggles, thermal gloves, and a lab apron.**
- **Hot objects may not appear to be hot.**
- **Possible danger of electrical shock exists.**

**LAB 14.1**

## Pre-Lab

1. State Charles's law.

2. Write the mathematical expression of Charles's law.

3. Write the mathematical expression used to convert Celsius temperature to Kelvin.

4. Read the entire laboratory activity. Form a hypothesis about how the volume of a gas will change as the temperature is changed. Record your hypothesis in the next column.

5. Summarize the procedures you will follow to test your hypothesis.

## Procedure

### Part A

1. Measure and record the temperature of the air in the room in **Data Table 1.**

2. Thoroughly clean and dry a 125-mL dropping bottle. Screw the cap onto the bottle, leaving the hinged cap open.

3. Use a ring stand and clamp to suspend the assembled dropping bottle in a 1000-mL beaker that is placed on a hot plate, as shown in **Figure A.**

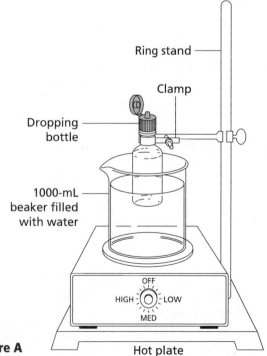

**Figure A**

4. Pour enough water into the beaker to cover at least 75 percent of the suspended bottle.

5. Heat the water to boiling. Then reduce the heat and continue boiling for about 5 minutes. Record the temperature of the boiling water in **Data Table 1.**

6. Close the hinged cap on the dropping bottle and immediately remove the bottle from the hot water. Cool the bottle by immersing it in another 1000-mL beaker containing tap water.

7. Stir the water until the temperature no longer changes and then record the temperature of the water.

8. Leave the bottle immersed in the water for 5 minutes. With the bottle and cap completely submerged, open the hinged cap and allow water to enter the bottle.

9. Hold the bottle in an inverted position, with the cap still open. Elevate or lower the bottle until the water level in the bottle is even with the water level in the beaker. Close the cap. The air in the bottle is now at atmospheric pressure.

10. Remove the bottle from the water and place it right side up on the lab desk.

11. The volume of water in the bottle is equal to the change in volume of the air as it cooled from the temperature of boiling water to the temperature of tap water. Use a graduated cylinder to accurately measure the volume of the water in the bottle.

12. To find the starting volume of air in the bottle, fill the bottle with water. Use the graduated cylinder to accurately measure the volume of the water in the bottle.

### Part B

Obtain a clean dropping bottle. Repeat Part A of this activity, only cool the dropping bottle in the boiling water this time by immersing it in a beaker of ice water instead of tap water.

## Hypothesis

_____

_____

_____

## Cleanup and Disposal

1. Return all lab equipment to its proper place.
2. Report any broken or damaged equipment.
3. Wash your hands thoroughly before leaving the lab.

## Data and Observations

| Data Table 1 | | |
|---|---|---|
| | **Part A** | **Part B** |
| Room temperature (°C) | | |
| Temperature of boiling water (°C) | | |
| Temperature of boiling water (K) | | |
| Final temperature of cooling water (°C) | | |
| Final temperature of cooling water (K) | | |
| Total volume of air in bottle at higher temperature (mL) | | |
| Change in volume of air in bottle (mL) | | |
| Volume of air at lower temperature (mL) | | |

## Analyze and Conclude

1. **Measuring and Using Numbers** Calculate the Kelvin temperatures of the water and record your answers in **Data Table 1.**

2. **Measuring and Using Numbers** Subtract the change in the volume of air in the bottle from the total volume of air in the bottle at a higher temperature to get the volume of air at a lower temperature. Record your answer in **Data Table 1.**

3. **Measuring and Using Numbers** Use the equation $\dfrac{V_1}{T_1} = \dfrac{V_2}{T_2}$ to calculate the expected volume of air when cooled in tap water.

_____

_____

4. **Comparing and Contrasting** Compare the expected final volume with the calculated final volume.

_____

_____

**5. Thinking Critically** What is the significance of elevating or lowering the bottle until the water level in the bottle is even with the water level in the beaker?

_____

_____

_____

**6. Predicting** Dry ice sublimes (changes from solid to gas) at $-78.5°$ C. Predict the volume of the gas in the bottle if the temperature of the air was reduced to that temperature.

_____

**7. Making and Using Graphs**

  **a.** Construct a graph of the data. Plot the volume of the gas at room temperature, in tap water, and in ice water on the *y*-axis. Plot the Kelvin temperatures on the *x*-axis. Extrapolate the line.

  **b.** At which temperature is the line predicted to cross the *x*-axis?

_____

  **c.** At which temperature did the line actually cross the *x*-axis?

_____

**8. Error Analysis** Account for any deviation between the predicted temperature line extrapolation and the actual extrapolated line temperature.

_____

_____

**Real-World Chemistry**

  **1.** Explain why bottled gas containers are equipped with a relief valve.

  **2.** Explain why bread rises when baked. (Hint: The action of yeast produces $CO_2$ gas.)

# Boyle's Law

**B**oyle's law states that the volume of a fixed amount of gas at a constant temperature is inversely proportional to the pressure, provided the temperature does not change. It has been observed that, at a constant temperature, doubling the pressure on a sample of gas reduces the volume by one-half. Conversely, halving the pressure on a sample of gas results in a doubling of the volume.

The graphical plot of pressure versus volume shows an inverse variation. In an inverse relationship, as the magnitude of one quantity increases, the magnitude of the second quantity decreases. This relationship may be expressed as

$$P_1V_1 = P_2V_2$$

where $P_1$ is the initial pressure, $V_1$ is the initial volume, $P_2$ is the second pressure, and $V_2$ is the second volume. Note that in this relationship, the product of pressure and volume is a constant, or,

$$PV = k$$

The procedure in this lab is done using an air sample over water, and water vapor will saturate and add to the pressure. So, the water vapor pressure must be subtracted from the barometric pressure. You will consult the *CRC Handbook of Chemistry and Physics* to determine water vapor pressure at the temperature of the water being used in the activity.

Additionally, the pressure equivalent of the heights of the water above and below the initial point must be calculated and either added to or subtracted from the corrected pressure for each case. Because mercury is 13.6 times as dense as water, any column of water can be converted to mm Hg, or torr, by dividing the water column height, in mm, by 13.6. Water is used instead of mercury because liquid mercury and its vapors are highly toxic and cannot be safely used in the classroom laboratory.

## Problem

For a sample of gas at a constant temperature, how does the product of pressure times volume compare at different pressures?

## Objectives

- **Measure** the volume of a gas (air) as the pressure varies.
- **Use numbers** to calculate corrected pressures and the product of pressure and volume.
- **Compare** the product of pressure and volume at different pressures and constant temperature.

## Materials

1000-mL beakers (2)
graduated cylinder
thermometer
stirring rod
barometer
eudiometer tube
leveling bulb
heavy-walled rubber tubing
*CRC Handbook of Chemistry and Physics*
meterstick

**LAB 14.2**

# LABORATORY MANUAL

## Safety Precautions

• **Always wear safety goggles, a lab apron, and gloves.**

## Pre-Lab

1. State Boyle's law in words.
2. Write the mathematical expression of Boyle's law.
3. Explain why water vapor pressure must be subtracted from the barometric pressure.
4. Explain why the pressure equivalent of the heights of the water above and below the initial point must be calculated by dividing the difference in heights by 13.6.
5. Read the entire laboratory activity. Form a hypothesis about how the volume of a gas will change as the temperature is changed. Record your hypothesis on page 111.

## Procedure

1. Obtain 500 mL of water at room temperature. If it is not at room temperature, heat or cool it until it measures the same temperature as the room.
2. Pour this water into a 1000-mL beaker.
3. Pour the water vigorously several times between two 1000-mL beakers to ensure that the water is saturated with air.
4. Stir the water slowly for 2 minutes. Do NOT use the thermometer as a stirring rod.
5. Record the temperature of the water in **Data Table 1.**
6. Assemble the apparatus as shown in **Figure A.**
7. Pour enough water into the leveling bulb to fill the bulb.
8. Disconnect the tubing from the eudiometer tube and allow water to run through the rubber tubing until the air is completely removed. Place your finger over the end of the tube.
9. Fill the eudiometer tube about one-third full of water and then reconnect the rubber tubing.
10. Reassemble the apparatus, as shown in **Figure A.**

**Figure A**

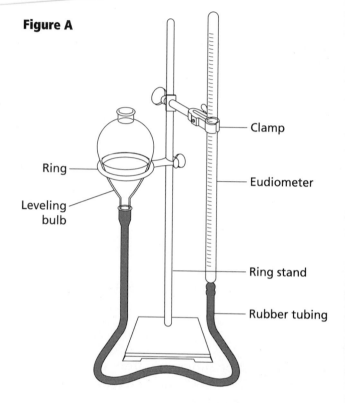

Clamp

Ring

Eudiometer

Leveling bulb

Ring stand

Rubber tubing

11. Check for leaks by raising and lowering the leveling bulb. If there are no leaks, the water level in the eudiometer should change at a constant rate. If leaks are present, check the connections and tighten as needed.
12. Adjust the leveling bulb and the eudiometer tube so that the levels of water in the tube and the bulb are the same.
13. Record the current barometric pressure in **Data Table 1.**
14. Record the volume of air in the eudiometer tube in **Data Table 2.**
15. Using the meterstick, lower the leveling bulb so that the level of water in the bulb is 250 mm below the water in the eudiometer.
16. Record the volume of air in the eudiometer tube in **Data Table 2.**
17. Lower the leveling bulb farther so that the level of water in the bulb is 500 mm below the water in the eudiometer.

18. Record the volume of air in the eudiometer tube in **Data Table 2.**

19. Raise the leveling bulb so that the level of water in the bulb is 250 mm meter above the water in the tube.

20. Record the volume of air in the eudiometer tube in **Data Table 2.**

21. Raise the leveling bulb farther so that the level of water in the bulb is 500 mm above the water in the tube.

22. Record the volume of air in the eudiometer tube in **Data Table 2.**

## Hypothesis

_____

_____

_____

## Cleanup and Disposal

1. Return all lab equipment to its proper place.

2. Report any broken or damaged equipment.

3. Wash your hands thoroughly before leaving the laboratory.

## Data and Observations

| Data Table 1 | |
| --- | --- |
| Water temperature (room temperature in °C) | |
| Barometric pressure (torr) | |
| Vapor pressure of water at current room temperature (torr) | |

| Data Table 2 | | | | |
| --- | --- | --- | --- | --- |
| **Water levels** | **Volume of air (mL)** $V$ | **Hg equivalent of water column (torr)** | **Corrected pressure of dry air (torr)** $P$ | **PV for dry gas (torr × mL)** |
| Levels equal | | — | | |
| Bulb is 250 mm below | | | | |
| Bulb is 500 mm below | | | | |
| Bulb is 250 mm above | | | | |
| Bulb is 500 mm above | | | | |

## Analyze and Conclude

1. **Making and Using Tables** Use the _CRC Handbook of Chemistry and Physics_ to look up water vapor pressure at the temperature of the water being used in the activity. Record the answer in **Data Table 1.**

2. **Measuring and Using Numbers** Calculate the mercury equivalent of changing the height of the water column by raising and lowering the leveling bulb. Record your answers in **Data Table 2.** (You will not have an equivalent value when the levels are equal.)

3. **Measuring and Using Numbers** Using the pressure data from **Data Table 1,** calculate the pressure of the dry air when the levels of the water in the leveling bulb and tube are the same. Record your answer in **Data Table 2.**

4. **Measuring and Using Numbers** Calculate the corrected pressure of dry air for each position of the leveling bulb by using this corrected pressure of dry air and subtracting or adding the pressure equivalent of the heights of the water above and below the initial point. Record your answers in **Data Table 2.**

5. **Measuring and Using Numbers** Use the relationship $PV = k$ to calculate the constant for each of the sets of data. Record your answers in **Data Table 2.**

6. **Thinking Critically** What is the significance of dividing the water level difference in each step by 13.6?

_____

_____

_____

7. **Thinking Critically** What is the significance of subtracting water vapor pressure in each step?

_____

_____

_____

8. **Predicting** What would be the value of $PV$ if the bulb was lowered so that the water in the bulb was 1 meter below the water level in the tube? Explain.

_____

_____

9. **Predicting** At which pressures would the volume of the gas be less than the original volume?

_____

_____

10. **Acquiring and Analyzing Data** What happens to the volume of the gas as the pressure increases?

_____

_____

11. **Error Analysis** Compare the $PV = k$ data for each trial. Account for any discrepancies.

_____

_____

## Real-World Chemistry

1. Compute the amount of pressure that would be needed to compress 4 liters of gas at 760 torr to 1 liter of gas. (Assume the temperature remains constant.)

2. Explain why SCUBA divers are taught to not hold their breath while ascending in water.

**LAB 15.1 LABORATORY MANUAL**

# Making a Solubility Curve

Use with
Section 15.1

A solution is a homogeneous mixture of a solute in a solvent. Solvents, however, are only able to dissolve (solvate) a limited amount of solute. As solute is added to a solvent and the solution is being formed, the solvent has an ever-decreasing ability to dissolve more solute. As long as the solvent is able to dissolve more solute, the solution is unsaturated. When the solvent can no longer dissolve additional solute, the solution is saturated. Any additional solute added will collect on the bottom of the container and remain undissolved. The amount of solute that can be dissolved in a given amount of solvent at a specific temperature and pressure is defined as the solubility of the solute.

Solubility is dependent upon temperature. Generally, solvents at lower temperatures cannot dissolve as much solute as solvents at higher temperatures. In this activity, you will determine the solubility of a salt at different temperatures and will plot a solubility curve for the solute.

## Problem

How do you determine the solubility curve for a given salt?

## Objectives

- **Prepare** a saturated solution in ice water.
- **Graph** solubility as a function of temperature and **observe** how the solubility changes with changing temperature.

## Materials

sodium chloride (NaCl)
potassium chloride (KCl)
ammonium chloride (NH$_4$Cl)
lithium sulfate (Li$_2$SO$_4$)
distilled water
400-mL beakers (2)
100-mL graduated cylinder

thermometer
hot plate
scoop
stirring rod
balance
weighing papers (4)
watch glass
metal pan filled with ice
graph paper (2 sheets)

## Safety Precautions

- **Always wear safety goggles and a lab apron.**
- **Never taste any substance used in the lab.**
- **Use caution around hot items.**

## Pre-Lab

1. How will you know when the solution is saturated?

2. Why is a mixture of ice and water used to make the freezing ice-water bath?

3. Why must a saturated solution be obtained in order to make a solubility curve?

4. Read over the entire laboratory activity. Hypothesize what will happen to the solubility when a saturated solution is heated. Record your hypothesis on page 114.

## Procedure

1. Select one of the four salts to test and record its identity in **Data Table 1.**

2. Using a graduated cylinder, measure 200 mL of water into a 400-mL beaker.

3. Using a balance, measure 100 g of ice. Add the ice to the beaker and insert the stirring rod. Stir the ice and water mixture for 1 minute, then use the thermometer to measure the temperature of the mixture. **CAUTION: Do not use the thermometer to stir the mixture.**

4. When the temperature is a constant 0°C, remove the thermometer and the stirring rod. Place a watch glass over the beaker. Pour the cold water into a second 400-mL beaker. If all the ice melts before the 0°C temperature is reached, add more ice. Do not transfer any ice to the new beaker.

5. Record the volume of the cold water in the second beaker in **Data Table 1.** Place the beaker in a pan containing ice. Surround the breaker with additional ice. Use the thermometer to measure the temperature of the water. Record the temperature in **Data Table 1.**

6. Using the balance, measure 5.0 g of the selected salt and add it to the water in the beaker. Stir the mixture until the solid is dissolved.

7. Repeat step 6 until no more of the salt will dissolve. The solution is now saturated. Make sure to keep track of the total mass of the salt added to the water. Any excess solid will remain on the bottom of the beaker. Record the amount of salt added to make the saturated solution in **Data Table 1.**

8. Remove the beaker form the pan and carefully dry the outside of the beaker with a paper towel. Place the beaker on the hot plate.

9. Using the thermometer to measure the temperature of the solution in the beaker, heat the solution to 20°C. Remove and replace the beaker from the hot plate as needed to maintain a constant 20°C temperature.

10. When the undissolved solid from the saturated solution dissolves, add another 5.0 g of the salt to the water. Stir until the salt dissolves. Continue adding the salt at 5.0-g increments until no more solid will dissolve in the water. The solution is saturated again. Any excess solid will remain on the bottom of the beaker. Record the amount of solid added to make the saturated solution in **Data Table 1.**

11. Repeat steps 9 and 10 at temperatures of 50°C and 80°C. **CAUTION: The beaker is hot.**

12. Remove the beaker from the hot plate and gently set it on the lab bench to cool.

13. Plot a graph of the mass of salt dissolved versus temperature. Draw a best-fit smooth curve through the data points. With the help of your teacher, obtain solubility data from the other groups in your class for the remaining three salts. Graph this data on your graph to obtain a family of solubility curves.

## Hypothesis

_____

_____

_____

_____

## Cleanup and Disposal

1. Turn off the hot plate and allow it to cool.

2. Make sure all glassware is cool before emptying the contents.

3. Place all chemicals in appropriately labeled waste containers.

4. Return all lab equipment to its proper place.

5. Clean up your work area.

## Data and Observations

| | Data Table 1 | | | |
|---|---|---|---|---|
| | **Identity of salt** | | | |
| **Temperature (°C)** | **Mass of salt added to make a saturated solution (g)** | | | |
| | | | | |
| | | | | |
| | | | | |
| | | | | |

## Analyze and Conclude

1. **Observing and Inferring** What happened to the solubility of the salt as the temperature increased?

   _____

   _____

   _____

2. **Comparing and Contrasting** The solubility of which of the four salts is the most temperature dependent?

   _____

   _____

3. **Predicting** What would happen to the solubility of each salt if it was tested at temperatures above 80°C?

   _____

   _____

   _____

4. **Thinking Critically** Why was the excess ice removed from the water before any salt was added?

   _____

   _____

   _____

**5.** **Error Analysis** Compare the results of this lab with the predictions of your hypothesis. Explain possible reasons for any disagreement.

_____

_____

_____

_____

## Real-World Chemistry

**1.** In a dishwasher, the temperature of the water is very hot. Explain why it is better to use hot water in a dishwasher rather than cold water.

**2.** Unlike solids for which solubility in a liquid generally increases with increasing temperature, the solubility of a gas in a liquid usually decreases as the temperature increases. Knowing this, explain why you should never heat a can containing a carbonated soft drink.

## LAB 15.2 LABORATORY MANUAL

# Freezing Point Depression

**Use with
Section 15.3**

**D**issolving a solute in a solvent changes several properties of the solvent, including the freezing point, the boiling point, and the vapor pressure. These changes in the physical properties of a solvent by the addition of a solute are known collectively as colligative properties. In this activity, the colligative property of freezing point depression will be investigated.

## Problem

What is the freezing point depression constant of naphthalene?

## Objectives

- **Make and use graphs** to find the freezing point of naphthalene.
- **Measure and use numbers** to determine the freezing point depression constant of naphthalene.

## Materials

naphthalene
1,4-dichlorobenzene
acetone
600-mL beaker
hot plate
large test tube with
   two-hole rubber
   stopper

thermometer
stirring wire
tripod stand and
   gauze
beaker tongs
balance
test-tube clamp

## Safety Precautions

- **Always wear safety goggles, a lab apron, and gloves.**
- **Avoid breathing in chemical vapors.**
- **Dispose of chemicals as instructed by your teacher.**
- **Acetone is flammable. It is slightly toxic by ingestion and inhalation.**
- **Naphthalene is moderately toxic by ingestion, inhalation, and skin contact.**
- **1,4-dichlorobenzene is a severe irritant to the eyes, skin, and respiratory tract and mildly toxic by ingestion.**

## Pre-Lab

The freezing point depression constant, $K_f$, is given by

$$\Delta T_f = K_f m$$

where $\Delta T_f$ = change in freezing point in °C, $K_f$ is the freezing point depression constant in °C·kg/mol, and $m$ is the molal concentration in mol/kg.

1. Read over the entire laboratory activity. Use the periodic table in your textbook to answer the following questions.

   **a.** What is the molar mass of caffeine ($C_8H_{10}N_4O_2$) in g/mol?

   **b.** How many moles of caffeine are there in 5.00 g of caffeine?

2. The density of water is 1.0 kg/L. What is the mass, in kg, of 250 mL of water?

3. What is the molal concentration, $m$, in mol/kg, of a solution of 5.0 g of caffeine in 250 mL of water?

4. The solution in question 3 freezes at $-0.192$°C. Because water normally freezes at 0°C, this means that the freezing point has decreased by 0.192°C. Thus, $\Delta T_f = -0.192$°C. What is the freezing point depression constant of water, $K_f$?

## Procedure

### Part A

1. Add about 400 mL of water to a 600-mL beaker. Using a hot plate, heat the water until it boils. **CAUTION: The hot plate and boiling water can cause burns.**

2. Read the directions in Laboratory Techniques at the beginning of this manual before inserting the thermometer. Insert the glass thermometer into one of the holes in the rubber stopper. **CAUTION: Follow the directions carefully. Be sure to lubricate the end of the thermometer with glycerol or soapy water before inserting it into the stopper. Do not force the thermometer, as it may shatter in your hand. If you have any difficulty, ask your teacher for help.**

3. Insert the stirring wire in the second hole of the rubber stopper. Set the rubber stopper assembly aside.

4. Measure the mass of the test tube to the nearest 0.01g and record the value in **Data Table 1.**

5. Add about 10 g of naphthalene to the test tube. Measure the mass of the test tube and the naphthalene and record the value in **Data Table 1.** Calculate the mass of the naphthalene and record the value in **Data Table 1.**

6. Use the test-tube clamp to hold the test tube vertically in the boiling water bath. Make sure all of the naphthalene is below the surface of the boiling water. When the naphthalene has melted, insert the rubber stopper assembly into the top of the test tube. **CAUTION: The test tube may be hot.** The thermometer should be immersed in the naphthalene. The stirring wire should loop around the thermometer. Move the stirring wire up and down to stir the contents of the test tube. Stir the naphthalene as it is being heated until all of the naphthalene has melted.

7. Remove the test tube from the boiling water bath by repositioning the test-tube clamp so that it is no longer over the beaker. **CAUTION: The test-tube clamp may be hot.** Monitor the temperature of the naphthalene as it cools. Continue stirring the naphthalene as it cools to ensure that the temperature is constant throughout.

8. When the temperature of the molten naphthalene has fallen to 90.0°C, begin recording the elapsed time and the temperature in **Data Table 2.** The first entry in **Data Table 2** will be the temperature of 90.0°C at an elapsed time of 0 sec. Take measurements every 30 s. Record all temperatures to the nearest 0.1°C.

9. In order to determine the freezing point accurately, the cooling curve must be observed both above and below the freezing point. Thus, continue recording the temperature even after the naphthalene has frozen. Stop making measurements once the temperature has dropped below 70°C.

### Part B

1. Reposition the test-tube clamp so that the test tube containing the solid naphthalene is again partially submerged in the boiling water bath. Heat the test tube until the naphthalene is melted and you can remove the thermometer and stirrer as a unit. **CAUTION: The thermometer, stirring wire, and test tube may be hot.** Do not discard the naphthalene. Remove all the naphthalene from the stopper, thermometer, and stirrer by washing them with acetone.

2. Measure the mass of the test tube and naphthalene again and calculate the mass of naphthalene remaining in the test tube. Record these values in **Data Table 1.**

3. Add about 1 g of 1,4-dichlorobenzene to the test tube. Measure the mass of the test tube and its contents, and calculate the mass of 1,4-dichlorobenzene that has been added. Record these values in **Data Table 1.**

4. Make sure that the stopper, thermometer, and stirrer are dry and free of acetone.

5. Repeat Part A, steps 2 and 3.

6. Repeat Part A, steps 6 through 9.

## Cleanup and Disposal

1. Dispose of the chemicals according to your teacher's directions.

2. Clean up your lab area and wash your hands.

**LAB 15.2**

# LABORATORY MANUAL

## Data and Observations

| Data Table 1 | | |
|---|---|---|
| | **Part A** | **Part B** |
| Mass of test tube (g) | | |
| Mass of test tube and naphthalene (g) | | |
| Mass of naphthalene (g) | | |
| Mass of test tube, naphthalene, and 1,4-dichlorobenzene (g) | — | |

| Data Table 2 | | |
|---|---|---|
| **Elapsed time (s)** | **Part A temperature (°C)** | **Part B temperature (°C)** |
| 0 | 90.0°C | 90.0°C |
| 30 | | |
| 60 | | |
| 90 | | |
| 120 | | |
| 150 | | |
| 180 | | |
| 210 | | |

1. Using graph paper and your data from Part A, construct a temperature (*y*-axis) versus time (*x*-axis) graph for the cooling of the naphthalene. Do not connect the data points. Label this graph "Cooling Curve of Pure Naphthalene."

2. The graph from question 1 should show two or possibly three distinct regions. These regions are distinguished by a change in the slope of the line that would pass through the data points. Draw a best fit straight line through the data points in each region. The points at which your best fit lines intersect yield an estimate for the freezing point of naphthalene. Record your estimate for the freezing point of naphthalene on the line below.

_____

3. Using graph paper and your data from Part B, construct a temperature (*y*-axis) versus time (*x*-axis) graph for the cooling of the naphthalene-1,4-dichlorobenzene solution. Do not connect the data points. Label this graph "Cooling Curve of Naphthalene and 1,4-dichlorobenzene Solution." Following the instructions in question 2, determine the freezing point of the solution in Part B. Record your estimate for the freezing point of the naphthalene-1,4-dichlorobenzene solution on the line below.

_____

# LABORATORY MANUAL

## Analyze and Conclude

### 1. Measuring and Using Numbers

**a.** What was the mass of naphthalene, in kilograms, used in Part B?

_____

**b.** The chemical formula for 1,4-dichlorobenzene is $C_6H_4Cl_2$. What is the molar mass of 1,4-dichlorobenzene?

_____

**c.** What was the molal concentration of 1,4-dichlorobenzene in naphthalene?

_____

_____

**d.** Label the freezing point of pure naphthalene from Part A, $T_A$. Label the freezing point of the 1,4-dichlorobenzene solution from Part B, $T_B$. Divide the difference between these two temperatures by the molal concentration of 1,4-dichlorobenzene to obtain the freezing point depression constant, $K_f$, for naphthalene.

_____

_____

### 2. Error Analysis Compare the freezing point depression values you calculated to the actual values. List several possible sources of error and explain how they may have affected the results.

_____

_____

### Real-World Chemistry

**1.** Why is it important to have antifreeze mixed with water in a car's radiator during the winter?

**2.** Explain how salting a road in the winter helps prevent the formation of ice.

# Heats of Solution and Reaction

Use with
Section 16.3

**T**wo types of processes commonly involve energy changes—chemical reactions and the dissolving process. Heat of reaction is the overall energy absorbed or released during a chemical reaction. Heat of solution is the overall energy absorbed or released during the solution process. Both are the difference between the energy absorbed to break bonds and the energy released when new bonds are formed. In this activity, you will investigate two examples of heat of solution and one example of heat of reaction.

The first example of heat of solution is the heat transferred when concentrated sulfuric acid ($H_2SO_4$) is added to water. The second is the dissolving of the ionic compound ammonium chloride ($NH_4Cl$) in water.

When an ionic compound dissolves in water, energy is needed to break the ionic bonds of the crystal. As the ions attach to the water molecules and become hydrated, energy is released. The process is endothermic if the energy needed to break the bonds is greater than the energy released when the ions attach to water. The reaction is exothermic if the energy needed to break the bonds is less than the energy released when the ions attach to water.

An example of a chemical reaction with a measurable energy change is the reaction of an acid and a base. In this activity, you will determine whether the reaction of hydrochloric acid (HCl) with sodium hydroxide (NaOH) absorbs or liberates heat.

## Problem

How do temperatures change during chemical reactions and the solution process?

## Objectives

- **Measure** the temperature changes of different processes.
- **Differentiate** between exothermic and endothermic processes.

## Materials

ammonium chloride ($NH_4Cl$)
18$M$ sulfuric acid ($H_2SO_4$)
1$M$ hydrochloric acid (HCl)
1$M$ sodium hydroxide (NaOH)

10-mL graduated cylinder
100-mL graduated cylinder
plastic-foam cups (3)
thermometer
balance
timer
stirring rod

## Safety Precautions

- Dispose of chemical wastes as directed by your teacher.
- Solutions may become very hot or very cold. Use caution when handling.
- Sulfuric and hydrochloric acids are toxic and corrosive to skin and react with metals.
- Dangerous spattering can result when diluting concentrated acids. Remember to add acid to water, never water to acid.
- Sodium hydroxide is toxic and corrosive to skin.
- Ammonium chloride is slightly toxic.
- Always wear safety goggles, a lab apron, and gloves.
- Mercury from mercury-based thermometers is toxic.
- Foam cups can be easily punctured, causing a chemical spill.

## Pre-Lab

1. Define *heat of reaction*.

2. Distinguish between exothermic and endothermic processes.

3. Read the entire laboratory activity. Form a hypothesis about how to distinguish exothermic and endothermic processes. Record your hypothesis on page 123.

4. Summarize the procedures you will follow to test your hypothesis.

5. Describe the anticipated temperature change of a system in which an exothermic process is taking place.

## Procedure

### Part A: Heat of Solution for Sulfuric Acid

1. Measure 45 mL of water. Pour the water into a foam cup.

2. Insert a thermometer into the water in the cup. After 2 min, read the temperature of the water. Record this initial temperature in **Data Table 1.**

3. Use a graduated cylinder to measure 8.0 mL $H_2SO_4$. Carefully pour the $H_2SO_4$ into the water in the foam cup. Cautiously without splashing, stir the solution with a stirring rod.

4. Measure and record the highest temperature attained.

5. Dispose of the acid solution as directed by your teacher.

### Part B: Heat of Solution for Ammonium Chloride

1. Measure 30 mL of water. Pour the water into a foam cup.

2. Insert a thermometer into the cup of water. After 2 min, read the temperature of the water. Record this initial temperature in **Data Table 2.**

3. Measure 5 g of ammonium chloride ($NH_4Cl$) crystals on a piece of weighing paper. Carefully pour the ammonium chloride from the weighing paper into the water in the foam cup. Cautiously without splashing, stir the solution with a clean stirring rod.

4. Measure and record the lowest temperature attained.

5. Dispose of the solution as directed by your teacher.

### Part C: Heat of Reaction

1. Use a graduated cylinder to measure 20 mL of $1M$ HCl. Pour the acid into a foam cup.

2. Insert a thermometer into the cup of acid. After 2 min, read the temperature of the acid. Record this initial temperature in **Data Table 3.**

3. Use a graduated cylinder to measure 10 mL of $1M$ NaOH. Carefully pour the sodium hydroxide (NaOH) solution into the acid in the foam cup. Cautiously without splashing, stir the solution with a clean stirring rod.

4. Measure and record the new temperature attained.

5. Dispose of the solution as directed by your teacher.

**LAB 16.1**  **LABORATORY MANUAL**

## Hypothesis

_____

_____

_____

## Cleanup and Disposal

1. Dispose of materials as directed by your teacher.
2. Return all lab equipment to its proper place.
3. Report any broken or damaged equipment.
4. Wash your hands thoroughly with soap or detergent before leaving the lab.

## Data and Observations

| Data Table 1 | |
|---|---|
| **Part A: Heat of Solution for Sulfuric Acid** | |
| Initial water temperature (°C) | |
| Water temperature after adding $H_2SO_4$ (°C) | |
| Temperature change (°C) | |
| Exothermic or endothermic? | |

| Data Table 2 | |
|---|---|
| **Part B: Heat of Solution for Ammonium Chloride** | |
| Initial water temperature (°C) | |
| Water temperature after adding $NH_4Cl$ (°C) | |
| Temperature change (°C) | |
| Exothermic or endothermic? | |

| Data Table 3 | |
|---|---|
| **Part C: Heat of Reaction** | |
| Initial acid temperature (°C) | |
| Temperature after adding NaOH (°C) | |
| Temperature change (°C) | |
| Exothermic or endothermic? | |

LAB **16.1**

**LABORATORY MANUAL**

## Analyze and Conclude

1. **Using Numbers** Calculate and record in the data tables the temperature changes of the three processes.

2. **Observing and Inferring** What observation allowed you to compare the heat flow in the three reactions?

_____

_____

_____

3. **Interpreting Data** What is the experimental evidence that indicates whether each reaction is exothermic or endothermic?

_____

_____

_____

4. **Making a Prediction** Would the temperature change in Part A be different if the same amount of water but less sulfuric acid had been used? Explain.

_____

_____

5. **Drawing Conclusions** In Part B, energy is needed to break the ionic bonds of the crystal. As the ions attach to water molecules and become hydrated, energy is released. Explain how you might conclude that more energy is being used to break bonds than is being released as the ions attach to water.

_____

_____

_____

6. **Error Analysis** To test your hypothesis in this activity, was it important that the amounts of reactants and the temperatures be measured with accuracy and precision? Explain.

_____

_____

### Real-World Chemistry

1. Explain how a "cold pack," often used in emergency or sports medicine, works.

2. Combustion of fuels is an exothermic reaction. Explain how the heat energy from this type of reaction is often used to do useful work.

3. Explain why it would not be practical to air-condition a home or business by using an endothermic chemical reaction.

# Heat of Combustion of Candle Wax

**Use with Section 16.3**

The amount of heat released by the complete combustion of one mole of a substance is defined as the heat of combustion, $\Delta H_{comb}$. The amount of heat released may be measured in calories (cal) or in joules (J). A calorie is the amount of heat needed to raise the temperature of one gram of water one degree Celsius. The SI unit of heat is the joule. One joule is equal to 4.184 calories.

If a sample of pure carbon is burned in oxygen, the reaction is as follows.

$$C(s) + O_2(g) \rightarrow CO_2(g) \quad \Delta H_{comb} = -393.5 \text{ kJ}$$

Some additional heats of combustion are provided in the table.

In this activity, you will calculate the heat of combustion of the fuel in a candle. The burning candle will heat a measured quantity of water. Using the specific heat of water, the mass of the water, and the increase in temperature, you can calculate the amount of heat released by the burning candle using the following relationship:

| Heats of Combustion | | |
|---|---|---|
| **Substance** | **Formula** | **$\Delta H_{comb}$ (kJ/mol)** |
| Methane (g) | $CH_4$ | $-890.3$ |
| Propane (g) | $C_3H_8$ | $-2219.9$ |
| Butane (g) | $C_4H_{10}$ | $-3536.1$ |
| Octane (l) | $C_8H_{18}$ | $-5450.8$ |

quantity of heat in calories =
     (mass of water)(change of temperature)(specific heat of water),

where the specific heat of water is 1 cal/(g·°C). You can then calculate the quantity of heat released per gram of candle wax and multiply by the molar mass of candle wax to obtain the heat of combustion ($\Delta H_{comb}$) in kJ/mol.

## Problem

How can you measure the heat released by a burning candle and calculate the heat of combustion of candle wax?

## Objectives

- **Measure** the change in temperature of a mass of water during a combustion reaction.
- **Calculate** the amount of heat released during a combustion reaction.
- **Calculate** the energy released per mole of reactant during a combustion reaction.

## Materials

candle
small metal can
large metal can
1/2-in. steel nuts (4)
thermometer
balance
felt-tip marker
metric ruler

paper clips (3)
disposable butane
   lighter or matches
ring stand
ring
thermometer clamp
glass stirring rod

**LAB 16.2**

## Safety Precautions

- Always wear safety goggles, a lab apron, and gloves.
- Dispose of wax wastes as directed by your teacher.
- Hot objects may not appear to be hot.
- Open flames may ignite clothing or hair.
- Mercury from mercury-based thermometers is toxic.

## Pre-Lab

1. Define *heat of combustion* and *calorie*.

2. State the relationship between (a) calories and joules and (b) calories, mass of water, change of temperature, and specific heat.

3. Define exothermic and endothermic reactions. What is the sign of $\Delta H$ for an exothermic reaction? An endothermic reaction?

4. Explain how you can calculate the heat of combustion if you know the number of calories released, the mass of substance burned, and the molar mass of the substance.

5. Read the entire laboratory activity. Form a hypothesis about how to measure the amount of heat released in a chemical reaction. Record your hypothesis on page 127.

## Procedure

1. Light a candle and drip a few drops of molten wax onto a can lid. Attach the candle to the lid while the wax is liquid and blow out the candle.

2. Use a marker to place a line 3 cm below the top of the candle wax.

3. Determine the mass of the candle and lid and record this value in **Data Table 1**.

4. Refer to **Figure A** as you set up the apparatus. Unbend three paper clips so that they are each in the shape of an S-hook. Use the paper clips to attach the small can to the ring.

5. Position the candle assembly under the small can and adjust the ring so that the bottom of the can is 4 or 5 cm above the top of the unlighted candle.

6. Unhook the small can. Measure the mass of the can and record this value in **Data Table 1**.

7. Fill the can approximately half full of distilled water.

8. Measure and record in **Data Table 1** the mass of the can and the water.

**Figure A**

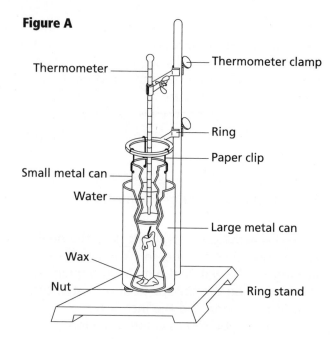

9. Place the large can over the candle.

10. Raise the large can off the base of the ring stand and insert the four nuts evenly spaced under the can. This will allow air needed for the combustion of the candle to enter around the base of the can.

11. Record the initial temperature of the water in **Data Table 1**. Use a butane lighter to light the candle.

12. Immediately replace the small can and water in its previous position.

13. While the candle heats the water, gently stir the water with a glass stirring rod.

14. Continue to burn the candle until the wax is consumed to the 3-cm mark made in step 2.

15. Blow out the candle and record in **Data Table 1** the final temperature of the water.

16. Measure and record in **Data Table 1** the mass of the candle assembly.

17. Repeat steps 2 to 16, except this time make the marker line 5 cm below the top of the candle.

**LAB 16.2**

## Hypothesis

_____

_____

_____

## Cleanup and Disposal

1. Return all lab equipment to its proper place.
2. Report any broken or damaged equipment.
3. Wash your hands thoroughly before leaving the lab.

## Data and Observations

| Data Table 1 | | |
|---|---|---|
| | **Trial 1 (3 cm)** | **Trial 2 (5 cm)** |
| Initial mass of candle assembly (g) | | |
| Final mass of candle assembly (g) | | |
| Mass of candle burned (g) | | |
| Mass of small can and water (g) | | |
| Mass of empty small can (g) | | |
| Mass of water (g) | | |
| Final temperature of water (°C) | | |
| Initial temperature of water (°C) | | |
| Temperature change of water (°C) | | |

1. Calculate and record in **Data Table 1** the mass of candle burned in each trial.
2. Calculate and record in **Data Table 1** the mass of water used in each trial.
3. Calculate the temperature change of the water for each trial.

## Analyze and Conclude

1. **Measuring and Using Numbers** Calculate the number of calories of heat absorbed by the water used in each trial.




2. **Measuring and Using Numbers** For each trial, calculate the heat released per gram of candle wax.

3. **Measuring and Using Numbers** Assume that the formula for the wax in the candle is $C_{32}H_{66}$. Calculate the molar mass of the wax.

4. **Applying Concepts** Write the equation for the combustion of one mole of candle wax ($C_{32}H_{66}$).

_____

5. **Measuring and Using Numbers** Calculate the number of kilocalories of heat released per mole of $C_{32}H_{66}$ for each trial.

6. **Measuring and Using Numbers** Convert the number of kilocalories per mole to kilojoules per mole for each trial. What is the $\Delta H_{comb}$ for candle wax in kJ/mol?

7. **Drawing a Conclusion** Compare the heat of combustion you obtained with the values in the table on page 125. Explain any trend you observe.

_____

_____

8. **Thinking Critically** Why were two trials performed?

_____

9. **Error Analysis** Explain possible sources of error in this activity.

_____

_____

## Real-World Chemistry

1. Explain why it is recommended that people traveling by car in cold climates carry a candle and matches as part of emergency survival equipment.

2. Diesel engines are often used in large trucks and heavy equipment because the diesel fuel produces more heat per liter than does gasoline. What does this imply about the nature of the molecules of diesel fuel, as compared to the molecules that make up gasoline?

**LAB 17.1 LABORATORY MANUAL**

# The Rate of a Reaction

**Use with
Section 17.2**

**A** chemical equation shows that as a chemical reaction takes place, reactants are changed into products. The reaction rate of a chemical reaction is often expressed as the change in concentration of a reactant or a product in a unit amount of time. In this activity, the reaction rate will be calculated from the amount of time it takes for a given amount of magnesium (Mg) to react completely with hydrochloric acid (HCl).

## Problem

What is the relationship between temperature and reaction rate? What is the relationship between concentration and reaction rate?

## Objectives

- **Measure** the amount of time it takes for a uniform strip of Mg ribbon to react completely with HCl under varying conditions.
- **Graph** the data.
- **Infer** the relationships between reaction rates and varied temperatures and concentrations.

## Materials

magnesium ribbon
sandpaper
1$M$ hydrochloric acid (HCl)
3$M$ hydrochloric acid (HCl)
ice
test tubes (8)
250-mL beakers (4)
10-mL graduated cylinder

thermometer
stirring rod
Bunsen burner
clock or timer
ruler
scissors
ring stand
iron ring
wire gauze

## Safety Precautions

- Always wear safety goggles, a lab apron, and gloves.
- Hot objects may not appear to be hot.
- Hydrochloric acid is toxic, corrosive to skin, and reacts with metals.
- Open flames may ignite hair or loose clothing.

## Pre-Lab

1. Define *reaction rate*.
2. Write the mathematical equation used to determine the average rate of a chemical reaction. What factor is held constant? What are the variables?
3. Read the entire laboratory activity. Form a hypothesis about how an increase in temperature will affect reaction rate. Form a second hypothesis about how an increase in concentration will affect reaction rate. Record your hypotheses on page 130.
4. Summarize the procedures you will follow to test your hypotheses.

## Procedure

Clean a 30-cm strip of magnesium ribbon with sandpaper. Cut the ribbon into 3.0-cm pieces.

### Part A: Effect of Temperature

1. Pour 10 mL of 1.0$M$ hydrochloric acid into a clean, dry test tube.
2. Place the test tube in a 250-mL beaker that contains 150 mL of ice water.
3. Wait 3 min. Measure the temperature of the acid and record it in the **Part A Data Table.**
4. Remove the thermometer from the acid and place a piece of magnesium ribbon into the acid. Use

Chemistry: Matter and Change • Chapter 17 **129**

the stirring rod to keep the magnesium completely submerged throughout the reaction.

**5.** Starting as soon as the magnesium is in contact with the acid, measure the time required for the magnesium to react completely. Record the reaction time.

**6.** Measure and record the temperature of the acid after the reaction.

**7.** Set up a hot-water bath and repeat the experiment at temperatures of about 25°C, 50°C, and 100°C.

### Part B: Effect of Concentration

**1.** Pour 10 mL of 3.0*M* hydrochloric acid into a clean, dry test tube.

**2.** Place the test tube in a 250-mL beaker that contains 150 mL of tap water.

**3.** Wait 3 min, then place a piece of magnesium ribbon into the acid. Use the stirring rod to keep the magnesium completely submerged throughout the reaction.

**4.** Starting as soon as the magnesium is in contact with the acid, measure the time required for the magnesium to react completely. Record the reaction time in the **Part B Data Table**.

**5.** Prepare the following solutions and pour each into a separate, clean, dry test tube: 4.0 mL of

tap water and 6.0 mL of 3.0*M* HCl; 7.0 mL of tap water and 3.0 mL of 3.0*M* HCl; 9.0 mL of tap water and 1.0 mL of 3.0*M* HCl.

**6.** Place each test tube in a 250-mL beaker that contains 150 mL of tap water.

**7.** Repeat steps 3 and 4 for each test tube.

## Hypotheses

_____

_____

_____

_____

## Cleanup and Disposal

**1.** Be sure the gas supply for the Bunsen burner is turned off.

**2.** Dispose of materials as directed by your teacher.

**3.** Return all lab equipment to its proper place. Report any broken or damaged equipment.

**4.** Wash your hands thoroughly before leaving the lab.

## Data and Observations

| | | | Part A Data Table | | |
|---|---|---|---|---|---|
| Tube | Initial temperature (°C) | Final temperature (°C) | Average temperature (°C) | Reaction time (s) | Rate of reaction |
| 1 | | | | | |
| 2 | | | | | |
| 3 | | | | | |
| 4 | | | | | |

| Part B Data Table | | | |
| --- | --- | --- | --- |
| Tube | Acid | Reaction time (s) | Rate of reaction |
| 1 | 10 mL 3.0M HCl, 0.0 mL water | | |
| 2 | 6.0 mL 3.0M HCl, 4.0 mL water | | |
| 3 | 3.0 mL 3.0M HCl, 7.0 mL water | | |
| 4 | 1.0 mL 3.0M HCl, 9.0 mL water | | |

**1.** Why is it necessary to clean the magnesium?

_____

_____

**2.** Why are the volume and molarity of the acid the same in each trial of Part A?

_____

_____

**3.** What effect does temperature have on reaction rate?

_____

_____

**4.** Why are the trials in Part B carried out in a beaker of water?

_____

_____

**5.** What effect does concentration have on reaction rate?

_____

_____

## Analyze and Conclude

**1. Using Numbers** Because the mass of magnesium is the same in each reaction, assume
the change in quantity to be 1. Thus, the rate of reaction is calculated by dividing 1 by the
reaction time. Calculate and record in the data tables the average temperature and the rate
of reaction for each tube in Part A and the rate of reaction for each tube in Part B. Why
was an average temperature used in Part A?

_____

_____

2. **Observing and Inferring** Did the reaction rate decrease, increase, or remain the same as the temperature of the acid solution increased? As the temperature of the acid solution decreased? Explain whether the reaction rates are directly proportional or inversely proportional to temperature.

_____

_____

_____

_____

3. **Graphing Data** On a sheet of graph paper, make a graph of temperature versus time, using the data from Part A. Then make a graph of concentration versus time, using the data from Part B. Were your hypotheses supported? Explain.

_____

_____

4. **Making a Prediction** Would you expect the reaction rate in Part A to increase if the acid was more concentrated? Explain why.

_____

_____

5. **Making a Prediction** Would you expect the graphs to have the same shapes if each magnesium strip was 6.0 cm long instead of 3.0 cm long?

_____

_____

6. **Error Analysis** What could you have done to improve the precision of the measurements?

_____

_____

_____

## Real-World Chemistry

1. What effect does acid rain have on the rate of corrosion of metals used in buildings, automobiles, and statues? How can concentration of the acid in the rain, and thus the rate of corrosion, be controlled?

2. Explain why refrigerated or frozen foods do not spoil as quickly as those left at room temperature.

3. For centuries, the production and destruction of ozone in Earth's ozone layer was constant. Explain why in recent decades the ozone has been depleted faster than it was replaced.

# Surface Area and Reaction Rate

**Use with Section 17.4**

In Lab 17.1, you learned about the effect of temperature and concentration on reaction rate. Another factor that affects reaction rate is the amount of surface area of the reactants. If a chemical reaction is to take place, the molecules of reactants must collide. Changing the amount of surface area modifies the rate of collision, and, thus, the rate of reaction. If surface area increases, collision frequency increases. If surface area decreases, so does the number of collisions. In this lab, you will examine the effect of surface area on rate of reaction. You will also determine how a combination of factors can affect reaction rate.

## Problem
What effect does surface area have on reaction rate? What effect does a combination of surface area and temperature have on reaction rate?

## Objectives
- **Determine** the effect of varying surface areas on reaction rates.
- **Measure** the rate of reaction.
- **Determine** the effect of more than one factor on reaction rates.

## Materials
effervescent antacid tablets (5)
25-mL graduated cylinder
test tubes (18)
test-tube rack
timer
mortar and pestle
stirring rod

## Safety Precautions

- **Always wear safety goggles and a lab apron.**
- **Hot objects may not appear to be hot.**
- **Do not eat or drink anything in a laboratory.**

## Pre-Lab

1. Summarize the collision theory and how surface area applies to reaction rates.
2. Read the entire laboratory activity. Form a hypothesis about how an increase in surface area will affect the reaction rate. Form a second hypothesis about how the rate of a reaction might be predicted. Record your hypotheses on page 134.
3. Summarize the procedures you will follow to test your hypotheses.
4. What factors are constant in this experiment?

## Procedure

1. Obtain five effervescent antacid tablets. Break each tablet into four equal pieces. One of these pieces will be used for each trial.
2. Measure exactly 15.0 mL of room-temperature tap water. Pour the water into a test tube.
3. Drop a piece of the antacid tablet into the water. Immediately start the timer. Stir the contents of the test tube throughout the reaction.
4. Measure the time until the reaction stops. Record this time in **Data Table 1.**
5. As another trial, repeat steps 2 through 4 for a second piece of tablet.

6. Take another piece of tablet and break it into several smaller pieces. Repeat steps 2 through 5, using the smaller pieces of tablet.

7. Use a mortar and pestle to grind a piece of tablet into a powder. Repeat steps 2 through 5, using the powdered tablet.

8. Repeat steps 2 through 7 using cold water.

9. Repeat steps 2 through 7 using very warm water.

## Cleanup and Disposal

1. Pour the solutions down the drain.

2. Wash all test tubes and stirring rods.

3. Return all lab equipment to its proper place. Report any broken or damaged equipment.

4. Wash your hands thoroughly before leaving the lab.

## Hypotheses

_____

_____

_____

## Data and Observations

| Data Table 1 | | | | |
| --- | --- | --- | --- | --- |
| **Time (s)** | | | | |
| **Particle size** | **Trial number** | **Water temperature** | | |
| | | **Room temperature** | **Cold** | **Warm** |
| One piece | 1 | | | |
| | 2 | | | |
| | Average | | | |
| Several pieces | 1 | | | |
| | 2 | | | |
| | Average | | | |
| Crushed | 1 | | | |
| | 2 | | | |
| | Average | | | |

**LAB 17.2**                                                        **LABORATORY MANUAL**

## Analyze and Conclude

1. **Using Numbers** Average the times for each set of two trials. Record these values in **Data Table 1.**

2. **Observing** What evidence did you observe to indicate that a reaction had taken place?

_____

_____

3. **Inferring** What relationship exists between reaction time and reaction rate?

_____

_____

4. **Drawing Conclusions** Write statements that summarize the results of the lab activity.

_____

_____

_____

_____

5. **Predicting** Can relative reaction rates be predicted with certainty when more than one factor that affects reaction rate is involved? Explain.

_____

_____

_____

6. **Drawing Conclusions** How does the collision theory explain the reaction times?

_____

_____

_____

7. **Error Analysis** Were your hypotheses supported? Explain. What could you have done to improve the accuracy of the predictions?

_____

_____

_____

**Real-World Chemistry**

**1.** Why does painting metallic objects that contain iron help prevent formation of rust?

**2.** How might particle size of reactants be varied to promote the sale of a product designed to neutralize stomach acids?

**LAB 18.1 LABORATORY MANUAL**

# Reversible Reactions

**Use with
Section 18.2**

In some chemical reactions, the reactants are not entirely converted to products. This is because as the products form, they react to re-form the reactants in a reverse reaction.

When the rate of the forward reaction is equal to the rate of the reverse reaction, the system is said to be at equilibrium. At equilibrium, the forward and the reverse reactions proceed at the same rate, so the concentrations of the reactants and products do not change.

LeChâtelier's principle states that if a system at equilibrium is subjected to a stress, the equilibrium will shift in a direction that will relieve the stress. One such stress is a change of concentration. In this activity, you will see how changing the concentration of a reactant or product creates a new equilibrium.

## Problem

How does a change in the concentration of a reactant or product affect a system at equilibrium?

## Objective

**Determine** shifts of equilibrium brought about by changes in concentration.

## Materials

12$M$ hydrochloric acid (HCl)
6$M$ hydrochloric acid (HCl)
0.1$M$ iron(III) chloride (FeCl$_3$)
0.1$M$ potassium thiocyanate (KSCN)
0.1$M$ cobalt(II) chloride (CoCl$_2$)
saturated ammonium chloride solution (NH$_4$Cl)
saturated sodium chloride solution (NaCl)

ammonium chloride (NH$_4$Cl)
iron(III) chloride and potassium thiocyanate solution
ammonia (ammonium hydroxide and phenolphthalein) solution
10-mL graduated cylinder
test tubes (9)
dropping pipettes (2)
test-tube rack

## Safety Precautions

- **Always wear safety goggles, a lab apron, and gloves.**
- **Ammonium chloride is slightly toxic by ingestion.**
- **Ferric chloride is a skin irritant and is slightly toxic.**
- **Potassium thiocyanate, cobalt(II) chloride, and hydrochloric acid are toxic.**
- **Hydrochloric acid is corrosive to skin and reacts with metals.**
- **Ammonia is a respiratory irritant.**

**LAB 18.1**

## Pre-Lab

1. State LeChâtelier's principle.

2. In which direction will a reaction shift if there is an increase in the concentration of a reactant?

3. In which direction will a reaction shift if there is a decrease in the concentration of a reactant?

4. Read the entire laboratory activity. Form a hypothesis about how a stress on a system at equilibrium will cause a shift of the system. Record your hypothesis in the next column.

## Procedure

### Part A: Chloride Solution

1. Pour 3 mL of saturated sodium chloride solution into a clean test tube. Add 6 drops of $12M$ hydrochloric acid. Record your observations in **Data Table 1.**

2. Pour 3 mL of saturated ammonium chloride solution into a clean test tube. Add 6 drops of $12M$ hydrochloric acid. Record your observations in **Data Table 1.**

### Part B: Iron(III) Chloride and Potassium Thiocyanate Solutions

1. Pour 5 mL of iron(III) chloride and potassium thiocyanate solution into each of three clean test tubes.

2. To the first test tube, add 1 mL of $0.1M$ potassium thiocyanate solution. Observe and record the color change in **Data Table 1.**

3. To the second test tube, add 1 mL of $0.1M$ iron(III) chloride solution. Observe and record the color change in **Data Table 1.**

4. Use the third test tube as a control. Note and record the color of the solution.

### Part C: Cobalt Chloride Solution

1. Pour 2 mL of $0.1M$ cobalt(II) chloride solution into a clean test tube.

   a. Add 3 mL of $12M$ hydrochloric acid.

   b. Add water dropwise until the original color is restored.

   c. Record your observations in **Data Table 1.**

2. Pour 2 mL of $0.1M$ cobalt(II) chloride solution into a second clean test tube.

3. Pour 2 mL of $0.1M$ cobalt(II) chloride solution into a third clean test tube.

   a. Add about 1.5 g of ammonium chloride.

   b. Compare the colors of the contents of the second and third test tubes and record your observations in **Data Table 1.**

### Part D: Ammonia Solution

1. Pour 5 mL of the ammonia solution into another clean test tube.

   a. Add 10 drops of $6M$ hydrochloric acid and stir the solution.

   b. Record your observations in **Data Table 1.**

## Hypothesis

_____

_____

_____

## Cleanup and Disposal

1. Dispose of chemicals as instructed by your teacher.

2. Return all lab equipment to its proper place.

3. Wash your hands thoroughly with soap or detergent before leaving the lab.

## Data and Observations

| Data Table 1 | |
| --- | --- |
| Step number | Observation |
| Part A:  1 | |
| 2 | |
| Part B:  2 | |
| 3 | |
| 4 | |
| Part C:  1 | |
| 3 | |
| Part D:  1 | |

## Analyze and Conclude

### 1. Collecting and Interpreting Data

   **a.** In Part A, step 1, which ion concentration change is responsible for the equilibrium shift?

   _____

   **b.** In Part A, step 2, which ion concentration change is responsible for the equilibrium shift?

   _____

   **c.** In Part B, step 2, which ion concentration change is responsible for the equilibrium shift?

   _____

   **d.** In Part B, step 3, which ion concentration change is responsible for the equilibrium shift?

   _____

### 2. Observing and Inferring  Explain the meaning of a control, as used in Part B, step 4.

   _____

   _____

### 3. Collecting and Interpreting Data

   **a.** In Part C, step 1, which ion concentration change is responsible for the equilibrium shift?

   _____

   **b.** In Part C, step 3, which ion concentration change is responsible for the equilibrium shift?

   _____

   **c.** In Part D, step 1, which ion concentration change is responsible for the equilibrium shift?

   _____

4. **Drawing a Conclusion** The equilibrium system for the cobalt chloride solution may be expressed as follows:

$$4Cl^-(aq) + Co(H_2O)_6^{2+}(aq) \rightleftharpoons 6H_2O(l) + CoCl_4^{2-}(aq)$$
$$\text{(pink)} \qquad\qquad\qquad \text{(blue)}$$

Explain what happened to the concentration of each of the following ions when hydrochloric acid was added.

a. $Cl^-$

_____

b. $Co(H_2O)_6^{2+}$

_____

c. $CoCl_4^{2-}$

_____

5. **Predicting** Predict the effect of adding sodium hydroxide in place of hydrochloric acid to a saturated solution of sodium chloride. (See Part A, step 1.)

_____

_____

6. **Error Analysis** To what extent are accuracy and precision factors in this activity? Explain.

_____

_____

_____

## Real-World Chemistry

1. In the Haber process, nitrogen and hydrogen are combined to form ammonia according to the following reaction.

$$N_2(g) + 3\,H_2(g) \rightleftharpoons 2\,NH_3(g)$$

Explain what effect an increase in pressure would have on the yield of ammonia.

2. A process called ion exchange is often used to soften hard water. The equilibrium reaction may be represented like this:

$$2NaCl(s) + X^{2+}(aq) \rightleftharpoons XCl_2(aq) + 2Na^+(aq)$$

Water softened by this method contains extra sodium ions. Explain why people with hypertension (high blood pressure) should avoid drinking water softened by this type of ion exchange.

## LAB 18.2 LABORATORY MANUAL

# Equilibrium

**Use with Section 18.3**

**A** chemical reaction in which the products react to re-form the original reactants is called a reversible reaction. For example, club soda is a mixture of carbon dioxide gas and water. The water and carbon dioxide react forming carbonic acid ($H_2CO_3$). Carbonic acid decomposes to again form water and carbon dioxide. A state of equilibrium is reached in which the amounts of carbonic acid, water, and carbon dioxide remain constant. The overall reaction can be written as follows.

$$CO_2(g) + H_2O(l) \rightleftharpoons H_2CO_3(aq)$$

Chemical reactions that are reversible are said to be in dynamic equilibrium because opposite reactions take place simultaneously at the same rate. A system that is at equilibrium can be shifted toward either reactants or products if the system is subjected to a stress. Changes in concentration, temperature, or pressure are examples of stresses.

How can you know whether reactants or products are favored in a reaction at equilibrium? The answer depends upon the reaction. For the club soda reaction, a measurement of pH indicates the amount of acid present in a solution. The lower the pH, the more acid is present.

What happens to a reaction at equilibrium if one of the products is removed? The reaction goes to completion because a product is not available to react in the reverse direction.

## Problem

How does stress affect a system in equilibrium?

## Objectives

- **Analyze** a system at equilibrium.
- **Describe** the effect of a stress on an equilibrium system.
- **Compare** a system at equilibrium to a reaction that goes to completion.

## Materials

club soda (one bottle chilled, one bottle at room temperature)
test tubes (4)
test-tube rack
rubber stopper to fit test tube
test-tube clamp
Bunsen burner

10-mL graduated cylinder
pH paper or pH meter
0.5$M$ copper(II) sulfate ($CuSO_4$)
0.5$M$ sodium carbonate ($Na_2CO_3$)
1.0$M$ hydrochloric acid (HCl)

## Safety Precautions

- Always wear safety goggles, a lab apron, and gloves.
- Dispose of chemical wastes as directed by your teacher.
- Use caution when handling hot substances.
- Copper(II) sulfate is a tissue irritant and toxic.
- Hydrochloric acid is corrosive to skin and toxic and reacts with metals.
- Take care in using a Bunsen burner.
- When heating the solution in the test tube, be sure to heat slowly, pointing the open end of the test tube away from yourself or anyone else.

## Pre-Lab

1. Define *chemical equilibrium*.

2. Distinguish between a reversible reaction and a reaction that goes to completion.

3. Read the entire laboratory activity. Form a hypothesis about how a stress can be applied to club soda to shift the equilibrium. Form a second hypothesis about what substance can be removed from this reaction to prevent equilibrium. Record your hypotheses in the next column.

4. Write a generalized equation to show the relationship between reactants and products in a system at equilibrium.

5. Write a generalized equation to show the relationship between reactants and products in a reaction that goes to completion because of the formation of a precipitate.

## Procedure

### Part A: Equilibrium

1. Observe the contents of an unopened bottle of club soda at room temperature.

2. Observe the contents of an unopened bottle of refrigerated club soda. **CAUTION: Do not shake either bottle.**

3. Remove the caps from both bottles. Note what happens as the caps are loosened and then removed.

4. Pour 5 mL of room-temperature club soda into one clean, dry test tube and 5 mL of cold club soda into another clean, dry test tube.

5. After 2 minutes, test the pH of the club soda in each test tube. Record these values in **Data Table 1.**

6. Carefully heat the test tube of cold club soda to boiling. Allow the contents of the tube to cool to room temperature and again test and record the pH in **Data Table 1.**

### Part B: Forming a Precipitate

1. Pour about 5 mL of copper(II) sulfate solution into a clean test tube and add about 5 mL of sodium carbonate solution. Stopper and shake the test tube.

2. Allow the test tube to remain undisturbed until a clear liquid forms above the solid material (precipitate) at the bottom of the test tube.

### Part C: Forming a Gas

1. Pour about 5 mL of sodium carbonate solution into a clean test tube. Slowly add 5 mL of hydrochloric acid.

2. Observe the reaction that takes place.

## Hypotheses

_____

_____

_____

_____

## Cleanup and Disposal

1. Dispose of materials as directed by your teacher.

2. Return all lab equipment to its proper place.

3. Report any broken or damaged equipment.

4. Wash your hands thoroughly before leaving the lab.

## Data and Observations

| Data Table 1 | | |
|---|---|---|
| | Cold club soda | Room-temperature club soda |
| Initial pH | | |
| pH after heating | | |

1. Compare the appearance of the contents of the two unopened bottles of club soda.

_____

_____

_____

**2.** Describe what happens as the caps of the two bottles of club soda are loosened and then removed.

_____

_____

**3.** Describe the colors of the sodium carbonate solution and the copper(II) sulfate solution.

_____

_____

## Analyze and Conclude

### Part A: Equilibrium

**1. Observing and Inferring** Describe evidence that indicates that an equilibrium exists in an unopened bottle of club soda.

_____

_____

**2. Observing and Inferring** Describe the stress that caused an equilibrium shift when the bottle of club soda was opened.

_____

_____

**3. Collecting and Interpreting Data** Account for the pH of the club soda before heating and then after heating.

_____

_____

**4. Observing and Inferring** Describe the appearance of the club soda as it was being heated.

_____

_____

**5. Observing and Inferring** Describe the stress that caused an equilibrium shift when the club soda was heated.

_____

_____

**6. Observing and Inferring** What gas was released as the club soda was heated?

_____

**7. Drawing a Conclusion** Write a balanced equation for the reaction that took place as the club soda was heated.

_____

8. **Error Analysis** Do your results support your hypotheses? What sources of error might have been present?

_____

_____

## Part B: Forming a Precipitate

9. **Predicting** Write a balanced equation for the reaction that takes place when sodium carbonate and copper(II) sulfate solutions are mixed.

_____

10. **Observing and Inferring** Describe the appearance of the precipitate. What is the formula for this substance?

_____

_____

11. **Drawing a Conclusion** Explain why the reaction between sodium carbonate and copper(II) sulfate goes to completion.

_____

_____

## Part C: Forming a Gas

12. **Observing and Inferring** What evidence indicates that a reaction took place when hydrochloric acid was added to sodium carbonate solution?

_____

_____

13. **Predicting** Write a balanced equation for the reaction that took place when sodium carbonate solution and hydrochloric acid solution were mixed.

_____

14. **Drawing a Conclusion** Explain why the reaction between sodium carbonate and hydrochloric acid goes to completion.

_____

_____

## Real-World Chemistry

1. Explain why labels on bottles of carbonated beverages often recommend that the beverage be used by a certain date.

2. In the early 1900s, Fritz Haber discovered a process to "fix" free nitrogen into useful nitrogen-containing compounds, such as ammonia. Use LeChâtelier's principle to explain how an equilibrium can be shifted so that atmospheric nitrogen can be combined with hydrogen to produce ammonia according to this equation.

$$N_2(g) + 3H_2(g) \rightleftharpoons 2NH_3(g) + heat$$

# Acids, Bases, and Neutralization

**Use with Section 19.4**

**N**eutralization is a chemical reaction between an acid and a base that produces a salt and water.

$$\text{acid} + \text{base} \rightarrow \text{salt} + \text{water}$$

In an acid-base neutralization reaction, the hydronium (hydrogen) ions of the acidic solution react with the hydroxide ions in the basic solution. The reaction may be shown by this equation.

$$H_3O^+(aq) + OH^-(aq) \rightarrow H_2O(l)$$

Note that one mole of hydronium ions reacts with one mole of hydroxide ions. The solution is neutral when chemically equivalent amounts of acid and base are present.

Indicators are chemical dyes that change color with a change of pH. Litmus paper and phenolphthalein are two common indicators used in acid-base reactions. They are chosen because they change color at or very near solution neutrality. Litmus paper is red in acidic solutions and blue in basic solutions. Phenolphthalein is colorless in acidic solutions and turns red in basic solutions.

## Problem

What substance is formed during a neutralization reaction?

## Objectives

- **Compare** the color of an indicator in acidic solution to its color in a basic solution.
- **Classify** a solution as an acid or a base by observing the color of an indicator in that solution.
- **Observe** the change in color of an indicator when the solution changes from acidic to basic.
- **Draw a conclusion** about what substance is formed during the neutralization reaction of an acid and a base.

## Materials

1.00M hydrochloric acid (HCl)
1M Sulfuric acid ($H_2SO_4$)
1M acetic acid ($HC_2H_3O_2$)
1.00M sodium hydroxide (NaOH)
1M ammonium hydroxide ($NH_4OH$)
limewater— saturated calcium hydroxide ($Ca(OH)_2$) solution
phenolphthalein
blue litmus papers (6)

red litmus papers (6)
100-mL beakers (2)
10-mL graduated cylinder
test tubes (6)
test-tube rack
dropping pipette
Bunsen burner
striker
ring stand
ring
wire gauze
stirring rod
filter paper
evaporating dish

LAB 19.1

## Safety Precautions

- Always wear safety goggles, a lab apron, and gloves.
- Dispose of chemical wastes as directed by your teacher.
- Hydrochloric acid, sulfuric acid, and acetic acid are corrosive to skin and clothing.
- Hydrochloric acid, sulfuric acid, and acetic acid are toxic.
- Sodium hydroxide and ammonium hydroxide are caustic and toxic.
- Limewater is a tissue irritant.

## Pre-Lab

1. Define neutralization.

2. Compare the color of litmus paper in acidic and basic solutions.

3. Compare the color of phenolphthalein in acidic and basic solutions.

4. Read the entire laboratory activity. Form a hypothesis about how to know when an acid or a base has been neutralized. Record your hypothesis on page 147.

5. Summarize the procedures you will follow to test your hypothesis.

## Procedure

### Part A: Acids and Bases

1. Number six test tubes 1 through 6.

2. Pour about 1 mL of $1M$ hydrochloric acid (HCl) into test tube number 1.

3. Pour about 1 mL of $1M$ sulfuric acid ($H_2SO_4$) into test tube number 2.

4. Pour about 1 mL of $1M$ acetic acid ($HC_2H_3O_2$) into test tube number 3.

5. Pour about 1 mL of $1M$ sodium hydroxide (NaOH) into test tube number 4.

6. Pour about 1 mL of $1M$ ammonium hydroxide ($NH_4OH$) into test tube number 5.

7. Pour about 1 mL of limewater, saturated calcium hydroxide ($Ca(OH)_2$), into test tube number 6.

8. Place six pieces of red litmus paper and six pieces of blue litmus paper on a piece of filter paper.

9. Use a stirring rod to transfer 1 drop of hydrochloric acid (test tube number 1) to a piece of red litmus paper. Then transfer 1 drop of hydrochloric acid to a piece of blue litmus paper.

10. Record your observations in **Data Table 1.**

11. Rinse the stirring rod and repeat steps 9 and 10 for the remaining solutions. Be sure to rinse the stirring rod between solution tests.

12. Add 2 drops of phenolphthalein solution to each solution in each of the numbered test tubes.

13. Record your observations in the data table.

### Part B: Neutralization

1. Label a 100-mL beaker "acid" and pour about 15 mL of $1.00M$ hydrochloric acid (HCl) into the beaker.

2. Label another 100-mL beaker "base" and pour about 15 mL of $1.00M$ sodium hydroxide (NaOH) into the beaker.

3. Using the 10-mL graduated cylinder, measure 10.0 mL of hydrochloric acid (HCl) and pour it into a clean evaporating dish.

4. Add 2 drops of phenolphthalein solution to the acid in the evaporating dish.

5. Stir the acid and gradually add about 9 mL of $1.00M$ sodium hydroxide (NaOH).

6. Using a dropping pipette, add $1.00M$ sodium hydroxide (NaOH) drop by drop to the acid solution, stirring after each drop, until 1 drop of base causes the solution to remain a permanent red color.

**7.** Add 1 drop of 1.00*M* hydrochloric acid (HCl). The red color should disappear. If the red color does not disappear, add another drop.

**8.** Attach a ring to a ring stand and place a wire gauze on the ring. Place the evaporating dish on the wire gauze.

**9.** Use a Bunsen burner to slowly heat the contents of the evaporating dish to near dryness.

**10.** Allow the evaporating dish to cool and examine the contents.

## Hypothesis

_____

_____

## Cleanup and Disposal

**1.** Dispose of chemicals as instructed by your teacher.

**2.** Return all lab equipment to its proper place.

**3.** Report any broken or damaged equipment.

**4.** Wash your hands thoroughly before leaving the laboratory.

## Data and Observations

| Data Table 1 | | | | | |
|---|---|---|---|---|---|
| Test-tube number | Name of substance | Color of blue litmus | Color of red litmus | Color of phenolphthalein | Acid or base? |
| 1 | Hydrochloric acid | | | | |
| 2 | Sulfuric acid | | | | |
| 3 | Acetic acid | | | | |
| 4 | Sodium hydroxide | | | | |
| 5 | Ammonium hydroxide | | | | |
| 6 | Calcium hydroxide | | | | |

## Analyze and Conclude

**1. Applying Concepts** Describe how litmus paper may be used to differentiate between an acid and a base.

_____

_____

**2. Classifying** Complete the last column of **Data Table 1.**

**3. Applying Concepts** Describe how phenolphthalein may be used to differentiate between an acid and a base.

_____

_____

**4. Observing and Inferring** Explain why the phenolphthalein remained colorless when 10.0 mL of 1.00*M* hydrochloric acid and about 9 mL of 1.00*M* sodium hydroxide were mixed.

_____

_____

**5. Observing and Inferring** What is the significance of the permanent red color change in step 6?

_____

_____

**6. Observing and Inferring** Why was a drop of 1.00*M* hydrochloric acid added to make the red color disappear in step 7?

_____

_____

**7. Observing and Inferring** Describe the solid residue remaining after heating the contents of the evaporating dish to near dryness.

_____

_____

**8. Drawing a Conclusion** Identify the solid residue remaining after heating the contents of the evaporating dish to near dryness.

_____

**9. Measuring and Using Numbers** Write a balanced chemical equation for the reaction between hydrochloric acid and sodium hydroxide.

_____

**10. Predicting** What quantity of 2.00*M* sodium hydroxide would be needed to neutralize 10.0 mL of 1.00*M* hydrochloric acid? Explain.

_____

**11. Error Analysis** Compare your answers in **Data Table 1** to the answers of other students in your class. What are some reasons that the answers might be different?

_____

_____

## Real-World Chemistry

**1.** Explain the difference between using antacids and acid inhibitors in the treatment of excess stomach acid.

**2.** Explain why neutralization of soil is important in the agricultural economy.

# Determining the Percent of Acetic Acid in Vinegar

**Use with Section 19.4**

Titration is a procedure used for determining the concentration of an acid or a base by neutralizing a known volume of the acid or base with a solution of a standard base or an acid. A standard solution is one whose molarity has been accurately determined experimentally.

In a titration, one solution is added slowly to the other until the equivalence point is reached. At the equivalence point of a neutralization reaction, the moles of acid and moles of base are equal. An indicator, placed in the reaction mixture, tells you by means of a color change, when the equivalence point has been reached. Your experimental data—the volume and molarity of the standard solution and the volume of the unknown acid or base solution—are all that you need to calculate the molarity of the unknown acid or base.

In this activity, you will first standardize a NaOH solution by using the solution to titrate a known mass of oxalic acid ($H_2C_2O_4$). Then, you will use your standardized solution to titrate a sample of vinegar. Vinegar is a solution of acetic acid ($HC_2H_3O_2$). From your titration data, you will be able to calculate the number of moles and the mass of the acetic acid in your vinegar sample and determine the percent of acetic acid in vinegar.

## Problem

What is the percent of acetic acid in vinegar?

## Objectives

- **Prepare** a solution of NaOH.
- **Determine** the molarity of the NaOH solution.
- **Determine** the percent of acetic acid in vinegar.

## Materials

sodium hydroxide pellets (NaOH)
acetic acid solution (white vinegar)
oxalic acid ($H_2C_2O_4 \cdot 2H_2O$)
phenolphthalein solution
250-mL Erlenmeyer flasks (2)
250-mL beaker
250-mL plastic bottle with screw top

100-mL graduated cylinder
ring stand
burette
burette clamp
balance
label
distilled water

## Safety Precautions

- **Always wear safety goggles, gloves, and a lab apron.**
- **Oxalic acid and sodium hydroxide are toxic.**
- **Sodium hydroxide is caustic, and oxalic acid is corrosive.**
- **Wipe up any water spills to avoid slippage.**

## Pre-Lab

1. Briefly explain what happens in a neutralization reaction.

2. What is a standard solution?

3. State the equation used to determine percent error.

4. Read the entire laboratory activity. Form a hypothesis about using a standard solution to determine the concentration of another solution. Record your hypothesis on page 151.

**LAB 19.2**

## Procedure

### Part A: Standardizing an NaOH Solution

1. Label a clean 250-mL plastic bottle *Standard NaOH Solution*. Write your name and the date of preparation on the label.

2. In the 250-mL plastic bottle, dissolve about 50 NaOH pellets in 200 mL of distilled water. **CAUTION: Sodium hydroxide is caustic.**

3. Set up the burette, burette clamp, and 250-mL Erlenmeyer flask as shown in **Figure A.**

**Figure A**

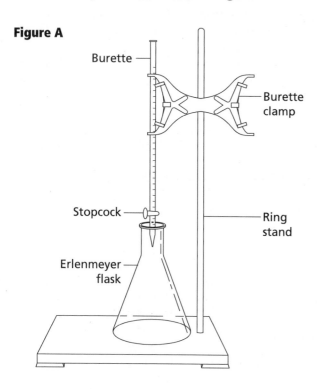

Burette

Burette clamp

Stopcock

Ring stand

Erlenmeyer flask

4. Prepare the burette by rinsing it with tap water. Then rinse it with distilled water, and finally with 5 to 10 mL of your NaOH solution.

5. Close the stopcock of the burette and pour enough NaOH solution into the burette so that the NaOH level is around the 5-mL mark.

6. To eliminate any air in the burette tip, place a *waste* beaker under the burette. Open the stop-cock and fill the tip of the burette. A drop or two of NaOH may run out into the waste beaker.

7. Record the initial volume of NaOH in **Data Table 1.**

8. Clean and rinse a 250-mL Erlenmeyer flask with distilled water. Measure the mass of the empty flask and record it in **Data Table 1.**

9. Add about 1.0 g of oxalic acid to the flask and measure its mass again. Record the mass of the flask and acid in **Data Table 1.**

10. Pour about 50 mL of distilled water into the flask containing the acid. Gently swirl the flask until the oxalic acid dissolves.

11. Add 3 drops of phenolphthalein solution to the flask containing the acid solution. Place the flask under the burette so that the tip of the burette is 1–2 cm inside the mouth of the flask.

12. Begin the titration by allowing small amounts of the NaOH to flow into the flask containing the acid. Swirl the flask to allow the base and acid to mix.

13. When the pink color of the indicator begins to take longer to disappear, you are close to the equivalence point. Adjust the stopcock of the burette so that the base runs into the acid drop-wise.

14. Continue to add drops of base until a permanent light pink color is obtained. Record the final volume of the NaOH solution in **Data Table 1.**

### Part B: Determining the Percent of Acid in Vinegar

1. Measure the mass of a second clean 250-mL Erlenmeyer flask and record its mass in **Data Table 2.**

2. Pour about 30 mL of vinegar into the flask, and measure the mass of the flask and vinegar. Record the mass in **Data Table 2.**

3. Refill the burette with NaOH solution so that the level of the solution is at approximately the 5-mL mark. Record this initial volume in **Data Table 2.**

4. Add the sodium hydroxide solution to the acid solution, following steps 11 through 14 in Part A. Record the final volume of NaOH used in **Data Table 2.**

**LAB 19.2**

## Hypothesis

_____

_____

_____

_____

## Cleanup and Disposal

**1.** Dispose of used chemicals and return excess chemicals as instructed by your teacher.

**2.** Return all lab equipment to its proper place.

**3.** Clean up your lab area and wash your hands thoroughly before leaving the lab.

## Data and Observations

| Data Table 1 | |
|---|---|
| Mass of flask and oxalic acid (g) | |
| Mass of empty flask (g) | |
| Mass of oxalic acid (g) | |
| Moles of oxalic acid (mol) | |
| Final volume of NaOH (mL) | |
| Initial volume of NaOH (mL) | |
| Volume of NaOH used (mL) | |
| Moles of NaOH (mol) | |
| Molarity of NaOH (*M*) | |

| Data Table 2 | |
|---|---|
| Mass of flask and vinegar (g) | |
| Mass of empty flask (g) | |
| Mass of vinegar (g) | |
| Final volume of NaOH (mL) | |
| Initial volume of NaOH (mL) | |
| Volume of NaOH used (mL) | |
| Mass of acetic acid (g) | |
| Percentage of acetic acid in vinegar solution | |

**1.** Complete **Data Table 1** by calculating the following:
   **a.** The mass of oxalic acid used to standardize the NaOH solution in Part A
   **b.** The volume of NaOH solution used to neutralize the oxalic acid

**2.** Complete **Data table 2** by calculating the following:
   **a.** The mass of the vinegar sample
   **b.** The volume of NaOH required to neutralize the acetic acid in the vinegar sample

## Analyze and Conclude

**1. Measuring and Using Numbers** From the mass of oxalic acid used and the molar mass of oxalic acid, determine and record the number of moles of oxalic acid.

_____

_____

**2. Applying Concepts** Write the equation for the reaction of oxalic acid ($H_2C_2O_4$) with NaOH. What is the ratio of moles of NaOH to moles of $H_2C_2O_4$?

_____

_____

3. **Applying Concepts** Use the moles of oxalic acid calculated in question 1 and the mole ratio from question 2 to determine the moles of NaOH.

_____

4. **Measuring and Using Numbers** Convert the volume of NaOH used in mL to L of NaOH and determine the moles of NaOH per liter. Record your result in **Data Table 1** as the molarity of NaOH (*M*).

_____

_____

5. **Measuring and Using Numbers** Use the molarity of the NaOH solution and the volume of NaOH used in part B to determine the moles of NaOH used to titrate the acetic acid in the vinegar sample.

_____

6. **Applying Concepts** Write the equation for the neutralization of acetic acid ($HC_2H_3O_2$). What is the ratio of moles of NaOH to moles of acetic acid? How many moles of acetic acid are in the vinegar sample?

_____

_____

_____

7. **Measuring and Using Numbers** Use the moles of acetic acid and the molar mass of acetic acid to calculate the mass of acetic acid in the vinegar sample.

_____

_____

8. **Measuring and Using Numbers** Use the mass of acetic acid and the total mass of the vinegar sample to calculate the percent acetic acid in vinegar.

_____

_____

9. **Error Analysis** Calculate the percent error of the experimental result using the actual value supplied by your teacher. Use the equation percent error = (deviation/correct answer) × 100. Explain what errors could have contributed to any deviation.

_____

_____

### Real-World Chemistry

1. Explain how titration might be used to determine the effects of acid rain on the environment.

2. Explain how titration might be used for medical testing.

**LAB 20.1 LABORATORY MANUAL**

# Electron-Losing Tendencies of Metals

Use with
Section 20.1

**A** chemical species that is able to reduce the oxidation state of another species by donating electrons is called a reducing agent. A strong reducing agent has a low electronegativity. In this lab, you will review the electronegativities of several metals, use the information to predict the relative strengths of the metals as reducing agents, and then perform two experiments to verify your predictions.

## Problem

How do you determine which of two metals is the stronger reducing agent?

## Objectives

- **Predict** the relative strengths of several metals as reducing agents.
- **Experiment** to verify the prediction.

## Materials

test tubes (3)
test-tube rack
grease pencil
10-mL graduated cylinder
50-mL graduated cylinder
forceps
zinc nitrate solution ($Zn(NO_3)_2$)
copper(II) nitrate solution ($Cu(NO_3)_2$)
magnesium nitrate solution ($Mg(NO_3)_2$)

zinc (Zn) metal strips (3)
copper (Cu) metal strips (3)
magnesium (Mg) ribbon strips (5)
calcium (Ca) (2 small chunks)
steel wool or fine sandpaper
250-mL beaker
phenolphthalein indicator
dropper
1.0$M$ hydrochloric acid (HCl)

## Safety Precautions

- **Always wear safety goggles, gloves, and a lab apron.**
- **Phenolphthalein solution is toxic and flammable. Be sure no open flames are in the lab when phenolphthalein solution is in use.**
- **Calcium is corrosive and harmful to human tissue.**
- **Copper(II) nitrate is moderately toxic.**
- **Zinc nitrate is a severe body tissue irritant.**
- **Magnesium nitrate is a skin and eye irritant.**

## Pre-Lab

1. Locate magnesium, calcium, copper, and zinc on the periodic table. Which three are in the same period? Which two are in the same group?

2. The electronegativity of aluminum is 1.61 and that of silver is 1.93. Which of these two metals is the stronger reducing agent?

3. Read the entire laboratory activity. Form a hypothesis about the relative strengths of these four metals as reducing agents, from strongest to weakest. Record your hypothesis on page 154.

4. Summarize the procedure you will use to test your hypothesis.

## Procedure

### Part A

**1.** Clean the strips of zinc, copper, and magnesium with the steel wool or sandpaper.

**2.** Place three test tubes in the rack, and label their places in the rack with the names of the three solutions.

**3.** Measure 5 mL of tap water into the graduated cylinder. Pour the water into one of the test tubes. Use the grease pencil to mark the test tube at the 5-mL level. Discard the water. Repeat for the other two test tubes.

**4.** Fill the three test tubes to the 5-mL level with their respective solutions.

**5.** Place a zinc strip in each of the test tubes.

**6.** After about 5 minutes, record your observations in **Data Table 1.** Describe any evidence of a reaction. If there is no reaction, write "NR."

**7.** Pour the contents of the test tubes into a beaker. Using forceps, remove the zinc strips. Rinse them with water and dry with paper towels. Rinse the test tubes thoroughly with water. Discard the used solutions as directed by your teacher.

**8.** Repeat steps 5 through 7, first with copper, then with magnesium.

### Part B

**1.** Put 15 mL of distilled water in a test tube and 50 mL of distilled water in a 250-mL beaker.

**2.** Place 2 drops of phenolphthalein in both the test tube and the beaker.

**3.** Place a strip of magnesium ribbon in the test tube.

**4.** Using forceps, obtain a small piece of calcium and place it in the beaker.

**5.** Observe the reactions for about 5 minutes. If you see no reaction, write "NR." Put the reaction aside until the next day and observe it again. Record your observations in **Data Table 2.**

**6.** Repeat steps 1 through 5, using 1.0$M$ HCl instead of water.

## Hypothesis

_____

_____

## Cleanup and Disposal

**1.** Dispose of the used metals and solutions according to your teacher's directions.

**2.** Return all lab equipment to its proper place.

**3.** Wash your hands thoroughly before leaving the lab.

## Data and Observations

| Data Table 1 | | | |
|---|---|---|---|
| Element | Zn(NO$_3$)$_2$ | Cu(NO$_3$)$_2$ | Mg(NO$_3$)$_2$ |
| Cu | | | |
| Mg | | | |
| Zn | | | |

| Data Table 2 | | |
|---|---|---|
| Element | Reaction with H$_2$O | Reaction with HCl |
| Mg | | |
| Ca | | |

**LAB 20.1**

## Analyze and Conclude

1. **Communicating** Write equations for all of the reactions that you observed. For each one, identify the reducing agent by circling it. Write nothing for the combinations in which no reaction takes place.

_____

_____

_____

_____

_____

_____

_____

2. **Observing and Inferring** Examine the equations you wrote for Part B. Why was the phenolphthalein added to the distilled water?

_____

_____

3. **Applying Concepts** All these reactions are of the same type. What type is it?

_____

4. **Sequencing** Order the metals in Part A by strength as a reducing agent, strongest to weakest. Which of the two metals in Part B is the stronger reducing agent?

_____

5. **Comparing and Contrasting** Use your results from parts A and B and list the four metals, from strongest reducing agent to weakest.

_____

6. **Using Numbers** What are the electronegativities of the four metals used? (Refer to Figure 9-15 on page 263 of the textbook.) Do these figures support your experimental results?

_____

_____

7. **Interpreting Data** In Part B, what could be done to quantify the results of each reaction?

_____

_____

8. **Predicting** Do you think beryllium would be a stronger reducing agent than magnesium? Why?

_____

_____

9. **Comparing and Contrasting** Look up the electronegativities of beryllium and zinc. Which of the two is the stronger reducing agent? Explain.

_____

_____

10. **Error Analysis** Do the strengths of the four metals as reducing agents support your hypothesis? Make a statement relating your results to your hypothesis.

_____

_____

_____

## Real-World Chemistry

1. Why do you think copper is commonly used for metallic sculptures that are located outside?

2. Why is calcium not found as a free element in nature?

3. Zinc metal is often used to coat iron objects in a process called galvanizing. Which of these two metals do you think is more reactive? Explain.

## LAB 20.2 LABORATORY MANUAL

# Determining Oxidation Numbers

**Use with Section 20.2**

**O**xidation–reduction reactions are very important in chemistry. They are the basis of many products and processes, from batteries to photosynthesis and respiration. You know redox reactions involve an oxidation half-reaction in which electrons are lost and a reduction half-reaction in which electrons are gained. In order to use the chemistry of redox reactions, we need to know about the tendency of the ions involved in the half-reactions to gain electrons. This tendency is called the reduction potential. Tables of standard reduction potentials exist that provide quantitative information on electron movement in redox half-reactions. In this lab, you will use reduction potentials combined with gravimetric analysis to determine oxidation numbers of the involved substances.

## Problem

Can oxidation numbers be determined by analyzing the half-reactions and their tendency of electrons?

## Objectives

- **Investigate** and **quantify** the tendency of elements to gain electrons.
- **Determine** oxidation numbers of chemical substances.

## Materials

75-mL beakers (4)
10-cm long copper wire segments (2)
silver nitrate (AgNO$_3$)
potassium nitrate (KNO$_3$)

filter papers (2)
funnel
stirring rod
masking tape
distilled water

## Safety Precautions

- Always wear safety goggles, gloves, and a lab apron.
- Silver nitrate is caustic, highly toxic, and will stain skin.

## Pre-Lab

1. Write the equations for the chemical reactions for (a) the oxidation of Ag, K, and Cu, and (b) the reduction of Ag$^+$, K$^+$, Cu(I), and Cu(II).

2. Write the net ionic equation for (a) the reaction of copper solid with silver nitrate to form copper(II) nitrate and silver solid, and (b) the reaction of copper solid with potassium nitrate that would form copper(II) nitrate and potassium solid.

3. Read the entire laboratory activity. Recall your study of reactivity in Chapter 10. Which beaker(s) will show evidence of a chemical reaction? What substance is in the beaker(s) after the reaction?

4. Formulate a hypothesis as to how the lab activity can determine oxidation numbers. Record your hypothesis on page 158.

## Procedure

1. Measure 4 g of silver nitrate, record the exact mass, and place the sample in the first beaker. Label this beaker *1*.

2. Measure a 4-g sample of potassium nitrate, record the exact mass, and place the sample in the second beaker. Label this beaker *2*.

3. Add approximately 20 mL of water to beaker 1, containing silver nitrate, and stir until dissolved.

4. Add approximately 20 mL of water to beaker 2, containing potassium nitrate, and stir until dissolved.

5. Take a small piece of masking tape and use it to label each piece of wire. Write *Ag* on the wire to be used with the silver nitrate, and *K* on the wire to be used with the potassium nitrate.

6. Coil each piece of copper wire so that it will fit in the funnel and can be submerged in the solutions present in each beaker with only the label remaining out of the solution.

7. Weigh and record the mass of each piece of labeled copper wire.

8. Now place the copper wire labeled Ag in beaker 1 and the copper wire labeled K in beaker 2. Be careful not to submerge the label in the solution.

9. Record the time that the wires were submerged in the solutions.

10. With a pencil, carefully write *Ag* on one piece of filter paper and *K* on a second piece of filter paper.

11. Weigh each piece of filter paper and record the mass.

12. Fold each piece of filter paper into quarters in preparation for filtration.

13. After 20 minutes have passed (from step 9), describe the contents of each beaker.

14. Place the filter paper labeled K in the funnel and carefully remove the K wire and place in the funnel.

15. Place the funnel with the K copper wire in another beaker. Slightly lift the copper wire from the funnel and carefully pour the contents of beaker 2 over the copper wire, rinsing the wire.

16. Set the copper wire aside to dry. Remove the filter paper from the funnel and set it aside to dry.

17. Repeat steps 14 and 15 using the copper wire labeled Ag and rinsing the wire with the contents of beaker 1. Set both the copper wire and filter paper with residue aside to dry.

18. Once dry, weigh and record the masses of both the copper wire and filter paper (with possible residue) labeled K.

19. Once dry, weigh and record the masses of both the copper wire and filter paper (with possible residue) labeled Ag.

20. Complete the tables and calculations.

## Hypothesis

_____

_____

_____

## Cleanup and Disposal

1. All solutions can be poured down the drain and flushed with water.

2. The solids recovered may be placed in the solid waste container or collected for recycling.

3. Return all equipment to its proper place.

4. Clean up your workstation and wash your hands thoroughly with soap or detergent before leaving the lab.

**LAB 20.2**

## Data and Observations

| Data Table 1 | |
| --- | --- |
| **Beaker 1** | **Data values** |
| Mass of silver nitrate (g) | |
| Initial mass of copper wire (g) | |
| Final mass of copper wire (g) | |
| Mass of copper wire used in reaction (g) | |
| Formula weight of copper (g/mol) | |
| Moles of copper used in reaction (mol) | |
| Final mass of filter paper and Ag (g) | |
| Initial mass of filter paper (g) | |
| Mass of Ag on filter paper (g) | |
| Formula weight of Ag (g/mol) | |
| Moles of Ag on filter paper (mol) | |
| Divide moles of Ag by moles of Cu used | |
| Appearance of beaker 1 after 20 minutes | |

| Data Table 2 | |
| --- | --- |
| **Beaker 2** | **Data values** |
| Mass of potassium nitrate (g) | |
| Initial mass of copper wire (g) | |
| Final mass of copper wire (g) | |
| Mass of copper wire used in reaction (g) | |
| Formula weight of copper (g/mol) | |
| Moles of copper used in reaction (mol) | |
| Final mass of filter paper and substance (g) | |
| Initial mass of filter paper (g) | |
| Mass of substance on filter paper (g) | |
| Formula weight of K (g/mol) | |
| Moles of substance on filter paper (mol) | |
| Divide moles of K by moles of Cu used | |
| Appearance of beaker 2 after 20 minutes | |

## Analyze and Conclude

**1. Collecting and Interpreting Data** Did a reaction occur in beaker 1? In beaker 2?

_____

**2. Comparing and Contrasting** What is the ratio of moles of Ag formed to moles of Cu consumed in beaker 1?

_____

**3. Applying Concepts** If the reduction of Ag requires only one electron per atom, how many electrons per Cu atom were oxidized?

_____

**4. Drawing a Conclusion** What is the oxidation number of the Cu ion in solution?

_____

**5. Observing and Inferring** Use your knowledge of reactivity from Chapter 10 to infer why no reaction took place in beaker 2.

_____

_____

**6. Error Analysis** Compare your predictions to the experimental results. Explain any differences.

_____

_____

### Real-World Chemistry

**1.** Silver is an important element in photography. This is due to the oxidation–reduction reaction of silver bromide in the presence of light.

$$2AgBr + light \rightarrow 2Ag + Br_2$$

What substance is oxidized in this reaction? Which substance is reduced?

**2.** The amount of reduction is dependent on the wavelength (or energy) of the light. Violet light is the most energetic visible wavelength. It requires only 15 seconds to reduce the same amount of silver bromide that is reduced in 5.5 minutes with yellow light. Why is a red light used in most darkrooms?

**LAB 21.1 LABORATORY MANUAL**

# Electrolysis of Water

**W**ater has a remarkably complex structure. For the purposes of electrolysis, however, it is convenient to think of water as an aqueous solution of $H^+$ and $OH^-$ ions. In the presence of an anode, which has a surplus of electrons, the $H^+$ ions are attracted and they line up to receive electrons. Conversely, at an electron-hungry cathode, $OH^-$ ions line up to donate electrons.

To test for the presence of hydrogen, inject the gas to be tested into bubble solution. The resulting bubbles should ignite easily. To test for the presence of oxygen, insert a glowing splint into the gas. The splint should immediately ignite. In this lab, you will discover what happens when an electric current is passed through water.

## Problem

What happens when an electric current is passed through water?

## Objectives

- **Observe** the pH of water near the electrodes.
- **Collect** and **identify** the gases that evolve at the electrodes.
- **Draw conclusions** about the composition of water.

## Materials

solid bromothymol blue indicator (a few grains)
dilute sodium bicarbonate solution (10 mL)
dilute vinegar (10 mL)
glycerol (1 mL)
fine copper wire (20 cm)
2-cm piece of platinum wire or graphite pencil leads
silicone putty
wood splints (4)
5-mL disposable graduated pipettes (2)

5-mL disposable syringes (2)
25-mL beaker
100-mL beaker
small polypropylene transfer pipettes (2)
surgical rubber or silicone tubing (5 cm)
ring stand
clamps (2)
matches
6-V, 9-V, or 12-V DC source
wire leads for power source
glass stirring rod

## Safety Precautions

- **Always wear safety goggles and a lab apron.**
- **Use care around flames.**
- **Secure loose clothing and tie back long hair.**
- **Never place the pipettes in your mouth.**

## Pre-Lab

1. Write equations for the reactions at each electrode.

2. Hypothesize about the pH you would expect to observe at each electrode. What ratio of gases do you expect to observe? Record your hypothesis on page 163.

## Procedure

### Part A: Electrode Assembly

1. Cut a plastic graduated pipette into a piece that is 5-cm long. Similarly, cut a piece of surgical rubber tubing 4-cm long.

2. Thread a length of copper wire through a piece of the graduated pipette. Wrap an end of the copper wire around the end of one of the platinum or graphite electrodes, as shown in **Figure A, step 1.**

Platinum or graphite electrode

Copper wire

**Step 1**
Wrapping the wire

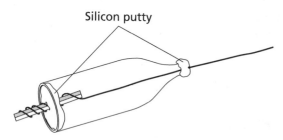

Silicon putty

**Step 2**
Sealing the ends

**Figure A**

3. Pull the copper wire and the electrode inside the length of pipette.

4. Seal the ends of the pipette using silicon putty, as shown in **Figure A, step 2**. This is the anode.

5. Assemble the electrodes as shown in **Figure B**. Note that the platinum or graphite electrode, as prepared above, serves as the anode. The cathode is copper wire mounted in a section of the pipette tube, which is then fitted over the end of a syringe. Surgical rubber tubing is used to seal the joint between the syringe tip and the pipette. The rubber tubing can be folded double to make the seal tighter. Silicon putty is used in the anode housing to ensure that the copper wire is not exposed in the anode.

## Part B: Electrolysis of Water

1. Place about 10 mL of water in a 25-mL beaker. Add a few grains of solid bromothymol blue. Stir until the bromothymol blue has dissolved.

2. If the solution is yellow, dip a glass stirring rod in dilute sodium bicarbonate solution. Transfer this solution to the indicator solution and stir. Continue adding dilute sodium bicarbonate solution until the solution turns green. If the solution is blue, carry out the same procedure with diluted vinegar until the solution turns green.

3. Lubricate the inner walls of the syringe with a few drops of glycerol.

4. Use the syringe of each assembly to fill the pipette tubing and about 1 mL of the syringe with the indicator solution. Make sure there are no air bubbles in either assembly.

5. Submerse the electrodes in the beaker of water and clamp them in position using a ring stand and two clamps.

6. Connect a DC battery to the electrodes. Remember that the cathode is the positive electrode.

7. The electrodes should start to bubble. If necessary, withdraw the syringe pistons from time to time to ensure that the gases collect in the syringes.

8. Allow the electrolysis to continue until you can see that gases have accumulated. Record the volume of gas collected at each electrode in **Data Table 1.**

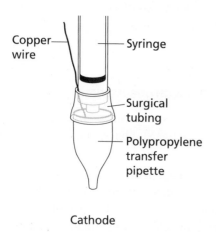

Copper wire — Syringe

— Surgical tubing

— Polypropylene transfer pipette

Cathode

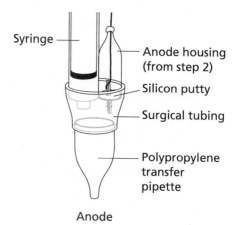

Syringe —

— Anode housing (from step 2)

— Silicon putty

— Surgical tubing

— Polypropylene transfer pipette

Anode

**Figure B**

**LAB 21.1**

## Hypothesis

_____

_____

_____

## Cleanup and Disposal

1. Dispose of materials as directed by your teacher.
2. Return all lab equipment to its proper place.
3. Wash your hands thoroughly with soap or detergent before leaving the lab.

## Data and Observations

1. The indicator bromothymol blue is green in a neutral solution, yellow in an acidic solution, and blue in a basic solution. Record in **Data Table 1** whether the electrolyte was acidic, neutral, or basic at each electrode.
2. Perform the tests discussed in the introduction to confirm the identity of the gases.

| Data Table 1: Measurements and Observations | | |
|---|---|---|
| **Electrode** | **Cathode (+)** | **Anode (−)** |
| Volume of gas | | |
| pH at electrode (acid or base) | | |
| Identity of gas | | |

## Analyze and Conclude

1. **Measuring and Using Numbers** What is the ratio of the volume of the gas produced at the cathode to that produced at the anode? Round your answer off to the nearest whole number.

_____

2. **Applying Concepts** Explain why this ratio has the value it has.

_____

_____

_____

3. **Applying Concepts** Is water oxidized or reduced at the cathode? At the anode? Why?

_____

_____

_____

**4. Thinking Critically** Explain the pH changes you observed.

_____

_____

_____

**5. Thinking Critically** Explain why care was taken not to expose the copper wire at the anode and why it didn't matter at the cathode.

_____

_____

_____

**6. Predicting** What would happen to the rate of gas production if you increased the voltage? Why?

_____

_____

**7. Predicting** What would happen to the rate of gas production if you moved the electrodes closer together? Why?

_____

_____

**8. Error Analysis** How accurately did you determine the gas volumes? What were possible sources of error in this activity?

_____

_____

_____

## Real-World Chemistry

One suggested application of solar energy is to use the electrical current that can be generated for the electrolysis of water. What product of the electrolysis would be most valuable as an energy source? Explain your choice.

# Electroplating

**Use with**
**Section 21.3**

Electroplating has a wide range of practical and decorative applications. In this lab, you will measure macroscopic quantities in order to say something about the microscopic nature of copper.

## Problem

How many electrons does a copper ion in copper sulfate solution take from a cathode in electroplating?

## Objectives

- **Compare** and **contrast** the mass lost by a copper anode to the mass gained by a metal object being plated at the cathode.
- **Measure** and **use numbers** to calculate how many electrons it takes to turn a copper ion in copper sulfate solution into a copper atom.

## Materials

metal object for plating (key or coin with drilled hole)
1-cm × 10-cm copper strip for use as anode
detergent solution
steel wool
5-cm #20–22 bare copper wire
tweezers
100-mL beakers (2)
250-mL beaker
3$M$ sodium hydroxide (NaOH)

3$M$ sulfuric acid (H$_2$SO$_4$)
plating solution
small glass rod
balance with 0.01 g precision
DC milliamp ammeter
12-V DC variable power supply
wires for circuit
alligator clips (2)
distilled water
paper towels

## Safety Precautions

- **Always wear safety goggles, a lab apron, and gloves.**
- **3$M$ NaOH is a strong base, and H$_2$SO$_4$ is a strong acid. Spills should be flushed with large amount of water, then neutralized with dilute vinegar. For eye-splashes, eyes should be washed in an eyewash, using tepid water, for 15 minutes. Then consult a doctor.**

## Pre-Lab

1. Write the cathode half-reaction equation.
2. Write the anode half-reaction equation.
3. Read the entire laboratory activity. Using the above equations to guide you, form a hypothesis about how many copper atoms you expect to lose from the copper anode for each copper atom deposited on the cathode. How many electrons do you expect to pass through the circuit for each copper atom deposited at the cathode? Record your hypothesis on page 166.

## Procedure

### Part A

1. These instructions will assume that you are plating a key. Clean the surfaces of the key and copper anode with steel wool.
2. Wash the key and copper anode with detergent and rinse with tap water.
3. Attach a 5-cm length of bare copper wire to the key. This will serve as a handle for further cleaning and plating.

**4.** Place 30 mL of 3*M* sodium hydroxide solution in a 100-mL beaker. Immerse the key and copper anode in the solution for a few minutes. Remove with tweezers and rinse with distilled water. **CAUTION: Avoid skin contact with sodium hydroxide.**

**5.** Place 30 mL of 3*M* sulfuric acid solution in a 100-mL beaker. Immerse the key and copper anode in the solution for a few minutes. Remove with tweezers and rinse with distilled water. **CAUTION: Avoid skin contact with sulfuric acid.**

## Part B

**1.** Place 200 mL of plating solution in the 250-mL beaker. The plating solution is a solution of copper sulfate, acidified with a little sulfuric acid.

**Figure A**

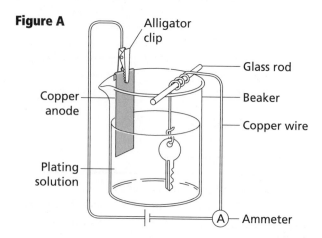

**2.** Place the copper anode in the beaker, bending the strip to fit over the edge of the beaker. Secure the copper strip to the beaker using an alligator clip. See **Figure A.**

**3.** Suspend the key in the solution using its copper wire handle and a small glass rod. See **Figure A.**

**4.** Without switching the power on, connect the power supply and ammeter in a circuit with the plating cell. The copper anode is connected, via the ammeter, to the positive (red) terminal of the power supply. The key acts as the cathode and is connected to the negative (black) terminal.

**5.** Have your teacher inspect the arrangement before proceeding.

**6.** Turn on the power supply and adjust it to 0.25 A (250 mA). Allow current to flow for about 5 minutes to prime the electrodes.

**7.** Turn off the power supply.

**8.** Remove the key and copper anode. Rinse with distilled water and blot dry with a clean paper towel.

## Part C

**1.** Find the mass of the copper anode to the nearest 0.001 g and record its mass in **Data Table 1.**

**2.** Find the mass of the key, together with its copper wire handle, to the nearest 0.001 g. Record the mass of this cathode assembly in **Data Table 1.**

**3.** Without switching on the power supply, follow steps 2 through 5 of Part B to reassemble the circuit.

**4.** To work out the actual number of electrons that leave the key while the plating occurs, you need to know two things: the current and the duration of the current flow. The current must be fixed at a steady value. Switch the power on, and simultaneously record the start time and immediately adjust the current to 0.25 A.

**5.** Keep the current at a steady value for about 30 minutes, then switch off the power supply and record the finish time.

**6.** Remove the key and copper anode. Rinse with distilled water and blot dry with a clean paper towel.

**7.** Repeat steps 1 and 2 of Part C.

## Hypothesis

_____

_____

## Cleanup and Disposal

**1.** *Carefully* return the three solutions to their correct storage bottles.

**2.** Disconnect the circuit, rinse and dry the beakers, and return everything to its correct place.

**3.** Wash your hands thoroughly with soap or detergent before leaving the lab.

**LAB 21.2**

## Data and Observations

Record the value of the current that you used for electroplating. _____

| Data Table 1 | | | |
|---|---|---|---|
| **Measurement** | **Start** | **End** | **Difference** |
| Mass of copper anode | | | |
| Mass of key (cathode) | | | |
| Time | | | |

## Analyze and Conclude

### 1. Measuring and Using Numbers

**a.** What is the difference between the final and initial mass of the key?

_____

**b.** The atomic mass of copper is 63.5, which is to say that 1 mole of copper has a mass of 63.5 g. How many moles of copper atoms were deposited on the key? Show your work and include units.

_____

_____

**c.** Multiply the number of moles of copper deposited by Avogadro's number $(6.02 \times 10^{23}$ atoms/mol$^{-1})$ to obtain the number of copper atoms deposited on the key.

_____

### 2. Measuring and Using Numbers

**a.** What mass of copper atoms was lost by the copper anode?

_____

**b.** How many moles of copper atoms were lost by the anode? Show your work.

_____

_____

**c.** What number of copper atoms was lost by the anode?

_____

### 3. Comparing and Contrasting How do your answers to questions 1a, 1b, and 1c compare to your answers to questions 2a, 2b, and 2c?

_____

_____

**4. Drawing a Conclusion** Use your answers to questions 1–3 to draw a conclusion relating the number of atoms lost by the anode to that gained by the cathode.

_____

_____

_____

**5. Measuring and Using Numbers** The total charge, in coulombs, passing any part of the circuit during the electroplating is equal to the product of the current (in amps, not milliamps) and the time (in seconds). Divide the total charge by the charge on an electron ($1.602 \times 10^{-19}$ coulombs) to find the total number of electrons passing any arbitrary point in the circuit. Show your work and include units.

_____

_____

_____

**6. Observing and Inferring** Explain the relationship between the number of electrons passing from the cathode and the number of copper atoms deposited on the key.

_____

_____

_____

_____

**7. Hypothesizing** Make a statement connecting your results to your hypothesis.

_____

_____

_____

_____

**8. Error Analysis** Was the increase in the mass of the key almost equal to the decrease in the mass of the copper anode? If not, what could be some sources of error?

_____

_____

_____

_____

**Real-World Chemistry**

**1.** What are some applications for electroplating?

**2.** What are some of the benefits of electroplating an item with a metal?

## LAB 22.1  LABORATORY MANUAL

# Isomerism

**T**wo or more substances that have the same molecular formula but different structures and properties are called isomers. Two main types of isomers exist. Structural isomers are ones in which the atoms are bonded in different orders. In stereoisomers, all the bonds in the molecule are the same, but the spatial arrangements are different.

To study molecules and isomers, chemists find the use of models helpful. Colored wooden or plastic balls are used to represent atoms. These balls have holes drilled in them according to the number of covalent bonds they will form. The holes are bored at angles that approximate the accepted bond angles.

Sticks and springs are used to represent bonds. Short sticks are generally used to connect carbon atoms with hydrogen atoms, while longer sticks are used to represent carbon-carbon single bonds. While single bonds are shown with sticks, double and triple bonds are shown with two springs and three springs, respectively.

While the sizes of the atoms are not proportionately correct, the models are useful to represent the arrangement of the atoms according to their bond angles. The models also demonstrate structural isomerism and stereoisomerism.

In this lab, you will work with models of molecules from the alkane family that have one, two, three, four, and five carbon atoms. Molecules in the alkane family are said to be saturated, which means they have only single covalent bonds between the carbon atoms.

Methane, $CH_4$, has one carbon atom. The next two members of the alkane family are ethane, $C_2H_6$, and propane, $C_3H_8$. Molecules of these compounds contain chains of two carbon atoms and three carbon atoms, respectively. Alkanes with more than three carbon atoms have more than one isomer. There are two structural formulas for butane, $C_4H_{10}$, and three structural formulas for pentane, $C_5H_{12}$.

## Problem

What are the shapes of some organic molecules? Can the same number of atoms be arranged differently?

## Objectives

- **Compare and contrast** the shapes of several organic molecules.
- **Draw** molecular structures for several organic compounds.
- **Formulate models** that show that the same number of atoms can be arranged differently.

## Materials

wooden or plastic molecular model set (ball and stick)
ruler
protractor

aluminum foil
sharp pencil
pliers
unlined paper (5 sheets)

**LAB 22.1**

## Safety Precautions

- Always wear safety goggles and a lab apron.
- Be careful not to pinch your skin with the pliers.

## Pre-Lab

1. What is the electron configuration of carbon? What is the electron configuration of hydrogen?

2. Define covalent bond.

3. How many covalent bonds will carbon normally form in a compound? How many covalent bonds will hydrogen normally form in a compound?

4. Read the entire laboratory activity. Form a hypothesis about the shapes of hydrocarbons and how the increase in the number of carbon atoms in a compound will affect the number of possible isomers. Record your hypothesis on page 171.

5. Summarize the procedures you will follow to test your hypotheses.

## Procedure

### Part A

1. Each hole that has been bored into the ball represents the potential for a single chemical bond. Count the number of holes present in the differently colored balls. Record your answers in **Data Table 1.**

2. On another sheet of paper, write out the electron configurations for carbon, hydrogen, nitrogen, oxygen, bromine, chlorine, and iodine.

3. On the basis of the number of holes and the electron configurations, identify the different colored balls as carbon, hydrogen, nitrogen, and oxygen. Label them in **Data Table 1.** (The colors of bromine, chlorine, and iodine have already been recorded for you.)

4. Record the electron configuration of each element and determine the number of unpaired electrons for each element in **Data Table 1.**

### Part B

1. Construct a model of methane, $CH_4$. The structural formula for methane, written on paper, is

2. Compare the model with the structural diagram.

3. Wrap a sheet of aluminum foil around the outside perimeter of your model. (Stretch the foil tightly from ball to ball.) Note the regular geometric shape of the model.

4. Now you will construct bromomethane. Remove one of the yellow (hydrogen) balls. Replace the ball with a ball representing the halogen, bromine. Note any differences in the general shapes of methane and bromomethane.

5. Remove the orange (bromine) ball and its wooden stick. Place the remainder of the model on a clean sheet of unlined paper so that the black (carbon) ball and two yellow balls are touching the paper.

6. On a clean sheet of paper, use a sharp pencil to trace the angle formed by the two sticks connecting the yellow (hydrogen) balls to the black (carbon) ball.

7. Remove the model and extend the lines until they intersect.

8. Use a protractor to measure the angle formed.

9. After your teacher has checked your work, disassemble the model.

### Part C

1. Construct a model of ethane, $C_2H_6$.

2. On another sheet of paper, draw the structural formula for ethane.

3. Hold one black ball in each hand. Attempt to rotate the carbon atoms around the carbon-carbon axis.

**4.** Construct a model of propane, $C_3H_8$.

**5.** Draw the structural formula for propane.

**6.** After your teacher has checked your work, disassemble the models.

**7.** Construct two different models of chloropropane, $C_3H_7Cl$.

**8.** Draw structural diagrams of these molecules.

**9.** After your teacher has checked your work, disassemble the models.

### Part D

**1.** Construct two different models of butane, $C_4H_{10}$.

**2.** Draw the structural formula for each isomer and label it with the correct IUPAC name.

**3.** After your teacher has checked your work, disassemble the models.

**4.** Construct three different isomers of pentane, $C_5H_{12}$.

**5.** Draw the structural formula for each isomer and label it with the correct IUPAC name.

**6.** After your teacher has checked your work, disassemble the models.

## Hypothesis

_____

_____

## Cleanup and Disposal

**1.** Be sure all sticks have been removed from the balls.

**2.** Neatly reassemble the model kit.

## Data and Observations

| | | | Data Table 1 | | |
|---|---|---|---|---|---|
| **Ball color** | **Number of holes** | **Identity of element** | **Electron configuration** | | **Number of unpaired electrons** |
| Red | | | | | |
| Orange | | bromine | | | |
| Yellow | | | | | |
| Green | | chlorine | | | |
| Blue | | | | | |
| Purple | | iodine | | | |
| Black | | | | | |

## Analyze and Conclude

**1. Observing and Inferring** How does the structural diagram of methane compare with the model?

_____

_____

**2. Observing and Inferring** Describe the geometric shape of the methane model when it is wrapped with aluminum foil.

_____

_____

**3. Observing and Inferring** Describe the rotation in the model of ethane.

_____

_____

**4. Observing and Inferring** Compare the shapes of the models of methane and bromomethane.

_____

_____

**5. Measuring and Using Numbers** Compare the measured bond angle in the methane molecule to the accepted bond angle, 109.5°. Account for any differences in the two values.

_____

_____

_____

**6. Drawing a Conclusion** Describe the relationship between the number of carbon atoms in an alkane and the number of possible isomers.

_____

_____

_____

**7. Error Analysis** Compare your isomers of butane and pentane with the isomers of other students in your class. Are the isomers the same or different? Describe any differences.

_____

_____

_____

## Real-World Chemistry

**1.** Methane is the major component of natural gas, while propane and butane are used as bottle-gas products. Research and compare the densities of methane, propane, and butane with that of air at STP. Which gas—natural gas or bottle-gas products—might you expect to rise in the air and which gas would you expect to settle to the ground?

**2.** Gasoline is a mixture of alkanes that generally have between 4 and 12 carbon atoms. It is liquid at room temperature. Paraffin wax is a mixture of hydrocarbons. Would you expect the number of carbons per typical molecule to be fewer or greater than the number of carbon atoms in any of the molecules that make up gasoline?

# The Ripening of Fruit with Ethene

**H**ave you ever tried to eat an unripe apple? Such an apple may appear green, have hard flesh, and have almost no taste. In fact, the flesh may taste sour. However, when you eat a ripe apple, everything is different. Such an apple generally appears red, although ripe apples may be colors other than red. The flesh is softer and tastes sweet. What happened during the ripening process to cause this change? Hydrocarbons provide the answer.

Hydrocarbons are the simplest organic compounds, containing only carbon and hydrogen. There are three families of hydrocarbons. The alkanes have only single bonds and are said to be saturated. Alkanes are very stable and generally unreactive. Alkenes and alkynes have multiple bonds between two adjacent carbon atoms and are said to be unsaturated. This unsaturation makes alkenes and alkynes more reactive than alkanes.

Several alkenes occur naturally in living organisms. Some of these alkenes act as hormones and control biological functions. Plants produce ethene as a hormone to stimulate flower and seed production and to ripen fruits. Ethene stimulates enzymes in the plants to convert starch and acids of unripe fruit into sugars. The enzymes also soften fruit by breaking down pectin in cell walls.

The plant produces ethene during its growth cycle. If the fruit is kept on the plant and allowed to ripen, the full development and ripening cycles can be observed. However, if farmers and growers wait until all the fruit is ripe before they ship it to stores, much fruit will be rotten and inedible by the time you purchase it. Ripening may be slowed by refrigeration; however, once ethene is produced, the process cannot be stopped. Generally, fruit is picked while green and the ripening process starts by exposing the unripe fruit to ethene in special gas-tight chambers.

Ethene is a colorless, odorless, and tasteless gas. Although it can be very dangerous in high concentrations, you will be using natural ethene produced in relatively low concentrations in this activity. You will test the effect of ethene on the ripening of fruit.

**LAB 22.2**

## Problem

What factors affect the rate at which fruit ripens?

## Objectives

- **Compare** and **contrast** fruit ripening in open and closed systems.
- **Observe** how a natural source of ethene ripens fruit.
- **Design experiments** that may cause fruit to ripen faster or slower.

## Materials

unripe bananas (9)
ripe apple
self-sealing plastic bags (2)
paper plates (3)

## Safety Precautions

- **Always wear safety goggles and a lab apron.**
- **Never eat or taste any substance used in the lab.**

## Pre-Lab

1. What is the active chemical in the ripening of fruit?
2. What is the structural formula for this chemical? Why should it be reactive?
3. How will you know when the bananas are ripe?
4. Read the entire laboratory activity. Form a hypothesis about which bananas will ripen first. Record your hypothesis in the next column.

## Procedure

1. Label the three paper plates with your name. Number the plates 1 through 3.
2. Pick out nine bananas that are unripe to the same degree. Divide the bananas into three groups of three bananas each. Be sure the bananas in all three groups are either attached or unattached at the stems.
3. Place each group of three bananas on a paper plate.
4. Examine each group of bananas. Record the appearance and firmness of each group in as much detail as possible on the Day-1 line in **Data Table 1.**
5. The bananas on plate number 1 will not be placed in a bag.
6. Place the second paper plate and bananas in a self-sealing plastic bag and seal it.

7. Place a ripe apple with the bananas on plate number 3. Place the plate, apple, and bananas in a self-sealing plastic bag and seal it.
8. Place all three plates of bananas side by side in an area designated by your teacher.
9. On day 2, examine each of the groups of bananas again. Record the appearance and firmness of each group in as much detail as possible on the Day-2 lines in **Data Table 1.** Do not open the bags unless instructed to do so by your teacher.
10. Record your observations each day until all the bananas have ripened.

## Hypothesis

_____

_____

_____

_____

## Cleanup and Disposal

1. Place all materials in the appropriate waste container.
2. Return all lab equipment to its proper place.
3. Clean up your work area.

## Data and Observations

| Data Table 1 | | | |
|---|---|---|---|
| **Day** | **Plate 1** | **Plate 2** | **Plate 3** |
| 1 | | | |
| 2 | | | |
| 3 | | | |
| 4 | | | |
| 5 | | | |
| 6 | | | |
| 7 | | | |
| 8 | | | |
| 9 | | | |
| 10 | | | |

## Analyze and Conclude

1. **Observing and Inferring** Why was plate 1 allowed to be open and plate 2 kept in a closed container?

_____

_____

2. **Comparing and Contrasting** What differences were observed between the three plates of fruit?

_____

_____

3. **Drawing a Conclusion** Why did the bananas on plate 2 ripen faster than those on plate 1?

_____

_____

4. **Drawing a Conclusion** Why did the bananas on plate 3 ripen faster than those on plate 2 or plate 1?

_____

_____

5. **Designing an Experiment/Identifying Variables** How could you have made the bananas ripen even faster?

_____

_____

6. **Designing an Experiment/Identifying Variables** How could you have slowed the ripening process?

_____

_____

7. **Error Analysis** Compare your results with those of other students in your class. Are they the same? What may be some reasons for differences?

_____

_____

### Real-World Chemistry

1. Suppose you wanted to ship bananas from Puerto Rico to New York and the time required for shipment was 8 days. Will you choose to ship ripe bananas or green bananas? Why?

2. You may have heard the saying "One bad apple will spoil the whole barrel." Based on the results of your experiment, do you think the statement may be true? Why?

**LAB 23.1** **LABORATORY MANUAL**

# The Characterization of Carbohydrates

Carbohydrates are either polyhydroxy aldehydes or ketones, or compounds that will yield polyhydroxy aldehydes or ketones upon hydrolysis. Carbohydrates are of major importance to both plants and animals. It is estimated that more than half of all the organic carbon atoms in the world are in the form of carbohydrate molecules. Carbohydrates are synthesized chiefly by chlorophyll-containing plants in a process called photosynthesis. Plants produce carbohydrates in the form of starch for energy storage, and in the form of cellulose for structural material. Starch and cellulose are both polymers made up of glucose units.

Carbohydrates are classified based upon the products formed when they are hydrolyzed. Monosaccharides are simple sugars that cannot be broken down into simpler sugars upon hydrolysis. Examples of monosaccharides are glucose, ribose, deoxyribose, and fructose. Disaccharides contain two monosaccharide units and yield two monosaccharides upon hydrolysis. Examples of disaccharides are lactose, maltose, and sucrose. Polysaccharides are polymers of monosaccharide units and yield many individual monosaccharides upon hydrolysis. Examples of polysaccharides are starch, glycogen, and cellulose.

Sugars can be classified as reducing or nonreducing based upon their ability to be oxidized. A reducing sugar is easily oxidized, and a nonreducing sugar cannot be oxidized. The term *reducing* is used to classify sugars because these compounds reduce the other chemical in the reaction. A common chemical test to distinguish between reducing and nonreducing sugars is the Benedict's test. In this test, copper(II) ion will be reduced to copper metal if a reducing sugar is present.

## Problem

How can you use a color test to distinguish between reducing and nonreducing sugars? How can you hydrolyze a nonreducing sugar and produce a reducing sugar?

## Objectives

- **Distinguish** reducing sugars from nonreducing sugars using a color test.
- **Convert** nonreducing sugars to reducing sugars.

## Materials

2% glucose solution (20 mL)
2% sucrose solution (20 mL)
2% fructose solution (20 mL)
2% starch solution (20 mL)
Benedict's solution (30 mL)
concentrated sulfuric acid (1 mL)

6M sodium hydroxide (NaOH) (5 mL)
red litmus paper
boiling chips
hot plate
250-mL beaker
10-mL graduated cylinder
test tubes (8)
test-tube rack
stirring rod
dropper
beaker tongs

## Safety Precautions

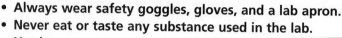

- Always wear safety goggles, gloves, and a lab apron.
- Never eat or taste any substance used in the lab.
- Hot items may not appear to be hot.

## Pre-Lab

1. What are the three major classes of carbohydrates?

2. What can be learned about sugars by performing the Benedict's test?

3. When you hydrolyze cellulose, what are the hydrolysis products?

4. Read over the entire laboratory activity. Form a hypothesis about what will happen when you mix the four sugars with the Benedict's solution. Record your hypothesis in the next column.

## Procedure

1. Set up a boiling-water bath by adding 150 mL of water to a 250-mL beaker. Add a few boiling chips to the water and place the beaker on the hot plate. Heat the water until it starts boiling.

2. Label eight test tubes as follows:
   Test tube 1: 1-glucose
   Test tube 2: 2-fructose
   Test tube 3: 3-sucrose
   Test tube 4: 4-starch
   Test tube 5: 5-sucrose
   Test tube 6: 6-starch
   Test tube 7: 7-sucrose
   Test tube 8: 8-starch

3. Place 5 mL of the solutions of glucose, fructose, sucrose, and starch into the appropriately labeled test tube, numbered 1 through 4. Add 4 mL of Benedict's solution to each test tube and shake each solution until thoroughly mixed. Place each test tube in the boiling-water bath and heat for 5 minutes. The four samples may be heated at the same time.

4. After 5 minutes of heating, remove the test tubes and place them in the test-tube rack to cool. Record your observations in **Data Table 1.** Note any color changes or precipitate that formed. Benedict's solution contains an oxidizing agent

that will react with reducing sugars, resulting in a brick-red, brown, green, or yellow precipitate. A precipitate of any of these colors is a positive test for the presence of a reducing sugar. A solution that does not change color or that does not produce a precipitate is a negative test.

5. Place 10 mL of sucrose solution and 10 mL of starch into test tubes 5 and 6. Add 2 drops of concentrated sulfuric acid to each solution and stir to mix thoroughly. Place the test tubes into the boiling-water bath and heat for 3 minutes. The samples may be heated at the same time.

6. After the 3-minute heating period, carefully add 15 drops of 6M NaOH solution to each test tube and stir. Using a stirring rod, test a drop from each solution with red litmus paper and record your observations in **Data Table 2.** If a solution turns the paper blue, the solution is basic. If the paper remains red, add NaOH one drop at a time, stirring after each addition, until you determine that the solution is basic by testing it with red litmus paper.

7. When the two solutions are basic, place 5 mL of the sucrose solution into test tube 7 and 5 mL of the starch solution into test tube 8. Add 4 mL of Benedict's solution to each test tube and stir or shake until thoroughly mixed. Place each test tube in the boiling-water bath. After 5 minutes of heating, remove the test tubes and place in the test-tube rack to cool. Record your observations in **Data Table 3.**

## Hypothesis

_____

_____

_____

_____

## Cleanup and Disposal

**1.** Turn off the hot plate and allow it to cool.

**2.** Use beaker tongs to remove the beaker from the hot plate. Allow it to cool before emptying the contents.

**3.** Place all chemicals in an appropriately labeled waste container.

**4.** Return all lab equipment to its proper place.

**5.** Clean up your work area and wash your hands thoroughly with soap or detergent before leaving the lab.

## Data and Observations

| Data Table 1: Benedict's Test | | |
|---|---|---|
| **Sugar** | **Volume of Benedict's solution (mL)** | **Observations** |
| starch | | |
| sucrose | | |
| glucose | | |
| fructose | | |

| Data Table 2: Hydrolysis | | | |
|---|---|---|---|
| **Sugar** | **Volume of solution (mL)** | **Amount of concentrated sulfuric acid (drops)** | **Amount of NaOH (drops)** |
| sucrose | | | |
| starch | | | |

| Data Table 3: Benedict's Test of Hydrolyzed Solutions | | |
|---|---|---|
| **Sugar** | **Volume of Benedict's solution (mL)** | **Observations** |
| starch | | |
| sucrose | | |

## Analyze and Conclude

**1. Observing and Inferring** Which of the solutions that you tested contained reducing sugars and which contained nonreducing sugars?

_____

_____

**2. Comparing and Contrasting** What observed differences were found between those sugars that are reducing and those that are nonreducing?

_____

_____

3. **Drawing a Conclusion** Write a word chemical equation to describe what happened during the hydrolysis of starch.

_____

_____

4. **Thinking Critically** Were reducing sugars detected in the hydrolyzed starch solution using the Benedict's test? Was this expected?

_____

_____

5. **Thinking Critically** Were reducing sugars found in the hydrolyzed sucrose solution using the Benedict's test? Was this expected?

_____

_____

6. **Error Analysis** What possible sources of error might account for unexpected results?

_____

_____

---

### Real-World Chemistry

1. Why would you want to use a color-change test to distinguish between the types of sugars?

2. When you place a piece of uncooked pasta in your mouth, there is very little taste. However, the longer the pasta remains in your mouth, the sweeter the taste becomes. Explain what is happening.

# Polymerization Reactions

**Use with Section 23.5**

**P**olymers are examples of organic compounds. However, the main difference between polymers and other organic compounds is the size of the polymer molecules. The molecular mass of most organic compounds is only a few hundred atomic mass units (for reference, atomic hydrogen has a mass of one atomic mass unit). The molecular masses of polymeric molecules range from thousands to millions of atomic mass units. Synthetic polymers include plastics and synthetic fibers, such as nylon and polyesters. Naturally occurring polymers include proteins, nucleic acids, polysaccharides, and rubber. The large size of a polymer molecule is attained by the repeated attachment of smaller molecules called monomers.

Polymers can be made from many repeating units of the same monomer. These may be represented by the sequence -A-A-A-A-A-A-A-A-. Other polymers contain chains of two different monomers that arrange in an alternating pattern. This sequence may be represented as -A-B-A-B-A-B-.

In the first part of this activity, you will prepare a polyester. As the name *polyester* implies, this polymer contains many ester functional groups. One technique for preparing an ester is by the reaction of a carboxylic acid with an alcohol. $RCOOH + R'OH \rightarrow RCOOR' + H_2O$

If the carboxylic acid has two carboxyl functional groups (a dicarboxylic acid) and if the alcohol has two hydroxyl functional groups (a diol), a polyester will result: $nHOOC—R—COOH + nHO—R'—OH \rightarrow$ $+OOC—R—COO—R'+_n + nH_2O$.

In the preparation of the polyester, you will react ethylene glycol, a diol, with phthalic anhydride. In this activity, phthalic anhydride will react similarly to the way phthalic acid (1,2-benzenedicarboxylic acid) reacts, resulting in the formation of a polyester. Phthalic acid and ethylene glycol are the A and B units of the A-B polymer: phthalic anhydride + ethylene glycol $\rightarrow$ polyester.

In the second part of this activity, you will prepare nylon, which is a polyamide with many amide functional groups. A common method for preparing amides is the reaction of a carboxylic-acid chloride with an amine, as in $RCOCl + R'NH_2 \rightarrow RCONHR' + HCl$.

In the preparation of nylon, you will react adipoyl chloride, a compound with two carbonyl-halogen functional groups, with hexamethylenediamine, a compound with two amine groups. Hexamethyenediamine is also known as 1,6-diaminohexane. Because each monomer has two reactive sites, a long chain of alternating units can form: $nClOC(CH_2)_4COCl + nH_2N(CH_2)_6NH_2 \rightarrow$ $+HN(CH_2)_6NHOC(CH_2)_4CO+_n + nH_2O$.

# LAB 23.2

## Problem

How can you make a polyester and a polyamide?

## Objectives

- **Prepare** a polyester from phthalic anhydride and ethylene glycol.
- **Prepare** a polyamide from adipoyl chloride and hexamethylenediamine.

## Materials

phthalic anhydride (2.0 g)
sodium acetate (0.1 g)
ethylene glycol (1 mL)
5% adipoyl chloride in cyclohexane (25 mL)
50% aqueous ethanol (10 mL)
5% aqueous solution of hexamethylenediamine (25 mL)
20% sodium hydroxide (NaOH) (1 mL)
scissors
copper wire

test tube
test-tube rack
10-mL graduated cylinder
50-mL graduated cylinder
150-mL beakers (2)
ring stand
clamp
Bunsen burner
striker or matches
balance
weighing papers (2)

## Safety Precautions

- **Always wear safety goggles, gloves, and a lab apron.**
- **Avoid skin contact with sodium hydroxide, phthalic anhydride, adipoyl chloride, or hexamethylenediamine.**
- **Handle the nylon with extreme caution so that any small bubbles of occluded liquid that form do not burst and squirt liquid on skin or clothing.**
- **Do not heat broken, chipped, or cracked glassware.**
- **Hot objects will not appear to be hot.**
- **Turn off the Bunsen burner when not in use.**
- **Avoid breathing in sodium acetate vapors—respiratory irritant.**
- **Conduct this lab under a fume hood.**

## Pre-Lab

1. Read the entire laboratory activity. Form a hypothesis about the number and identity of the functional groups present in each monomer. Form a second hypothesis about the type of polymer sequence that will be formed when the monomers join. Record your hypotheses on page 183.

2. Draw the structural formula for the polymer that you will prepare from phthalic anhydride and ethylene glycol.

3. Can a polyester be formed from the reaction of the two molecules shown below? If a polyester can be formed, draw the structural formula. If you think a polyester cannot be formed, explain why not.

$$H_3CCOOH \qquad H_3COH$$

## Procedure

### Part A: Preparation of a Polyester

1. Using a laboratory balance, measure the mass of a piece of weighing paper. Record this value in **Data Table 1**. Place 2.0 g of phthalic anhydride

on the weighing paper and record the combined mass in **Data Table 1**. Calculate the mass of phthalic anhydride and record this value as well. Place the phthalic anhydride in a clean test tube.

2. Using a laboratory balance, measure the mass of a second piece of weighing paper and record the mass in **Data Table 1**. Place 0.1 g of sodium acetate on the weighing paper and record the combined mass. Calculate the mass of sodium acetate and record this value in **Data Table 1**. Place the sodium acetate in the test tube containing the phthalic anhydride.

3. Measure 1.0 mL of ethylene glycol using a clean 10-mL graduated cylinder and place the ethylene glycol into a test tube. Record the amount used in **Data Table 1**. Shake the test tube gently to mix the contents.

4. Clamp the test tube to a ring stand using a clamp and heat gently using a Bunsen burner until the mixture appears to boil. Continue to heat the mixture gently for 5 additional minutes.

**5.** Once the 5-minute heating period has ended, turn off the gas flow to the burner. When the test tube has cooled to room temperature, test the brittleness and viscosity of the polymer using a stirring rod. Record your observations.

## Part B: Preparation of Nylon

**1.** Using a clean 50-mL graduated cylinder, measure 25 mL of a solution of adipoyl chloride in cyclohexane and pour it into a 150-mL beaker. Record the volume used in **Data Table 2.**

**2.** Clean the graduated cylinder and use it to measure 25 mL of the hexamethylenediamine solution. Pour this solution into a different 150-mL beaker. Record the amount used in **Data Table 2.** Add 10 drops of 20% sodium hydroxide to this beaker and mix gently. Record the number of drops used.

**3.** Carefully pour the adipoyl chloride solution down the inside wall of the beaker containing the hexamethylenediamine. This can best be done by tilting the beaker containing the hexamethylenediamine and pouring the adipoyl chloride solution down the inclined side. If this is done carefully, two layers will form.

**4.** A polymer film will immediately form where the two liquid layers meet. Using a copper wire with a hook at the end, gently pull the polymer strings from the walls of the beaker. Then, snag the polymer film at its center and draw it slowly upward so that the polymer forms continuously and produces a long rope.

**5.** Cut the polymer at the liquid-liquid interface using a pair of scissors. Place the rope in a 150-mL beaker and rinse the rope several times with water. Then remove the rope from the beaker and place on paper towels and allow to air dry.

**6.** Vigorously stir the remainder of the mixture with the stirring rod to form additional polymer. Pour off the remaining liquid into the waste container.

**7.** Wash the resulting solid with 10 mL of 50% aqueous ethanol. Measure the ethanol with a graduated cylinder. Pour off the liquid into the waste container.

**8.** Wash the solid with water and remove it from the beaker using your stirring rod. Place the solid

onto a paper towel and allow it to dry. Once your samples of nylon have dried, examine them and record your observations.

## Hypothesis

_____

_____

_____

_____

## Cleanup and Disposal

**1.** Turn off the gas to the Bunsen burner and allow all hot items to cool.

**2.** Place all chemicals in appropriately labeled waste containers.

**3.** Return all equipment to its proper place.

**4.** Clean up your work area and wash your hands with soap or detergent before leaving the lab.

## Data and Observations

| Data Table 1: Preparation of a Polyester | |
|---|---|
| Mass of phthalic anhydride and weighing paper (g) | |
| Mass of weighing paper (g) | |
| Mass of phthalic anhydride (g) | |
| Mass of sodium acetate and weighing paper (g) | |
| Mass of weighing paper (g) | |
| Mass of sodium acetate (g) | |
| Volume of ethylene glycol (mL) | |

**1.** Describe the viscosity and brittleness of the polymer prepared.

_____

_____

_____

_____

| Data Table 2: Preparation of Nylon | |
|---|---|
| Volume of adipoyl chloride solution (mL) | |
| Volume of hexamethylenedianmine (mL) | |
| Volume of NaOH solution (number of drops) | |

**2.** Describe the appearance of the nylon.

_____

_____

_____

_____

## Analyze and Conclude

**1. Comparing and Contrasting** Compare the appearance of the polyester with the appearance of the nylon.

_____

_____

**2. Predicting** Amino acids are the monomeric units that make up proteins. The reaction that joins amino acids is similar to the reaction used in the preparation of nylon. Two amino acids are shown below. Predict the structure of the molecule that will form when these two amino acids are joined.

$$H_2NCH_2COOH \qquad H_2NCH(CH_3)COOH$$

_____

_____

_____

_____

**3. Drawing a Conclusion** Consider what happened to the polyester as you heated it. What would you expect to happen to the viscosity of your polymer if you heated it more vigorously or for a longer time?

_____

_____

**4. Error Analysis** What sources of error could account for unusual results?

_____

_____

### Real-World Chemistry

**1.** Why would the polyester that you formed not work as well as nylon for making stockings?

**2.** Would you prefer to keep your milk in a polymer container or a glass container? Why?

**3.** A typical nylon fiber has a molecular mass of approximately 12 000 amu. Approximately how many monomer units are present in this fiber?

## LAB 24.1 LABORATORY MANUAL

# Denaturation

**Use with
Section 24.1**

**H**ydrogen bonds and other intermolecular attractions are important
in retaining the three-dimensional structure of certain proteins.
When the pH is lowered or the temperature is raised, these attractions
are disrupted, resulting in a change of the three-dimensional shape of
the protein.

Denaturation is a term used to describe the change of structure of
protein molecules in solution. The addition of heat or a decrease of pH
are methods of denaturing or changing the nature of the protein. An
example of denaturation is the hardening of an egg white when the
egg is boiled or fried.

In this activity, egg whites are used as an example of a protein.
Denaturing will be accomplished by lowering the pH and by increasing
the temperature.

### Problem

What happens to the
properties of a protein
once it undergoes
denaturation?

### Objectives

- **Observe** the change in
  properties of a protein
  due to heat.
- **Observe** the change in
  properties of a protein
  due to lowering of pH.

### Materials

$2M$ sulfuric acid
  ($H_2SO_4$)
$2M$ hydrochloric
  acid (HCl)
white vinegar, 5%
  acetic acid
  ($HC_2H_3O_2$)
$2M$ sodium hydrox-
  ide (NaOH)
egg white
Bunsen burner

10-mL graduated
  cylinder
stirring rods (5)
labels (6)
ring stand
ring
wire gauze
test tubes (6)
test-tube rack
striker or matches

## Safety Precautions

- **Always wear safety goggles, a lab apron, and gloves.**
- **Dispose of chemical wastes as directed by your teacher.**
- **Hot objects may not appear to be hot.**
- **Hydrochloric acid, sulfuric acid, and acetic acid are corrosive to skin.**
- **Sodium hydroxide is caustic.**
- **Use gloves when handling raw egg whites.**

## Pre-Lab

**1.** Briefly explain denaturation.

**2.** State two conditions that might cause a protein to
become denatured.

**3.** What is a control in an experiment?

**4.** Read the entire activity and form a hypothesis
about the effect that lowering the pH or raising
the temperature will have on the properties of a
protein. Record your hypothesis on page 186.

**LAB (24.1)**

## Procedure

1. Affix labels to six test tubes. Place your name on each label and number the test tubes *1* through *6*. Place the test tubes in a rack.

2. Pour 2 mL of egg white into each of six clean test tubes.

3. To test tube 1, add 10 mL of 2*M* hydrochloric acid (HCl) and stir using a stirring rod.

4. To test tube 2, add 10 mL of 2*M* sulfuric acid ($H_2SO_4$) and stir.

5. To test tube 3, add 10 mL of vinegar and stir.

6. To test tube 4, add 10 mL of 2*M* sodium hydroxide (NaOH) and stir.

7. Set up a hot-water bath. Place test tube 5 in the hot-water bath when the water boils and leave it in for 5 min.

8. Remove test tube 5 from the boiling water.

9. To test tube 6, add 10 mL of water. This tube serves as the control.

10. Observe what happens in each test tube and record this information in **Data Table 1**.

11. Place the test tubes in a secure place, as directed by your teacher.

12. After 24 hours, observe what happened in each test tube and record this information in **Data Table 1**.

## Hypothesis

_____

_____

_____

_____

## Cleanup and Disposal

1. Dispose of chemicals as instructed by your teacher.

2. Return all lab equipment to its proper place.

3. Wash your hands thoroughly before leaving the lab.

4. Neutralize excess acid and flush it down the drain. Neutralize excess NaOH and flush it down the drain.

## Data and Observations

| Data Table 1 | | | |
|---|---|---|---|
| Test-tube number | Treatment | Immediate observation | Observation 24 h later |
| 1 | HCl | | |
| 2 | $H_2SO_4$ | | |
| 3 | vinegar | | |
| 4 | NaOH | | |
| 5 | heat | | |
| 6 | control | | |

## Analyze and Conclude

1. **Observing and Inferring** What change of appearance did the egg white undergo when it became denatured?

_____

_____

**2. Observing and Inferring** Which substances caused a permanent change in the appearance of the egg white?

_____

_____

**3. Observing and Inferring** What type of pH change results in the denaturation of protein?

_____

**4. Observing and Inferring** How did a temperature change affect the properties of the protein?

_____

**5. Predicting** What was the function of test tube 6?

_____

_____

**6. Drawing a Conclusion** What happens to the properties of a protein when it undergoes denaturation?

_____

_____

**7. Drawing a Conclusion** Why was a second set of data recorded after 24 hours?

_____

_____

**8.** **Error Analysis** Compare the results of this lab with the predictions of your hypothesis. What possible sources of error might account for unusual results?

_____

_____

### Real-World Chemistry

**1.** The native people of the regions of Peru and Ecuador discovered that combining local seafood with citrus juices produced a "cooked" fish, called a seviche, that was firm and opaque. Why are lemon juices or lime juices used to marinate fish in the preparation of seviche?

**2.** Why might the lowering of blood pH cause the hemoglobin in blood to become unable to transport oxygen?

**LAB 24.2 LABORATORY MANUAL**

# Saturated and Unsaturated Fats

Use with
Section 24.3

**P**lants and animals both store energy in the bonds of chemical substances. The stored energy is used later. The energy stored in plant seeds is used to support rapid growth of the young plant after germination. Animals use the stored energy when food sources are not available.

Organisms store energy as fats and oils, which are mixtures of triglycerides. Triglycerides are esters of long chain carboxylic acids and glycerol. Each molecule of a triglyceride is made from one molecule of glycerol and three molecules of fatty acids.

The formula for a triglyceride may vary because (a) the length of the fatty acid chains may vary from 14 to 24 carbon atoms; (b) a triglyceride may contain as many as three different fatty acids; and (c) the bonding between adjacent carbon atoms may consist of combinations of single and/or double covalent bonds.

The general formula for a triglyceride is shown at the right. In this formula, R, R′, and R″ represent fatty acid chains. These groups may be identical to or different from each other.

In a saturated fatty acid, only single bonds are found between carbon atoms. The term *saturated* indicates that the carbon atoms of the chain contain all the hydrogen atoms that can be attached. Saturated fats contain only saturated fatty acid chains. A fatty acid with one or more double bonds in the chain is said to be unsaturated, that is, more hydrogen atoms can be attached. Unsaturated fats contain one double bond in the fatty acid chain. Polyunsaturated fats contain several double bonds.

General formula for a triglyceride

Lauric, myristic, palmitic, and stearic fatty acids make up most of the saturated fatty acids found in fats. Oleic acid, linoleic acid, and linolenic acid are the most abundant unsaturated fatty acids found in oils.

The main difference between oils and fats is that oils are liquid at room temperature and fats are solid at room temperature. Oils, such as olive oil or corn oil, usually come from plant sources and contain mainly unsaturated fatty acids. Fats, such as butter and lard, contain an abundance of saturated fatty acids and generally come from animal sources.

Saturated and unsaturated fatty acids have different chemical properties. Halogens can be easily added to fats that contain carbon-carbon double bonds. The reaction may be shown as $I_2 + \text{R-CH}=\text{CH-R}′ \rightarrow \text{R-CHI-CHI-R}′$.

In this activity, iodine solution is used to detect and estimate the degree of unsaturation in fats. The red-brown color of iodine will disappear when an iodine solution is added to an unsaturated fat. The red-brown color of the iodine will be retained when the solution is added to a saturated fat.

**LAB 24.2**

## Problem

What is the relative amount of saturated and unsaturated fatty acids in sample triglycerides?

## Objectives

- **Differentiate** between saturated fats and unsaturated fats.
- **Determine** the relative amount of saturation or unsaturation in samples of triglycerides.

## Materials

test tubes (9)
test-tube rack
10-mL graduated cylinder
dropper
glass stirring rod
coconut oil
butter
vegetable shortening

olive oil
corn oil
cottonseed oil
soybean oil
linseed oil
tincture of iodine
600-mL beaker
test-tube holder
hot plate

## Safety Precautions

- **Always wear safety goggles, a lab apron, and gloves.**
- **Dispose of chemical wastes as directed by your teacher.**
- **Broken glassware can easily puncture or slice skin.**
- **Tincture of iodine may be a tissue irritant.**
- **Iodine is toxic.**

## Pre-Lab

1. Explain how a saturated fat, an unsaturated fat, and a polyunsaturated fat are different.

2. What are two main differences between a fat and an oil?

3. Write an equation to show iodine reacting with an unsaturated hydrocarbon.

4. Read over the entire activity. Form a hypothesis about how a change in color of a halogen can be used to predict the degree of saturation of a fatty acid. Record your hypothesis in the next column.

## Procedure

1. Affix labels to nine test tubes. Place your name on each label and number the test tubes *1* through *9*.

2. Test tube 1 is a control. Add 1 mL of water to this test tube.

3. As detailed in **Data Table 1**, add 1 mL of each specified fat or oil to each of the remaining eight test tubes. Heat all tubes in a hot water bath until the solid fats melt.

4. Add 3 drops of tincture of iodine to each test tube.

5. Using a stirring rod, stir the contents of each test tube to evenly distribute the iodine. Clean the stirring rod between each tube.

6. Using a test-tube holder, return the test tubes to the rack and begin observing the color changes at 1-minute intervals for 3 minutes. In **Data Table 1,** record your observations using this code: 0 = no fading of iodine color; 1 = some fading of iodine color; and 2 = color of iodine completely gone.

7. Determine the degree of unsaturation based on the color changes. Use an arbitrary scale of 1 to 3, where 3 is the most unsaturated.

## Hypothesis

_____

_____

_____

_____

## Cleanup and Disposal

1. Dispose of chemicals as instructed by your teacher.

2. Return all lab equipment to its proper place.

3. Report any broken or damaged equipment.

4. Wash your hands thoroughly before leaving the lab.

**LAB 24.2**  **LABORATORY MANUAL**

## Data and Observations

| Data Table 1 | | | | | |
|---|---|---|---|---|---|
| Test-tube number | Material tested | Color after 1 min (0–2) | Color after 2 min (0–2) | Color after 3 min (0–2) | Degree of unsaturation (1–3) |
| 1 | control | | | | |
| 2 | olive oil | | | | |
| 3 | coconut oil | | | | |
| 4 | corn oil | | | | |
| 5 | cottonseed oil | | | | |
| 6 | soybean oil | | | | |
| 7 | linseed oil | | | | |
| 8 | melted butter | | | | |
| 9 | melted vegetable shortening | | | | |

## Analyze and Conclude

**1. Observing and Inferring** Which fats or oils showed a lesser fading of the iodine color?

_____

_____

**2. Observing and Inferring** Which fats or oils showed a greater fading of the iodine color?

_____

_____

**3. Observing and Inferring** What does the different degree of fading of the iodine color indicate about the bond patterns of the substances tested?

_____

_____

**4. Observing and Inferring** What type of bond pattern results in the greatest degree of color change of the iodine?

_____

**5. Thinking Critically** What was the function of test tube 1?

_____

_____

6. **Drawing a Conclusion** Do animal fats or vegetable oils generally contain the greater amount of saturated fat?

_____

_____

7. **Drawing a Conclusion** Why were observations made after 1, 2 and 3 minutes, respectively?

_____

_____

8. **Error Analysis** What possible sources of error may account for inaccurate results?

_____

_____

## Real-World Chemistry

1. Hydrogenation is the process of adding hydrogen to vegetable oils to make them solid. Explain what happens to the carbon-carbon bonds in the oils when the hydrogen is added.

2. Fats and oils react with oxygen from the air and produce aldehydes and acids that have unpleasant odors and tastes. Where in the fat molecules is the oxidation most likely to take place?

**LAB 25.1 LABORATORY MANUAL**

# Radioisotope Dating

The Zag meteorite fell in the western Sahara of Morocco in August 1998. This meteorite was unusual in that it contained small crystals of halite (table salt), which experts believe formed by the evaporation of brine (salt water). It is one of the few indications that liquid water, which is essential for the development of life, may have existed in the early solar system. The halite crystals in the meteorite had a remarkably high abundance of $^{128}$Xe, a decay product of a short-lived iodine isotope that has long been absent from the solar system. Scientists believe that the iodine existed when the halite crystals formed. The xenon formed when this iodine decayed. For this reason, the Zag meteorite is believed to be one of the oldest artifacts in the solar system. In this lab, you will use potassium-argon radiochemical dating to estimate the age of the Zag meteorite and the solar system.

## Problem

What is the age of the solar system?

## Objectives

**Determine** the age of the Zag meteorite, using potassium-argon (K-Ar) radiochemical dating.

## Materials

calculator
graph paper
  (4 sheets)

## Safety Precautions

Always wear safety goggles and a lab apron.

## Pre-Lab

1. Suppose the initial number of nuclei of a radioactive nuclide is $N_0$, and that the half-life is $T$. Then the amount of parent nuclei remaining at a time $t$ can be written as $N_1 = N_0(1/2)^{(t/T)}$. This relationship is called the **radioactive decay equation.** What is the number of daughter nuclei present at time $t$, expressed in terms of $N_0$ and $N_1$?

2. What is the ratio of daughter nuclei to parent nuclei at time $t$ expressed in terms of $N_0$ and $N_1$? Simplify the expression.

3. Use the radioactive decay equation to eliminate $N_0$ and $N_1$ from your answer to question 2.

4. $^{40}_{19}$K decays to $^{40}_{20}$Ar. $^{40}_{19}$K has a half-life of $1.25 \times 10^9$ years and decays by positron ($^{0}_{+1}\beta$) emission. Write the equation for this nuclear reaction.

## Procedure

1. **Data Table 1** shows a number of quantities that change with time in a radioactive system. Column one shows the time, expressed in units of the half-life of the radioactive parent. Column two shows the fraction of the original parent nuclei that remain after the indicated number of half-lives. Subtract the value in column two from 1.0 to obtain the fraction of the original parent nuclei that have decayed to daughter nuclei. The final column is the ratio of daughter nuclei to parent nuclei. Complete **Data Table 1.**

2. Plot a graph of daughter-to-parent ratio versus number of half-lives on the axes in **Figure A.** Draw a smooth curve through the points.

**3.** The ratio of $^{40}$Ar to $^{40}$K was measured for four samples from the Zag meteorite. The values obtained are shown in **Data Table 2.** Use your graph in **Figure A** to estimate how many half-lives (to the nearest tenth of a half-life) have passed since the meteorite was formed. Multiply the number of half-lives by $1.25 \times 10^9$ years, the half-life of $^{40}$K, to obtain an estimate of the age of the sample. Use the average value from the age determinations of all four samples to estimate the age of the meteorite.

## Data and Observations

| Data Table 1 | | | |
|---|---|---|---|
| **Parent and daughter nuclei data** | | | |
| **Number of half-lives** | **Parent fraction** | **Daughter fraction** | **Daughter-to-parent ratio** |
| 0 | 1 | | |
| 1 | 1/2 | | |
| 2 | 1/4 | | |
| 3 | 1/8 | | |
| 4 | 1/16 | | |

**Figure A**

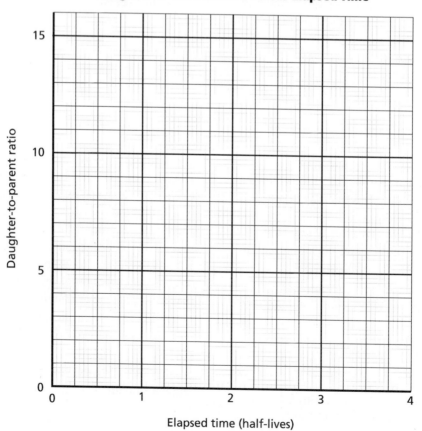

**Daughter-to-Parent Ratio Versus Elapsed Time**

Daughter-to-parent ratio (y-axis): 0, 5, 10, 15

Elapsed time (half-lives) (x-axis): 0, 1, 2, 3, 4

| Data Table 2 | | | |
| --- | --- | --- | --- |
| **Argon and potassium sample data** | | | |
| **Sample** | **$^{40}Ar/^{40}K$** | **Number of half-lives** | **Age ($10^9$ yr)** |
| A | 9.44 | | |
| B | 9.79 | | |
| C | 8.34 | | |
| D | 12.3 | | |

Average age ($10^9$ yr) = _____

## Analyze and Conclude

1. **Measuring and Using Numbers** What is the average age of the Zag meteorite (in years)?

   _____

2. **Thinking Critically** The K-Ar data for this experiment were obtained using a mass spectrometer. In this process, a small sample is heated with a laser until its constituent atoms vaporize and become ionized. A voltage is then applied that accelerates the charged ions towards a detector. The lightest ions reach the detector first, and the numbers of ions of each mass are identified and counted. There are a number of practical concerns that researchers must address in order to be confident that the measurements truly yield an accurate age for the object. List and explain a few possible concerns.

   _____

   _____

   _____

   _____

   _____

   _____

   _____

   _____

   _____

   _____

3. **Comparing and Contrasting** $^{14}C$ decays to $^{14}N$ with a half-life of 5730 years. This reaction is used for radiochemical dating of a certain class of terrestrial objects. How many half-lives of $^{40}C$ have passed since the Zag meteorite formed?

_____

_____

_____

_____

4. **Thinking Critically** Based on your answer to question 3, explain why radiochemical dating using carbon is an inappropriate technique for dating meteorites.

_____

_____

_____

_____

_____

_____

_____

_____

_____

## Real-World Chemistry

1. A sample of spruce wood taken from Two Creeks forest bed near Milwaukee, Wisconsin, is believed to date from the time of one of the last advances of the continental ice sheet into the United States. The ratio of $^{14}C$ to $^{12}C$ in the sample was found to be 0.2446 of the atmospheric value of this ratio. What is the daughter-to-parent ratio for the decay process in the sample?

2. What is the estimated age of the spruce wood sample? Show calculations that support your answer.

**LAB 25.2 LABORATORY MANUAL**

# Modeling Isotopes

**T**he defining characteristic of an atom of a chemical element is the number of protons in its nucleus. A given element may have different *isotopes*, which are nuclei with the same numbers of protons but different numbers of neutrons. For example, $^{12}C$ and $^{14}C$ are two isotopes of carbon. The nuclei of both isotopes contain six protons. However, $^{12}C$ has six neutrons, whereas $^{14}C$ has eight neutrons. In general, it is the number of protons and electrons that determines chemical properties of an element. Thus, the different isotopes of an element are usually chemically indistinguishable. These isotopes, however, have different masses.

Between 1962 and 1982, pennies were made of brass, which is an alloy composed of 95% copper and 5% zinc. In 1982, the rising price of copper led to a change in the composition of the penny. Beginning in 1982, pennies have been made of zinc plated with copper. These pennies contain 2.5% copper and 97.5% zinc. In this experiment, the two different types of pennies will represent two isotopes of an element.

## Problem

What is the isotopic composition of a collection of 100 pennies?

## Objectives

- **Determine** the isotopic composition of 100 pennies.
- **Apply** the lessons of the penny-isotope analogy to isotopic data.

## Materials

pennies (100)
balance

## Safety Precautions

**Always wear safety goggles and a lab apron in the lab.**

## Pre-Lab

1. What is an isotope?

2. The average atomic mass of the atoms of an element is what is known as a weighted average. In a weighted average, the value of each type of item is multiplied by the number of that type of item. The products are added, and the sum is divided by the total number of items. Use weighted average to solve the following problem: If you have four quarters, five dimes, and nine

pennies, what is the average value of the coins? Describe the procedure. Then calculate the answer.

3. Explain how the two different types of pennies are analogous to isotopes of an element.

4. Read the entire laboratory activity. Make a flow chart of the procedure you will follow.

**LAB 25.2**

## Procedure

**1.** Measure the mass of ten pre-1982 pennies to the nearest 0.01 g. Record your measurement in **Data Table 1.** Repeat for post-1982 pennies.

**2.** Using your data from step 1, calculate the average mass of one pre-1982 penny. Record this average mass in **Data Table 1.** Repeat for a post-1982 penny.

**3.** Obtain 100 pennies. Find the mass of the sample to the nearest 0.01 g. Record your measurement in **Data Table 2.**

**4.** Divide the sample of 100 pennies into pre-1982 and post-1982 pennies. Record the numbers of each in **Data Table 2.**

## Cleanup and Disposal

Follow your teacher's instructions for returning the coins.

## Data and Observations

| Data Table 1 | |
|---|---|
| **Mass of pennies** | |
| **Pennies** | **Mass (g)** |
| 10 pre-1982 | |
| 10 post-1982 | |
| 1 pre-1982 | |
| 1 post-1982 | |

| Data Table 2 | |
|---|---|
| **Data for 100-penny sample** | |
| Mass of 100 pennies (g) | |
| Number of pre-1982 pennies in 100-penny sample | |
| Number of post-1982 pennies in 100-penny sample | |
| Average mass of a penny in 100-penny sample (g) | |

## Analyze and Conclude

**1. Thinking Critically** In Procedure step 1, why did you measure the mass of ten pennies instead of the mass of one penny?

_____

_____

_____

**2. Measuring and Using Numbers** Divide the mass of 100 pennies in **Data Table 2** by 100 to find the average mass. Record your answer in **Data Table 2.**

**3. Measuring and Using Numbers** Using the mass of pre-1982 and post-1982 pennies from **Data Table 1** and the number of each type of penny from **Data Table 2,** calculate the average mass of a penny in the 100-penny sample. How does your answer compare to the average value calculated in question 2?

_____

_____

_____

4. **Comparing and Contrasting** How is the value you calculated in question 3 analogous to the atomic mass of the atoms in a sample of an element?

_____

_____

5. **Measuring and Using Numbers** Calculate the theoretical mass of a pre-1982 penny and a post-1982 penny.

**a.** The density of copper is 8.96 g/cm$^3$, and that of zinc is 7.13 g/cm$^3$. Using the compositions given in the introduction, the density of a pre-1982 penny is $(0.95)(8.96 \text{ g/cm}^3) + (0.05)(7.13 \text{ g/cm}^3) = 8.87 \text{ g/cm}^3$. Calculate the density of a post-1982 penny.

_____

_____

**b.** A typical penny has a diameter of 1.905 cm and a thickness of 0.124 cm. What is the volume in cm$^3$ of a typical penny? Hint: $V = (\pi r^2)(\text{thickness of penny})$

_____

_____

**c.** Using the density and volume values from questions 1 and 2, calculate the theoretical mass of a pre-1982 penny and the mass of a post-1982 penny.

_____

_____

6. **Making and Using Tables** Data Table 3 shows the isotopic mass and relative abundance for the most common isotopes of copper and zinc.

**a.** How many protons and neutrons are there in a $^{64}$Cu nucleus?

_____

**b.** How many protons and neutrons are there in a nucleus of $^{64}$Zn?

_____

| Data Table 3 | | | | |
|---|---|---|---|---|
| Isotope | Atomic number | Mass number | Isotopic mass (amu) | Relative abundance (%) |
| Copper-63 | 29 | 63 | 62.9298 | 69.09 |
| Copper-64 | 29 | 64 | 64.9278 | 30.91 |
| Zinc-64 | 30 | 64 | 63.9291 | 48.89 |
| Zinc-66 | 30 | 66 | 65.9260 | 27.81 |
| Zinc-67 | 30 | 67 | 66.9271 | 4.73 |
| Zinc-68 | 30 | 68 | 67.9249 | 18.57 |

## 7. Measuring and Using Numbers

**a.** Using the data in **Data Table 3,** calculate the atomic mass of copper.

_____

_____

**b.** Using the data in **Data Table 3,** calculate the atomic mass of zinc.

_____

_____

## 8. Applying Concepts  Use the values from **Data Table 1** and the answers from question 7 to calculate the following.

**a.** How many atoms of copper are in a pre-1982 penny? (Hint: Use Avogadro's number.)

_____

_____

**b.** How many atoms of zinc are in a pre-1982 penny?

_____

_____

_____

**c.** How many total atoms (copper and zinc) are in a pre-1982 penny?

_____

**d.** How many total atoms (copper and zinc) are in a post-1982 penny?

_____

_____

## 9. Error Analysis  Compare the mass of a pre-1982 penny and a post-1982 penny in **Data Table 1** to the answers of question 2c. What might have caused any differences?

_____

_____

_____

### Real-World Chemistry

A nuclear power plant that generates 1000 MW of power uses 3.2 kg per day of $^{235}U$. Naturally occurring uranium contains 0.7% $^{235}U$ and 99.7% $^{238}U$. What mass of natural uranium is required to keep the generator running for a day?

# Organisms That Break Down Oil

**Use with Section 26.2**

**O**il spills cause significant environmental problems. The largest spill in history was the deliberate release of oil into the Persian Gulf during the 1991 Gulf War. The second largest spill took place in 1979 when an exploratory well off the coast of Mexico released about 140 million gallons of oil.

Large oil spills near wells and from tankers pose the most vivid display of concern. However, oil pollution can also be seen in situations such as contaminated soil from automotive fuel spills, industrial spills, tank leaks, and household grease wastes.

Cleanup of major oil spills may be accomplished by physical, chemical, and biological methods. In this activity, you will focus on bioremediation, which is a method of using natural organisms to break down contaminants at the site.

There are naturally occurring microbes living in soil and water where contaminants are found. Some of these microbes break down hydrocarbons. The fungus *Penicillium* and the bacteria *Pseudomonas* are two such microbes. However, they are present in small amounts, and it would take many years to accomplish the cleanup. Biostimulation is the process of improving the area of concern by adding microorganisms and encouraging their growth. These microorganisms are natural. They have not been genetically engineered. The process simply increases the number of natural organisms at the site.

Density indicator strips are used to monitor the rate of microbial growth. These strips are attached to the culture vessel. As the microbes multiply, the solution becomes cloudy, obscuring some of the shaded strips. The degree of visibility of the shaded strips indicates the density of the microbes. In this activity, you will observe the bioremediation effectiveness of the fungus *Penicillium* and the bacteria *Pseudomonas* on a sample of oil.

## Problem

How effective are *Penicillium* and *Pseudomonas* for breaking down oil?

## Objectives

- **Observe** the effect of hydrocarbon-degrading microbes on oil.
- **Observe** microbes degrade oil.

## Materials

*Penicillium sp.* culture
*Pseudomonas sp.* culture
sterilizing, disinfectant solution
lightweight oil
nutrient fertilizer
density indicator strips (5)
paper towels
30-mL sterile culture test tubes with screw caps (3)
250-mL beaker
sterile 25-mL graduated cylinder
plastic dropping pipettes (4)
labels (4)
sterile distilled water

**LAB** 26.1

## Safety Precautions

- Always wear safety goggles, a lab apron, and gloves.
- Dispose of wastes as directed by your teacher.
- Organisms or living materials should always be treated and handled as if they were hazardous.
- Observe proper personal hygiene when handling microorganisms. Be sure to wear gloves and wash your hands with antibacterial soap or detergent after removing the gloves.

## Pre-Lab

1. Briefly explain bioremediation and biostimulation.

2. Explain why it is necessary to disinfect the work area.

3. Explain the function of the density indicator strips.

4. Read the entire laboratory activity. Form a hypothesis about the effect the microbes will have on the oil suspended in the water. Record your answer in the next column.

## Procedure

1. Use the disinfectant solution according to the manufacturer's directions to thoroughly clean and disinfect your work area. Wipe the area with paper towels and dispose of the towels as directed by your teacher. Wash your hands with antibacterial soap.

2. Affix labels to each of the sterile culture test tubes. Label them all with your name. Label one test tube *Penicillium*, the second test tube *Pseudomonas*, and the third test tube *control*. Place a label with your name, date, and class period on the 250-mL beaker.

3. Using a 25-mL graduated cylinder, pour 15 mL of distilled water into each sterile culture test tube.

4. Add 12 drops of oil to each test tube.

5. Add about 0.1 mL of nutrient fertilizer to each test tube.

6. The control test tube should not receive any additional materials. Being careful not to pick up other microbes by laying down equipment, add about 3 mL of *Penicillium* culture to the appropriate test tube. Add about 3 mL of

*Pseudomonas* culture to the *Pseudomonas* test tube.

7. Securely fasten the top on each test tube. Shake each tube gently to ensure thorough mixing of the contents.

8. Number the density strips from 1 to 5, with 1 being the lightest coloration. Secure the strips to the outside of each test tube so that the density strip is visible through the solution. The top set of bars should be just below the level of the liquid in the test tube.

9. Record the visibility of the density strips, the color of the liquid, and the general appearance of the contents of the test tube on **Data Table 1.**

10. Loosen the caps on the test tubes about half way and place them all in the labeled 250-mL beaker. Place the specimens in a warm location in the classroom. **CAUTION: Do not touch bacteria cultures.**

11. Repeat the same observations daily and record your observations on **Data Table 1** for a total of 5 days.

## Hypothesis

_____

_____

## Cleanup and Disposal

1. Dispose of materials as instructed by your teacher.

2. Return all lab equipment to its proper place.

3. Using the disinfectant solution, disinfect your work area.

4. Wash your hands thoroughly with antibacterial soap before leaving the lab.

## Data and Observations

| | | Data Table 1 | | |
|---|---|---|---|---|
| **Day** | **Test-tube contents** | **Density strip reading** | **Color of liquid** | **General appearance of test-tube contents** |
| 1 | control | | | |
| 1 | *Penicillium* | | | |
| 1 | *Pseudomonas* | | | |
| 2 | control | | | |
| 2 | *Penicillium* | | | |
| 2 | *Pseudomonas* | | | |
| 3 | control | | | |
| 3 | *Penicillium* | | | |
| 3 | *Pseudomonas* | | | |
| 4 | control | | | |
| 4 | *Penicillium* | | | |
| 4 | *Pseudomonas* | | | |
| 5 | control | | | |
| 5 | *Penicillium* | | | |
| 5 | *Pseudomonas* | | | |

## Analyze and Conclude

1. **Observing and Inferring** What changes occurred in each test tube as the 5 days progressed?

   _____

   _____

   _____

2. **Observing and Inferring** Did one organism break down the oil better than the other organism?

   _____

3. **Observing and Inferring** What happened to the cloudiness of the tubes as the 5 days progressed?

   _____

4. **Acquiring and Analyzing Information** What does an increase in the cloudiness of the system indicate?

   _____

5. **Acquiring and Analyzing Information** What did the changes in the color of the system and the general appearance indicate?

   _____

6. **Designing an Experiment/Identifying Variables** What was the function of the control test tube?

   _____

   _____

7. **Designing an Experiment/Identifying Variables** What was the purpose of shaking the test tubes and then leaving the caps partially opened?

   _____

   _____

8. **Error Analysis** Compare your results to those of other students in the class. What could be the cause of some differences?

   _____

   _____

### Real-World Chemistry

**1.** What effect might the use of microorganisms that are not native to a site have on the ecology?

**2.** Why might knowledge of pH be useful when using bioremediation techniques?

# Growth of Algae as a Function of Nitrogen Concentration

Use with
Section 26.2

Freshwater comes from many sources, including lakes, rivers, and municipal reservoirs. However, daily activities of life often leave these water sources polluted and unfit for personal consumption or use in industry.

Nitrogen and phosphorus compounds are among the most common pollutants. They contribute to pollution by causing algae and bacteria in the water to reproduce rapidly. When these organisms die, the decomposition process depletes oxygen in the water, killing fish and other aquatic life. In this lab, you will investigate the effect of nitrates on algae.

## Problem
How does the presence of nitrates in water affect the growth of algae?

## Objectives
- **Determine** how the level of nitrogen affects algal growth.
- **Identify** how much nitrogen is present in water, using algal growth as an indicator.

## Materials
algae culture
stock solutions of
  $0.3M$ NaNO$_3$,
  $0.6M$ NaNO$_3$, and
  $0.9M$ NaNO$_3$
unknown NaNO$_3$
  solution
distilled water
15-mm $\times$ 150-mm
  test tubes (5)

light source
aluminum foil
test-tube rack
dropper
china marker
10-mL graduated
  cylinder

## Safety Precautions

- **Always wear safety goggles and a lab apron.**
- **Never eat or taste any substance used in the lab.**
- **Wash your hands with soap or detergent thoroughly before leaving the lab.**

## Pre-Lab

1. What are sources of nitrogen and phosphorus pollution in Earth's freshwater?

2. Why is light needed for algal growth?

3. Read the entire laboratory activity. Hypothesize why the growth of algae may indicate the concentration of nitrogen pollutants in water. Record your hypothesis on page 206.

## Procedure

1. Using a china marker, label five test tubes as follows and place them in the test-tube rack. Label test tube 1, *Unknown*; test tube 2, $0.0M$ NaNO$_3$; test tube 3, $0.3M$ NaNO$_3$; test tube 4, $0.6M$ NaNO$_3$; and test tube 5, $0.9M$ NaNO$_3$.

2. Add 10 mL of unknown solution, supplied by your teacher, to test tube 1.

3. Add 10 mL of distilled water to test tube 2.

4. Add 10 mL of the appropriate $NaNO_3$ stock solution to each of test tubes 2, 3, and 4.

5. Place 10 drops of algal culture into each test tube, and cover the open end of all test tubes with a small piece of aluminum foil.

6. Record the appearance of each test tube in **Data Table 1.**

7. Place the test tubes under the light source as your teacher directs.

8. Check each test tube daily for 10 days, and record the appearance of each test tube in **Data Table 1.**

## Hypothesis

_____

_____

_____

_____

_____

## Cleanup and Disposal

1. Place all chemicals in the appropriately labeled waste container.

2. Dispose of the algae as your teacher directs.

3. Return all lab equipment to its proper place.

4. Clean up your work area.

## Data and Observations

| Data Table 1 | | | | | |
|---|---|---|---|---|---|
| Observations for each test tube | | | | | |
| Day | Test tube 1 | Test tube 2 | Test tube 3 | Test tube 4 | Test tube 5 |
| 1 | | | | | |
| 2 | | | | | |
| 3 | | | | | |
| 4 | | | | | |
| 5 | | | | | |
| 6 | | | | | |
| 7 | | | | | |
| 8 | | | | | |
| 9 | | | | | |
| 10 | | | | | |

## Analyze and Conclude

1. **Observing and Inferring** What happened in each test tube over the course of the 10 days?

_____

_____

_____

_____

2. **Comparing and Contrasting** What was the difference in sodium nitrate concentration among test tubes 2–5?

_____

_____

_____

_____

3. **Drawing a Conclusion** What can you conclude about the amount of algal growth and the nitrate concentration in test tubes 2–5?

_____

_____

_____

_____

4. **Drawing a Conclusion** What can you conclude about the amount of pollution, in the form of $NaNO_3$, that was present in the *Unknown*, test tube 1? Explain.

_____

_____

_____

_____

5. **Predicting** What would you predict to be the immediate response of algal growth if the amount of pollutants was allowed to keep increasing?

_____

_____

_____

_____

**6. Recognizing Cause and Effect** Why do nitrates increase growth of algae?

_____

_____

_____

_____

**7.** **Error Analysis** What could be done to improve the precision and accuracy of your investigation?

_____

_____

_____

_____

## Real-World Chemistry

**1.** Why is it not possible to completely eliminate algae blooms from the water supply?

**2.** In ponds where there are viable fish and plant populations, algae are seldom seen. Explain why this might happen.

**3.** People who have backyard ponds often keep snails and tadpoles in the ponds. Explain the purpose of these organisms.

# CREDITS

## Art Credits

Navta Associates: **22, 26, 33, 34, 37, 38, 58, 62, 94, 150, 162, 166, 194;** Glencoe: **x, xi, xii;**
MacArt Design: **2, 6, 54, 98, 102, 106, 110, 126**